FIRST WAVE

The story of Warrant Officer Reg Payne,
Royal Air Force Wireless Operator with 50 Squadron
during World War Two

by

Kenneth Ballantyne

Published by
Laundry Cottage Books

Laundry Cottage
Shawbirch Road
Admaston
Wellington
Shropshire
TF5 0AD

Tel: 01952 – 223931

Email: cenneach@westcoast13.wanadoo.co.uk

First published in Great Britain in 2013
by Laundry Cottage Books, Shawbirch Road,
Admaston, Wellington, Shropshire, TF5 0AD

ISBN 978-0-9550601-6-8

An environmentally friendly book, typeset, printed and bound in England
by www.printondemand-worldwide.com

Mixed Sources
Product group from well-managed forests, and other controlled sources
www.fsc.org Cert no. TT-COC-002641
FSC © 1996 Forest Stewardship Council

PEFC Certified
This product is from sustainably managed forests and controlled sources
PEFC www.pefc.org
PEFC/16-33-415

This book is made entirely of chain-of-custody materials

Other Titles published by Laundry Cottage Books

Another Dawn Another Dusk
ISBN 978-0-9550601-3-7

All the Things You Are
ISBN 978-0-9550601-4-4

The Journey
[Title no longer in print]

Also published by
Laundry Cottage Books in this series

The D-Day Dodger
Albert F Darlington
ISBN 978-0-9550601-2-0

Acknowledgements

I am deeply grateful to Reg Payne for allowing me to recount his life story in this book, for kindly sharing his very personal memories and experiences with me, and for allowing me to use his own material and personal photographs.

Wing Commander Peter Jacobs is the author of a number of books about the RAF, including *Stay the Distance*, the biography of Marshal of the Royal Air Force Sir Michael Beetham GCB, CBE, DFC, AFC, and *Bomb Aimer Over Berlin*, the biography of Flight Lieutenant Les Bartlett, DFM. I am particularly indebted to Peter for his great kindness and generosity in giving me unreserved permission to use whatever information I might need from these two books whilst writing *First Wave*. This has been particularly helpful when cross-referencing events, names, dates and places.

My thanks are also due to other people who have helped me with this book: to Sir Michael Beetham for generously allowing me to quote him on the cover of this book and to reproduce his photograph as a Flight Lieutenant in 1944; to Louise Bush of the Lincolnshire Aviation Museum for kindly making Lancaster NX611 'Just Jane' available to me so that I could photograph Reg at his wireless operator's position; to Ed Norman, archivist at 49 Sqn website, for kindly supplying me with the prisoner of war details for Reg's brother, Sgt William Arthur Payne, and to Squadron Leader Richard Head for thoughtfully sending me the photograph of the remaining Beetham crew at RAF Waddington in 1977.

The remaining photographs are from my own collection.

Once more my very grateful thanks go to Sue Browning of Sue Browning Editing and Proofreading for kindly correcting my literary waywardness and grammatical inexactitudes, and for guiding the flow of this story through the pitfalls of writing. I should also add my apologies to Sue if I have dabbled with the manuscript after she returned it to me and in so doing take full responsibility for any consequential errors.

Like my previous titles, this book could not have been written had it not been for the immense and enduring help, support and encouragement from my wife, Elaine who took care of everything else whilst I locked myself away to write.

Kenneth Ballantyne

Dedication

For my brother Sergeant William Arthur Payne,
Wireless Operator with 49 Squadron,
Royal Air Force, Bomber Command,
and for everybody who served with
50 Squadron on the ground and in the air during
the Second World War.

Bibliography

All the Things You Are; Kenneth Ballantyne; Laundry Cottage Books

Another Dawn Another Dusk; Kenneth Ballantyne; Laundry Cottage Books

Bomb Aimer Over Berlin; Peter Jacobs; Pen and Sword Aviation

Bomber Command; Max Hastings; Pan Books

London 1914-17: The Zeppelin Menace; Ian Castle; Osprey Publications

RAF Handbook 1939-1945; David Wragg; Sutton Publishing

RAF Skellingthorpe, Lancaster Station at War 1941-1945; Derek Brammer; Tucann Books

The Bomber Command War Diaries; Martin Middlebrook & Chris Everitt; Midland Publishing Ltd

The Dambuster Who Cracked the Dam; Arthur G Thorning; Pen & Sword Aviation;

War on the Home Front, 1939-1945; Juliet Gardiner; Carlton Books in association with the Imperial War Museum

Contents

Introduction

Bomber Command's offensive during World War Two was not simply a military strategy to defeat the enemy but a strategic imperative to secure the survival of the British nation. The ultimate cost in the lives of the young men who carried out that strategy was beyond anyone's comprehension at the beginning. Had it been foreseen with any certainty, Bomber Command would not have had the war it did. The prevailing wisdom pre-war was 'the bomber will always get through', and whilst that was demonstrably true, it was not so in the way that had been envisaged, and a realistic calculation of the scale of losses to achieve that end was not put into the equation because they didn't know what they would be.

Winston Churchill recognised, even during the Battle of Britain, that whilst Fighter Command could defend the skies over Britain, it needed a substantial bomber force to take the fight to the enemy in his homeland. Once the immediate threat of invasion had receded in the autumn of 1940, the political process to divert vast resources to build up that bomber force began, and the initiative and drive came from the very top of government; the Prime Minister.

All aircrew were volunteers, and patriotic young men from the four corners of the British Empire queued up to offer themselves; most were posted to Bomber Command and most of those would not survive a tour of thirty operations. A staggering total 55,573 of those young volunteers were killed flying with Bomber Command and a further 9,784 became prisoners of war. From the unsustainable early daylight attacks upon well-defended military targets flying inadequate, lightly armed and out-dated aircraft to the massed night-time raids on German cities in four-engine heavy bombers, Bomber Command took the war to the enemy. As a consequence,

Hitler increasingly had to divert essential and ultimately diminishing resources to defend the Reich. In the end, a million men and 55,000 anti-aircraft guns were kept back for homeland defences. His aircraft production was dominated by the need to produce fighters to defend the German people from the almost nightly bombing attacks. Had Bomber Command not forced Hitler to defend German air space, he would have been free to develop his own heavy bombers and larger, more lethal Vengeance weapons with which to pulverise the people of these islands and produce a different outcome.

The Luftwaffe bombing of 1940-42 showed at Coventry, Hull, Clydeside, Liverpool, Southampton and most other British cities, as well as London, what havoc could be wrought by relatively light twin-engine bombers. Heavy bombers would have devastated the cities of Britain, which, because of the shape of the country and their proximity to our major rivers, were always a lot easier for the Luftwaffe to locate with rudimentary navigation aids, even in the blackout of 1940, than German cities deep inside Europe were for the RAF throughout the war.

Only by getting into one is it really possible to understand how cramped the conditions were in a bomber, how difficult it must have been to escape when it was on fire and falling out of the sky. The Lincolnshire Aviation Museum at East Kirkby has one of only three working Lancasters in the world and hopes that one day NX611 'Just Jane' will fly again. In the meantime, a taxi run in this aircraft can be booked in advance and give some idea of just how cramped these bombers were under operational conditions with the airmen wearing their bulky flying kit. Sometimes they had only seconds to get out before the aircraft blew up, as happened to Reg's brother, or before it began to tumble out of control from the sky, as happened to Reg; and sometimes they didn't get out at all, like Christopher Panton, lost on the Nuremberg raid of 30th/31st March 1944 and in whose memory his brothers Fred and Harold have created the museum.

Bomber Command aircrew were amongst the most highly trained of any in the Allied Armed Forces. It took two years to train an entire crew. Individual crews chose their own members because the life of each man was in the care of all the others. A look at contemporary photographs tells its own story; young, fresh-faced and keen whilst training, those same airmen were strained, drawn and middle-aged long before they got to the end of their tour, a feat which fewer than one in four achieved. Reg Payne was one of those, but the crew that started out was not the same crew that finished.

Kenneth Ballantyne
Laundry Cottage
8th May 2013

FIRST WAVE
Chapter One

" The Angel that presided o'er my birth
Said, 'Little creature, formed of joy and mirth,
Go love without the help of anything on earth "'
' The Angel that presided o'er my birth';
- William Blake

The wind moaned mournfully around the corners of the house and the freezing rain lashed against the window panes of my parents' bedroom with an unrelenting rhythm. On that bitterly cold stormy night my mother struggled through her second labour to give me the life that I have. My first encounter with the world was the stout arm of the local midwife who had assisted mother, followed by her equally stout slap on my bottom, which had the desired effect and induced an indignant cry from me as I filled my lungs with air. Gently wrapped in a warm blanket, I sought the comfort and protection of my mother's arms as the midwife allowed my father to enter his own bedroom to greet his second son and congratulate his wife: it was Sunday 11th March 1923.

Home births were still the general rule then but I had arrived into a world so very different from the one which I see around me today in almost every conceivable way. Sometimes it is difficult to believe that only ninety years separates me from that late winter's night.

Two years earlier, my elder brother Arthur, who we always called Art, had been greeted by the same mid-wife when he too had been born in that small bedroom at 19 Washington Square, Kettering. In 1921, the house had been brand new, part of Kettering's modern council housing estate built to provide homes in Prime Minister David Lloyd George's 'land fit for the returning heroes' of the Great War; we were the lucky ones, because for so many it was the unfulfilled dream of an empty promise. Some nineteen months after me, on 26th November 1924, Art and I had a baby sister, Doris. Around 1928, we had a baby brother, but he died within a few weeks. Although this was heartbreaking for us as a family, it was not unusual in the days of high child mortality rates before antibiotics and penicillin in particular, and before the National Health Service, still the envy of the world. Our little brother Brian arrived on 5th January 1940.

My earliest memory is at about four years of age when I wandered off alone into Kettering, attracted by the sound of the steam engines on the railway at the bottom of Northampton Road. Completely oblivious to the worry which I had caused to my parents, I had obviously had a very informative and exciting time out on my own watching the trains go by, although by late afternoon I must have been feeling hungry because I was found pottering along Stamford Road, not far from home, though undoubtedly lost. A man riding a bicycle who had been searching for me coasted up and stopped beside me. "Hello, young Reg. Are you all right? Your mum is very worried about you." I just smiled in reply, but I do remember that I did like his bicycle. "Come on, my lad, let's get you home." And with that, he picked me up and put me on the cross-bar of his bike and set off back to Washington Square. That ride was the best part of the day.

Inevitably the day came round when I started school, and on that first day I played at the sand table in the infants' class of St. Mary's in Fuller Street for a long time; it was my introduction to nine years of formal education. I quickly outgrew the infants and was glad to move up to the junior school section, which was much more interesting. The headmaster here was Mr Shepardson, who had a particular liking for all things to do with pond life. Tadpoles, frogs, newts, water-boatmen, larvae of all sorts and the plants which grew there were his fascination and he infected us with his enthusiasm. Part of our curriculum was to collect specimens for his various aquaria, which he kept in the main hall. Small groups of children would each be assigned to a particular tank and to care for its contents. It was a wonderful way to learn about the natural world on our doorstep, but I don't suppose OFSTED would have approved!

The paddling pool in Rockingham Road Park was a great attraction to us, especially in the summer, and I learned to swim very young. As I got a little older, along with my pals, I would play in the Ise Brook near to Mr West's farm, known as The Mill. Parts of the brook were quite deep and we loved to swim in it during the good weather. Consequently, by the time we were old enough to join the swimming classes at school, we were already accomplished 'water babies' and in my last year at the juniors I was part of the school swimming team.

Football was, of course, an important part of our play activities. There were about thirty boys living around Washington Square, which had an open green in the middle where the children played. No-one had a real leather football, they were far too expensive, and so we used a pig's bladder which we got from the Co-op slaughter house at the back of the Central Hall. The slaughter man would blow it up and tie the ends for us; it made a great substitute for a ball and I don't remember one ever bursting. With so many lads around the Square, there was always a game of football to be had and by the time I was ten years old I had made the school football team. We played our matches on a Saturday morning against all the other local schools as far away as Corby, and home games were on the Headlands playing fields. The football for these games was leather and very heavy when wet, but we didn't know anything different then so never thought about it. I do doubt, though, whether today's highly paid footballers would look half as good if they had to play with a leather ball instead of the light weight plastic ones they use. It just makes me realise how much better the likes of Stanley Matthews, Duncan Edwards, Billy Wright and all those others really were compared with today's players.

Eric, one of farmer West's sons, was a great friend and was also in our team so we practised on his father's field along the Valley Walk. Mr Simms, our trainer, would keep those of us in the team behind in the main hall after school on a Friday evening before a match. We would roll down our socks, we all wore short trousers, of course, and Mr Simms would rub horse liniment on our legs to protect them from the cold during the game the next day. I have to smile at this memory now because today there would be parental outrage and poor Mr Simms would lose his job, even though he was actually taking care of us and looking after our welfare. At that time, however, nobody thought anything of it other than exactly what it was, our trainer preparing us for the game, and none of us ever came to any harm; it never even entered our heads that we would do, or our parents' heads, for that matter.

Mr Simms was actually a very kind and caring man. The parents of one or two of us in the team could not afford to buy a pair of football boots and so he bought us each a pair out of his own money at the cost of four shillings and six pence per pair, 22½p today, and our parents repaid him at the rate of sixpence a week for the next nine weeks.

As well as the banks of the Ise Brook, the Valley Walk was a beautiful area of trees and open meadows bursting with wild flowers, insects, butterflies and birds, including the ground-nesting Lapwings, which we always called Peewits because of the cry they made as they circled above us when we got too close to their nests. Mr Shepardson had taught me well and the Ise Brook was where I spent most of my free time. It was wonderfully clean water which was teeming with fish and other wildlife, as well as being home to dozens of water voles. There was many a time when, as I sat quietly at the side of the brook on a still summer evening, the air heavy with the scent of honeysuckle and the soft buzzing of the bumble bees seeking out its nectar, I would hear a gentle plop in the water and see a little brown head forging across the surface, its tiny bow wave barely visible, before disappearing into a hole in the bank. It is so sad that the water vole, immortalised as Ratty by Kenneth Grahame in *The Wind in the Willows* has forever gone from the Ise.

There were pike in the brook, too, some as long as eighteen inches, so we would creep along the bank to the deeper pools and gaze down at one of them lying on the bottom like a dead leaf pointing slightly upwards. Then, after we had watched it for a while, captivated by its camouflage, someone would stamp on the bank and the fish would be gone in an instant, so fast that, try as we might, we couldn't see it go, only a cloud of mud left behind.

There was a small dam made from a sheet of heavy metal on the Ise which raised the normal water level about a foot on the upstream side. One evening, when together with some friends I was passing the dam, I could see what seemed to be hundreds of fish all milling around in the water of the lower level, just in front of the dam. They were perch and were trying to get further upstream, presumably to spawn, but the water level was too low and the dam was barring their way. The local refuse tip was close by, so we scrambled over the fence and searched around until we found two or three bucket-sized tin cans. Thus, suitably armed with the necessary equipment, we returned to the brook and started to scoop up the fish, which was very easy to do as there were so many of them in such a small area. Then, with each can full, we carried them over the dam and set them free on the top side, watching as with unspoken thanks and a flick of their tails they darted away into the deeper water and the flow of the stream.

At one point in the brook there was a large pool which was the outflow point for the water from the sewage works and was home to eels. The water being discharged into the brook had been through a purification process and must have been very clean because I never remember anyone being ill from swimming in the Ise Brook, which supported so much wildlife and always looked crystal clear. The sewage works was along Valley Walk Road and one of our neighbours a couple of doors away had a lodger who worked there. This lodger had perfected the art of catching eels from this pool and there was many an evening when I would go round to their house and see two or three large eels still alive, curled up in the kitchen sink which was full of water. The eels made wonderful eating as they are very tasty, and even today some fish and chip shops sell them as 'rock salmon'.

Corporal punishment was something that was handed out at home and at school more or less in equal measure as a part of growing up, part of the learning curve. If you did something wrong and got caught, you knew what the penalty was likely to be; it was as simple as that. Although it hurt at the time, it didn't do me any harm and it taught me either not to do it again or to be more careful not to get caught. The pendulum of corporal punishment has, however, swung a very long way from when my father was a child. Whether it has swung too far is still a matter of great debate, but certainly my parents would not have recognised the arguments against it and there appears to be no happy medium. Dad had been born at the very end of the nineteenth century when Queen Victoria was still alive and had been brought up on the maxim of 'spare the rod and spoil the child'. Perhaps today we see the real truth in that maxim and the consequences of having completely abandoned it in repeated anti-social behaviour which simply didn't happen when I was young because the community didn't countenance it.

On the long winter evenings when the weather was too bad for us to go out to play, we would sit around the fire at home with my parents, and when dad was in the right mood, he would tell us of some of the things that he used to get up to when he was young before the Great War. Once, when he was about fifteen, he had been playing with his friends when some of them started to throw stones at the passing trains. This would have been around 1913. It wasn't long before the train drivers reported this hooliganism to Kettering station and the police very quickly came and rounded up the culprits, including dad, who swore that he didn't throw any stones. Nevertheless, as one of the oldest in the group, it was thought that he should have stopped the others and was therefore just as much to blame as those who had thrown the stones.

The punishment decided upon was eight lashes of the birch on the back, not to be given by the police but by dad's father, who was duly summoned to the police station. My grandfather was handed the birch and told to get on with it. After eight strokes, the police sergeant said that the first two strokes had not been hard enough and so dad had to be given another eight strokes. Undoubtedly, this was a harsh punishment, but throwing stones at passing trains was just as dangerous then as it is now, probably more so with open windows and non-toughened glass. The police officers and my grandfather were even more a product of the Victorian age than were my own parents.

Nevertheless, Dad was fairly free and easy with his leather belt and there were many occasions when he would give us all a thrashing if we had misbehaved. It wasn't that he was particularly cruel to us, because he wasn't; it was just the way it was. Art and I, however, had a secret weapon against dad that we would occasionally use if we thought that it would save our backsides – when the moment of retribution arrived and he started to pull his belt through the loops of his trousers, we would push our little sister Doris forward to be the first to receive the punishment. Just once in a while it worked; he would relent and we would get away with it.

My father was not a big man but grew up tough in a hard and unforgiving world. When the Great War came, he enlisted in the Army and went off to fight on the Western Front, where survival was not just a battle against the Germans, but against the elements and the appalling conditions of the trenches. His hard upbringing prepared him for that experience and helped him to survive it, as twenty years later mine would help me, too.

In the 1920s and 1930s when I was growing up, there was no television and we didn't really have a wireless set either. In 1933, though, dad did acquire a radio speaker. This he hired from Paul Taylor, the radio and bicycle shop in Kettering, for one shilling a week and, by flicking a two-way switch it would give us one of two programmes, the BBC National Programme or Radio Luxembourg. Wireless sets were relatively expensive at this time, but these speakers did the same job and Paul Taylor must have had them set up all over Kettering.

It was around this time that I got my first real glimpse of the future. In June 1919, John Alcock and Glaswegian Arthur Whitten (Teddie) Brown had become the first men to fly non-stop across the Atlantic when they flew a converted Great War Vickers Vimy bomber from Newfoundland to Connemara on the west coast of Ireland. The flight was far from trouble free in the freezing air above the ocean and on several occasions Brown, with no parachute, had to climb out onto the wings to break off the ice that had formed there. Even the landing was something of a mishap when Alcock put the aircraft down in what he thought was a lush green field but was actually a bog. Nevertheless, both men emerged unhurt and were knighted by Edward VII upon their return to England.

A few weeks later, the airship R-34 flew from East Fortune in Scotland to New York and then back again. The future of long-distance travel for fee-paying passengers seemed to be with airships, and in 1923 Ramsay MacDonald's Labour government commissioned two craft under the Imperial Airship Scheme to be built to the same specification, to assess their future viability for transporting mail and passengers throughout the British Empire. The immense 777 foot long R-101, the largest flying craft in the world at the time, was built at Cardington in Bedfordshire by the Air Ministry team, whilst the slightly smaller R-100, at 709 foot, was built by Vickers at Howden in Yorkshire.

The two teams were in competition with each other to see who could build the best airship, in the knowledge that only one team would survive and so they did not share any technical or development information. Vickers, however, had two gifted young engineers on their team who would become household names. The first, Barnes Wallis, who would invent the 'bouncing bomb' for the Dambusters' raid in May 1943, was to head up the design team, while the other, Nevil Shute Norway, better known as the author Nevil Shute, would be the chief technical calculator.

The two airships took six years to build, and at some time during the summer of 1930 I remember seeing them both, on separate occasions, go gliding gracefully by overhead. By then, both airships were stationed at Cardington in the vast hangars there, but disaster awaited. On 4th October 1930, the R-101 left Cardington for Karachi only to crash in northern France at 2.07am in the early hours of the following morning, having run into a local storm, killing all but six of the fifty-four passengers and crew. Amongst the dead were Lord Thomson, the Secretary of State for Air, Sir Sefton Brancker, the Director of Civil Aviation, and Lieutenant Colonel VC Richmond, the R-101's designer. Airship production in Britain was brought to an abrupt halt; the R-100 was scrapped and all development effort was put towards the aeroplane.

The Germans continued with their airship programme, probably as a cover for their military aircraft development and for a short time the *Hindenburg* enjoyed much popularity. However, on the evening of 6th May 1937 she succumbed to the same fate as the R-101 when she caught fire at her docking station in New Jersey. The age of the great airships was over.

The trouble for Britain was that during the 1920s we had lost six years of aeroplane development opportunity whilst concentrating on airships. Then, after the Wall Street crash, the years of the great depression had followed and there was precious little government money put into catching up on those lost years, a decision which would cost the RAF dear in the early years of World War Two when facing an enemy which had developed its aircraft technology and then tested it during the Spanish Civil War.

In 1931 I had a pet jackdaw. They made very good pets and were quite popular because they could be taught to speak. In the spring of that year when I was eight, I climbed up a tree and took a young jackdaw from its nest just before it was fledged. I had made it a cage which I hung high up in our porch and I would feed it bread and milk and taught it to answer to its name – Jack of course. Jack was very tame and would fly around the garden and land on the house roof, but I had to put him in his cage before I went to school each day. One thing he loved to do was to stand under the cold running water tap in the kitchen sink, but occasionally he would then fly onto the table and shake his feathers which mum didn't like. Sometimes when dad went off to work after lunch, Jack would follow him and land on his shoulder, so dad would have to run back with him. One morning however, no matter how much I called him, he wouldn't come down off the roof and I had to go to school and leave him there. When I got back home that evening Jack was gone and I never saw him again; he had returned to the wild where he belonged.

Although I did not have a job as a newspaper boy, around this time I would accompany my friends who delivered the Evening Telegraph and help them finish the round in half the time. Sometimes the round went to the far side of town where the very big houses were and occasionally we would be called back and given a penny by the more generous owners. Clutching the penny, on the way home we would call at the butchers on the corner of Stamford Road and Fuller Street which stayed open until well after eight o'clock. In the shed at the back of the shop the butcher made his faggots and a penny would buy one of these freshly made delights which we would hungrily eat out of the paper whilst sitting on the wall outside the shop.

One of the rounds went out as far as the village of Rushton which was about five miles from Kettering. The round was from WH Smith on Kettering railway station and was given to any of the young lads who had left school at fourteen but not yet in a factory job. One of these lads lived near me in Washington Square and I would help him with this round. Smith's supplied him with a heavy red bicycle with a carrier over the back wheel and in the winter it was necessary to have lights on the bike otherwise the police would have stopped us and reported Smith's. The lights were two small paraffin lamps showing red to the rear and white to the front, like miniature ships' lamps. As we cycled out to Rushton, I would sit astride the carrier and in the winter be able to warm my hands on the rear lamp. There was a village hall in Rushton which always had a coke stove burning in the winter and we would go in there after the round was done to have a warm before setting off back home. With us both riding on the bike, I had to be ready to jump off quickly if we saw a policeman as two on a bicycle, unless a tandem, was, and still is, against the law. The police knew that the paper boys often rode two on a bike and would stop us if they could, so I had to keep a sharp look out.

When I was older, I would also help Eric West with the farm milk round after school. We did this on push bikes, with a small churn of milk hanging between us from the handle bars. At each house we delivered to, we would use the half pint ladle to measure out the milk into the jugs brought out from the house. It had its fringe benefits though because on the hot summer evenings during the round we would stop and dip the ladle into the churn and have a lovely cool drink of fresh milk, barely an hour out of the cow.

Whenever we could, we were out of doors playing games and running about or off along the Valley Walk. Only wealthy people had cars before the war and so as children we walked everywhere or else rode a bicycle. Consequently we were all very fit and it was most unusual to see a child who was over-weight. Apart from time spent in school lessons or reading at home, we always seemed to be on the go. There were plenty of team games to be played either on the green or around the neighbourhood. 'Release', 'Stig-Stag' and 'Catty and Stick' were three popular games. 'Release', which was much better played in the dark and involved a lighted street lamp, was always a favourite during the winter evenings.

The local refuse tip close to the Valley Walk was a readily available source for all sorts of free materials for our various activities of which canoe making for use on the Ise Brook during the summer months was a favourite. After the gates had been closed and the men who worked there had gone home, we would slip under the fence and scavenge around for the basic materials; timber and canvas or roofing felt. Once obtained, these hitherto discarded items would be made into simple one-man canoes which we spent many happy hours paddling up and down the brook.

The central area of Washington Square was open space, a traditional piece of green on which various community events took place and where as children we spent much of our free time playing. There was never any homework to do from school so once lessons were finished for the day, our time was our own. It wasn't all play time however, as we had jobs to do at home to help mum and dad. There were about thirty children living around the Square and so the green was a favourite place for a game of football, other ball games and for kite flying. We made all our own kites and one popular addition when flying them at night was to give them a fiery tail. With so many boot and shoe manufacturers in the town, there was always plenty of waste rubber and leather to be retrieved from the factories or the refuse tip. So these sources were duly visited and, having gathered some waste rubber, we would cut it up into strips, tie a piece to the end of the kite's tail and then light it. The smell was awful, but the kite was soon airborne and the smell with it. As the kite played on the wind high above our heads we could see the glowing rubber on the tails and in the right conditions gleefully watched the sparks shower down around Washington Square, although this was a somewhat less attractive spectacle to the householders whose roofs were underneath the molten rubber, which left quite a mess.

The cinema was then just as much as it is now an opportunity to escape from reality and enter the world of fantasy. When I started going to the children's matinees at the Empire cinema, they were still showing silent films with sub-titles. I was really too young to be able to read most of what was on the screen, but Art would read it out for me and the other smaller children. Many of the children's films were serialised so that we would have to go again the following week to find out how our hero had escaped from his latest predicament. The cinema was also an important source of news and information for adults. Through Pathé News, the latest national and international events, celebrity trivia and sporting highlights were brought in pictures and commentary to an audience without television or twenty-four-hour news programmes. Although the events portrayed were usually several days old at best, they were nevertheless an important source of visual information and particularly so in the late 1930s as the war approached.

These were the days when most people smoked, when lighting a cigarette was as essential to the plot of a film script as were the words, when children could go to the corner shop and buy a packet of five Senior Service or Woodbine "for me dad". It was also the golden age of the cigarette card. Collections of fifty or more in a series were available from the manufacturers of all the leading brands of the day. Players, WD & HO Wills, Imperial, Gallaghers and others put these picture cards in their cigarette packets, pictures which covered a wide range of subjects, including aeroplanes, kings and queens, film stars, motor cars, birds, ships, sports people; almost anything. Of course, we avidly collected these cards, which we called 'photos' [pronounced 'foatees'], and were always ready to swap our doubles. Now, every so often, one of these complete collections of cards will turn up on the BBC's Antiques Roadshow and I am always surprised at how much the rarer collections are worth.

Computers, iPods, iPads, iPhones and X-boxes were not even the stuff of science fiction; instead we made our own entertainment and I think that we were much happier for it, too, even though we had so little money to spend. We did, though, read a great deal and the children's comic magazines of the day were very popular. So, having read the Hotspur, the Rover or the Adventure I would then swap it for one of the others amongst my friends. Many a time there would be a knock at the door in the evening and mum would tell me that there was a lad wanting to know if I had any comics to swap.

We were certainly not well-off, but there were many families much poorer than us, and my parents managed their money very carefully. There were no quarterly bills; everything was paid for in cash at the time of purchase, or weekly. I don't think that my mum or my dad ever had a bank account. Mum and Dad both worked, as did most people in Kettering before the war, in the boot and shoe manufacturing trade; for dad it was at the Freeman, Hardy & Willis factory. He was paid in cash and he in turn paid all the bills in cash; that was the way it was. Clothes generally were bought by weekly payment through a club, as were any larger items. The gas was on a penny meter and when the gasman came to empty it on his regular round, he would stack the pennies on the kitchen table in shilling piles. Mum always had a small rebate from this and there was usually a penny or ha'penny for Art, Doris and me.

Even when the three of us were quite small, our mother worked at Allan & Caswells, which was the boot factory at the top of the street. We always looked forward to Friday nights when we would meet her coming from work; Friday was pay day and she would give us each a penny from her wages to spend on sweeties or whatever we wanted. However, we were only allowed to spend up to a ha'penny on Friday night, the rest had to last us through the week. It wasn't for nothing, though, as Art, Doris and I all had jobs to do when we got home from school each day, which was often before either mum or dad got in from work, and one of my main tasks was to make sure that a fire had been lit in the grate.

The electricity was also on a meter but this took shillings not pennies and there was no rebate. The rent for the house was paid weekly to the Council, and from the age of about ten it was my job to take the fourteen shillings [70p today] down to the Council, offices which were opposite Marks & Spencer in Kettering. Payment to the baker who delivered the bread to us every morning was an altogether more informal affair. He would call to collect his money fairly late on a Saturday evening; however, very often by the time he was due to call my parents had gone out to the North Park Club for a drink, leaving us three young children alone in the house. Presently, the baker would arrive, walk in through the back door, which was never locked, and come into the dining room where we were sitting by the fire.

He would greet us with a cheery "Hello", walk over to the mantelpiece, lift up the large vase which stood there, retrieve the money which mum had left underneath it, always the right amount, and then, with an equally sunny "Cheerio", he would leave us and go on to his next customer. Neither the baker, my parents nor we children gave the circumstances of this weekly visitation the slightest thought. Rather like Mr Simms the football trainer, this would cause such consternation today that Social Services would probably take us away. But these were very different times, communities were small and tight, people took care of each other and there was nothing unusual in what my parents did; it was normal behaviour then. Times change.

"Art, Doris & Reg in early 1926"

"Adults l-r, mum, Aunt Nell & dad with Art & Betty standing, Reg & Doris kneeling"

"St Mary's School football team 1933. Reg sitting front left. Mr Simms at the back"

Chapter Two

"I slip, I slide, I gloom, I glance,
Among my skimming swallows;
I make the netted sunbeam dance
Against my sandy shallows."

- From '*The Brook*'; Alfred, Lord Tennyson

In 1934 I moved up to the seniors, which for me was the Parish Church School in Dalkeith Place. However, instead of a ten-minute walk to school, it was now twice as far and with coming home for lunch each day it meant that I spent nearly one and a half hours every day walking to and fro. The school had a very good choir, which I joined, although it did mean practising after hours. Nevertheless, we did well and lifted the shield at various eisteddfods quite a few times. Mr Loake was the music master, and when we were practising, his son would come in and play the piano for us. It was also at this school that I was introduced to Shakespeare.

Thinking again of how times have changed, our school was close to the road and, although there weren't many cars or lorries on the road, every now and then a funeral would go by. Whenever this happened, our teacher would make us stand to attention until the procession had gone by. Policemen on duty in the street would salute a funeral as it went by, too. I can't remember the last time I saw that happen except on state occasions.

In the winter evenings, before the snow and ice came, we would roller-skate up and down Barnwell Street. All the children had roller skates and no-one complained about us playing in the street. It was the same for the girls, too, as they were always running around playing their own games like skipping, hopscotch, chase, What's the Time Mr Wolf and so on. It's what children did then. However, all this walking to and from school and active play was typical of the era before children went everywhere in cars and when added to the time spent playing football and doing PT at school, it is no wonder that as a generation we were very fit when growing up.

Whatever the causes of global warming may be, there is no doubt that there is a significant difference in the seasons of Britain now from the way they were during the first half of the twentieth century. This is not just a view of the past through rose-coloured glasses but a reality from the activities which we enjoyed as children then but which are simply not predictably possible now. The summers were sunnier and the winters were much colder, with more snowfall over a prolonged period.

Every early winter the Ise Brook would fill up and overflow onto its small flood plain as it wound its way through the valley towards Wicksteed Park. The rain would keep the brook full until the winter frosts came and then the flood water would freeze solid; it made a wonderful rink for us and we skated for hours in safety. Even the dark evenings of school days didn't stop this exciting pastime. We would go into the nearby refuse tip and pick up drums of various sizes, fill them with any combustible material we could find there, wood, roofing felt, paper, anything that would burn, place them around the edge of the ice, set them alight and start skating.

It was very rare that the ice would crack and break because it was so thick from the constant freezing temperatures, but if it did, the worst that would happen was that whoever fell through would get their legs wet as the water was only a foot or so deep. Nearly all youngsters, and many adults, too, owned a pair of ice skates, most of which had been bought from the Sports & Rubber Company at the top of Gold Street in Kettering. Another regular winter pastime was to go sledging on the steep slope of Mill Road, below Fuller Street. There was hardly any traffic then and the Council certainly didn't waste money on gritting the roads.

Evidence of this change in our climate can be seen in the news broadcasts today; a week of freezing temperatures or a couple of inches of snow hits the headlines and the country struggles to function. When I was growing up, such winter weather would have been considered a mild spell. Six inches of snow would regularly fall overnight and the temperature would not rise above freezing for weeks, but life simply carried on. Part of that was that there was much less dependency upon electricity and particularly upon the motor car. People walked or bicycled short distances to work rather than drive forty miles each way. The railways were used for longer commuting journeys, but again there was little use of electricity on them outside London and the South East. Instead, the trains were pulled by steam engines, the points and signals were all manually operated and the railway companies employed linemen whose job it was to keep the track clear of snow and leaves and the points and signals free from ice. In the golden age of railways, they didn't suffer from the wrong kind of snow.

To help us to keep warm when we were out playing at the weekends during the long winter months, we dug a tunnel into the side of a piece of waste ground along the Valley Walk and then formed a chamber at the end large enough for four or five boys to crouch in. Later we improved this by building a small stove in the chamber, complete with a piece of pipe recovered from the refuse tip to form a chimney. When we lit the fire in the stove we found that, although some of the smoke went up the pipe, most of it came into the chamber as there wasn't enough draw on the fire. Of course, by the time I got home my clothes stank of wood smoke and this would result in a smack around the ear from one or other of my parents, who had to work hard to buy those clothes for me.

New Year's Day 1937 was bright, sunny and cold. The crisp frozen snow lay deep on the ground and as I lay in bed I could see my breath condensing as I breathed out into the chill air of my bedroom; I didn't want to get up and leave the warmth of the covers, but the fire had to be lit before mum and dad got up. This was the year that I would turn fourteen and leave school at Easter. Art was already working at the Maypole stores and it was time for me to look for work, too.

I had already been to the Boot & Shoe works in Havelock Road to see if they had vacancies coming up at Easter, but as soon as it opened again on Monday, 4th January after the New Year holiday weekend, I went to see if they had any news for me. However, I was told that they had my name and address and would let me know if they had any suitable vacancies. I was disappointed, but, in any event, fate had other plans for me.

One dismal morning in early February, Mr Loake introduced us to a man I instantly recognised as Mr Swingler, the local secretary for the Royal British Legion. The Midland Region Headquarters was being moved from Bristol to Kettering and Mr Swingler, after telling us a little about the work of the RBL, said that he was looking for two suitable boys to work in the records office. I was very interested and asked to be considered. "Hello, Reg Payne, I didn't know that you were here. I'd be very pleased to put you forward for an interview, although it won't be with me."

Mr Swingler lived very near to us and that was how he knew me and my parents. True to his word, a few days later, he called at the house to tell me to go for an interview with Captain Bates, the Midland Region Benevolent Agent. The interview was the usual sort of thing to assess my basic educational standard and suitability, in particular my neatness of writing and figures. I wasn't told how I got on at the time, but within the week I received a letter at home, which itself was quite a novelty, offering me the job and asking me to write back if I wanted to accept it, starting after Easter. I certainly did as this was a very good job to have and it paid very well; my wages would be seventeen shillings and six pence a week. At this time the usual wages for a fourteen-year-old boy would be ten shillings a week.

So, on Monday, 12th April 1937, I entered the front hall of Avenue House in Rockingham Road and became part of the world of work. I also became the envy of all my friends because, not only was I paid very well, but I didn't start until 9.30am, whereas most workers had been at work for two hours by then. It later transpired that my generous wages were the result of an error; the RBL had thought that I was sixteen and had paid me accordingly; however, I didn't have to repay the extra money.

We had over 300,000 files to look after, and a huge backlog in the processing of applications by members for help from the Legion had built up during the period of the move. The elderly chief clerk was very slow and eventually had a nervous breakdown. By then I had been joined by another young lad and, with the help of one of the women from the upstairs office, we set about getting through the backlog and bringing the whole system into order. The three of us were so efficient at this that soon there wasn't enough work for two clerks and I was moved from being full time in the filing room to spending each afternoon working in the accounts office.

Now that I was earning, I was able to give my wages to mum each week for my keep. She let me have three shillings for myself and also bought me a new bicycle to get to work on. It was a Humber and cost £4-19s-6d, although with three-speed gears it would have been an extra pound.

During the summer of 1937, with the farmer's permission, we spent a lot of our weekends camping in one of his fields near Islip Mill. Like everyone else, my working week at the British Legion included Saturday mornings, but after lunch, off we went to collect our sleeping bags, tents and cooking pots from the barn on the farm where we kept them and set about pitching camp. We would cut away the turf from a small area and then build and light the camp fire, which would burn all weekend and on which we would cook our food. Some of the lads, including my brother Art, had to work until eight o'clock on Saturday evening and so the rest of us would usually walk along to the road to meet them around nine.

We passed the time canoeing and swimming in the river and gravel pits nearby or watching the abundance of wildlife that was always around us. As Sunday evening began to draw close, the fire was let out and then, just to be sure, we would douse it with water from the river before replacing the turf clods that we had lifted the day before. When we left, there were hardly any signs that we had been there at all.

The news coming out of Germany was increasingly serious. I was really still too young to fully understand the implications of all that was happening, but after the Nazis' 1936 Nuremberg Rally and the start of the Spanish Civil War, I realised that dad was becoming ever more concerned about the situation in Europe. He had been through the horrors of the trenches and didn't want his sons to have to do the same. The radio speaker was always switched to the BBC at news time and we would all sit and listen in silence whilst the news reader brought the country up to date.

The Olympics had been staged in Berlin during August 1936 and the news included short accounts of the major events and the results. The black American athlete Jesse Owens, grandson of a slave, was the star of the Games and shattered Hitler's Aryan race propaganda when he won gold medals in the 100 metre, 200 metre and 4 x 100 metre races, together with the long jump, a feat not equalled until Carl Lewis repeated it in the 1984 Olympics.

Hitler's intention at the Games was to shake hands only with the German medallists, but the Olympic officials told him that he would shake hands with all the medallists or none at all; he chose the latter. After Owens had won the 100 metre final, Hitler left the stadium, and it was generally reported that he had done so to snub the American, who was asked at the time what he thought about Hitler leaving. He is reported to have replied, "*Hitler had a certain time to come to the stadium and a certain time to leave. It happened he had to leave before the victory ceremony after the 100 metres, but before he left I was on my way to a broadcast and passed near his box. He waved at me and I waved back. I think it was bad taste to criticise the 'man of the hour' in another country.*"

Back home in the United States, racial discrimination was widespread and Owens received no official recognition for his achievements from President Franklin D Roosevelt or his successor Harry Truman. It was not until Dwight Eisenhower became president after the war that Jesse Owens received the recognition that he deserved. When asked how he felt, Owens tellingly replied, *"Hitler didn't snub me; it was FDR who snubbed me. The President didn't even send me a telegram."* Hitler, though, had sent Owens a commemorative inscribed photograph of himself. In private, however, the German Chancellor had been incensed that a Negro athlete had excelled so outstandingly at the Games. Perhaps this all says more about the character of Jesse Owens than of the politicians of the day.

Despite Stanley Baldwin and then Neville Chamberlain following a foreign policy of appeasement towards the Nazis, the British government was slowly waking up to the warnings which Winston Churchill had been giving for some considerable time, and by early 1937 had begun to make serious preparations for the increasingly likely war with Germany.

During the Great War, and particularly from 1916 onwards, aircraft had been shown to be of critical importance as a weapon and represented the future of warfare. The zeppelin bombing raids over London and the South East between 1915 and 1917 had demonstrated that future wars would involve the civilian population more than ever before through large-scale bombing raids. Some two hundred people had been killed by these zeppelin raids, the first of which was as early as 31st May 1915 when number 16, Alkham Road in Stoke Newington became the first property in Britain ever to be bombed from an aircraft and, although no-one suffered any serious injuries there, shortly afterwards seven people died and thirty-five were injured in Hackney and Stratford in the East End before the airship left London and made its escape.

At first, the zeppelins flew too high for the early fighters of the Royal Flying Corps, but once more advanced aircraft were developed, the airship crews were doomed and the final raid took place on 19th October 1917, a raid which claimed the lives of another thirty-three people.

The government, and the Air Ministry in particular, realised that in future wars air superiority would be critical and that the ability to bomb the enemy's homeland would be an essential requirement. This conclusion was borne out during the 1930s with the development of twin-engine bombers, which were much faster, more manoeuvrable and had a greater range than zeppelins. The devastating effect of bombers on civilians and the attendant huge numbers of casualties had been demonstrated by the Nazis in the Spanish conflict.

As well as having an attacking force, we also needed a defence force. In April 1937, the Air Raid Wardens' Service [ARP] was formed and by the time of the Munich crisis in September the following year some 700,000 men and women had volunteered, many of the men being Great War veterans.

With 1938 came more bad news. The clouds of war were gathering thick and fast over Europe. The then Home Secretary, Sir Samuel Hoare, knew the value of women's voluntary work, and so, on 16th May founded the Women's Voluntary Service for Air Raid Precautions, the WVS. He appointed the redoubtable Lady Reading, who had been a nurse during the 1914-18 war, as its head. As soon as the war came, their role quickly changed, becoming as diversified as the jobs they undertook, and by 1941 the ranks of the WVS had swelled to over a million women. They helped to evacuate one and a half million children and nursing mothers from the cities, provided food and clothing for refugees arriving here from Europe, and helped displaced families after bombing raids by organising rest centres, washing facilities, food preparation and a clothing bank for those who had lost everything. They worked with local authorities administering mobile mortuaries, co-ordinated recycling facilities and supported the other Civil Defence services with mobile canteens. The involvement of the WVS was as limitless as the energy of its members, almost all of whom were volunteers and even had to buy their own uniform. Intended to be disbanded in 1947, the WVS received the Royal Warrant in 1966 and is still going strong today.

By the autumn, the gradual and inexorable drift towards war was becoming an irresistible force. With the looming Munich crisis coming to a head in September, it was time to mobilise women into uniform. The Women's Army Auxiliary Corps had been founded in 1917 and served with the British Army until 1921. On 9th September, whilst Prime Minister Neville Chamberlain prepared for the Munich Conference with Hitler at the end of the month to negotiate a lasting peace, the Women's Auxiliary Territorial Service, the ATS, was re-formed. The earliest women's voluntary corps, the First Aid Nursing Yeomanry [the FANY], was affiliated to the ATS and, although not part of it, would produce some outstandingly courageous women as Special Operations Executive [SOE] agents, including Nancy Wake, the most highly decorated allied woman of the war, Odette Sansome, and Violette Szabo. The ATS fulfilled a very wide range of duties but were kept particularly busy during the early years of the war as searchlight crews and anti-aircraft battery crews. After D-Day, many ATS women went over to Normandy supporting the advancing troops.

Despite the build-up to war, we tried to carry on as normal and enjoy whatever peacetime there was left. During the summer of 1938 we regularly camped at the weekend in a field at Denford, which was somewhat better than at Islip because there was a spring nearby where we could get fresh drinking water without having to boil it first. The farmer's wife was very kind to us here and would sometimes invite us up to the farm, where she had set up a table in the yard and would give us tea and homemade cake.

In early 1939 there was an outbreak of typhoid in Kettering. My brother Art and the man next door were two of its first victims. I remember going to visit Art in the isolation hospital along the Rockingham Road, but we were not allowed to go in so had to simply see him through the closed windows and try to have some sort of conversation. Kettering had been suffering from a water shortage during the late 1930s and a new steel water pipe was laid to the town's pumping station from Wicksteed Park Lake which may have been the source of the typhoid. Typhoid was not uncommon in the days before the purification which gives us the clean drinking water that we take so much for granted now, and many of Britain's towns and cities had suffered similar outbreaks over the years. Art and our neighbour survived, but since they had both worked with food before their illness, they were now not allowed to do so again and became unemployed.

Perhaps because I was working at the British Legion offices, or perhaps because I was growing up, or perhaps simply because it was unavoidable, I was becoming increasingly absorbed by the news and the political developments that were taking place in Europe and the activities of the Nazis in particular. Some of the news I got from listening to the BBC National Programme through our speaker at home, other news I heard at the RBL, where the prospect of another war with Germany was viewed with dread and incredulity. However, the most graphic view of the world's current affairs came through the Pathé Newsreels which were shown at the pictures.

Although Neville Chamberlain had returned from his meeting in Munich with Hitler at the end of the previous September with an agreement that he had famously referred to as 'peace for our time', it very soon became clear that it wasn't. Gas masks had continued to be issued to the whole civilian population and there was talk of children being evacuated from the cities soon. Hitler's response to peace for our time became clear on St. Valentine's Day 1939, when he launched the world's largest battleship, the *Bismarck*. In Britain, by the spring it had become commonplace to see RAF aircraft flying over the countryside and Kettering was no exception.

In March, German troops entered Czechoslovakia as Hitler declared that it had ceased to exist, in clear violation of the Munich Agreement. He also demanded the return of Danzig and the 'Polish Corridor' to the Reich; the final pieces for war were falling into place. But March 1939 was also my sixteenth birthday and I began to realise that it wasn't only the world around me that was changing; I was, too. I became increasingly conscious of girls and their natural attraction. This in turn made me much more conscious of my own appearance and I started to take a greater pride in my clothes, even to the extent of being measured for a tailor-made suit to go out in.

One day, my sister Doris came home from work and, with a blush and a giggle, said that a girl she worked with had told her that she would like me to take her to the pictures one Saturday evening. I vaguely knew the girl and this was to be my very first date and a big step in growing up. Doreen was very pretty and I said that I would take her, so the next Saturday I met her close to where she lived and we went to see whatever film was showing. Girls grow up quicker than boys and she clearly had greater expectations of me than I had of myself. I didn't hold her hand during the film or kiss her; I didn't even walk her home afterwards, which was not very gallant of me; unsurprisingly, she didn't ask me to take her out again.

In April, Britain signed the mutual assistance pact with Poland and the stage was set. By now recognising that the Munich Agreement was a worthless piece of paper and that war with Germany was inevitable, the Government passed the Military Training Act, which required all men aged twenty and twenty-one to register for six months' military training. The Act was designed to quickly create and equip a substantial standing army and also made exemptions for those in the reserved occupations listed as farmers, scientists, merchant seamen, railway workers, utility workers [gas, water and electricity], miners and dockers. Neither Art nor I was old enough to be affected by this Act but it was another indication of the rapidly deteriorating situation in Europe and of the impending war.

As the spring turned to summer, the sense of a looming conflict grew stronger. Wherever you went, whomever you spoke to, sooner or later the conversation would turn to the subject of war. In the spring it was "Do you think there really will be another war with Germany?" By the summer, it was "When do you think the war will start?"

On 20th June, the Women's Auxiliary Air Force, the WAAF, was formed. Women had first served in the air force as the WRAF when the amalgamation of the Royal Flying Corps and the Royal Naval Flying Service on 1st April 1918 created the Royal Air Force. The WRAF was disbanded in 1920. Unlike the ATS, which was a separate women's unit, WAAFs served within the main body of the RAF on individual stations. The first Director of the WAAF was Katherine Trefusis-Forbes, who had served in the Women's Volunteer Reserve in the Great War.

As well as more traditional female roles, WAAFs undertook work as drivers, parachute packers, cooks, mechanics, fitters, electricians, engineers, barrage balloon crews, code breakers, radar controllers and plotters, aerial photography interpreters, pilots with the Air Transport Auxiliary and as SOE agents. One of the most courageous who had transferred from the FANY was Noor Inayat Khan, the first woman to go into occupied Europe as an agent. She was captured, tortured and executed by the Gestapo in Dachau concentration camp.

June was also the month that the Women's Land Army [WLA] was re-formed. It had first been created in 1917 to help combat the U-boat blockade which so nearly strangled us during the Great War, when Britain only held enough food for about three weeks; it is a good job that we didn't know that within two years we would be in an even worse position with less than a fortnight's food supply in the country. The WLA was disbanded in 1919 but the government at least remembered the great contribution it had made in the last war and now re-formed it with women once more in charge.

Many farmers were reluctant to take on these Land Girls but soon came to value the work they did, work which was hard by any measure. There was little mechanisation on farms; Shires and Clydesdale horses provided the motive power, with almost everything from milking to harvesting done by hand. Only the larger farms had a small tractor and even they kept horses too.

July saw the Women's Royal Naval Service, the WRNS, re-formed. Like the WLA, the WRNS had been formed in 1917 when the Navy was the first of the Services to recruit women, but it was disbanded two years later when peace returned. Women in the WRNS were known as Wrens and served at home and overseas as drivers, cooks, administrative staff, radar and communication operators, weather forecasters and code breakers at Bletchley Park. Wrens also staffed the Naval Censorship Branch and many were involved with the planning operations for the invasion of Europe. Those who spoke other languages, especially German and French were posted to coastal stations where they intercepted and translated enemy signals. Others operated small tugs and harbour craft ferrying sailors to and from ships anchored away from the quayside. In all, Wrens carried out some two hundred different jobs for the Navy. Women were going to be involved in this war like never before; indeed, the whole population was going to be involved like never before.

"Art & Reg [left] in their front garden 1936"

"Reg with his hand made model of a Short Bros Empire flying boat, summer 1939"

Chapter Three

"They went with songs to the battle, they were young,
Straight of limb, true of eye, steady and aglow.
They were staunch to the end against odds uncounted,
They fell with their faces to the foe."
- From 'For the Fallen'; Lawrence Binyon

At 11 o'clock on the morning of Sunday, 3rd September 1939, the Third Reich brought the world into which I had been born and through which I had enjoyed my childhood to a shattering end: nothing would ever be quite the same again. On that Sunday morning, we were all home from church early and sitting close to the radio speaker in our kitchen. We already knew from the newspapers and the radio that two days earlier the Germans had invaded Poland and about the terrible mass bombing of Warsaw and how the Polish Army and Air Force had been destroyed; we also knew that the British government had given Hitler an ultimatum to withdraw from Poland by 11 o'clock on this fateful morning or Britain would go to war.

Prayers had been said in church for a peaceful solution, but I don't think that anyone really thought that there was now any possibility of one. We didn't have long to wait for confirmation of those fears. At 11.15am, the BBC announcer Alvar Lidell introduced Neville Chamberlain who told an expectant nation that we were now at war with Germany. The implications of the Prime Minister's announcement had a much greater impact upon my parents' generation because the Great War was still so fresh in their memories, having finished barely twenty years earlier and they knew what war with Germany involved.

We expected the Luftwaffe to arrive at any moment to bomb our cities with the same devastating effect that we had seen reported on the Pathé News in the cinemas during the Spanish Civil War, but it didn't happen. Orders went out that we were to carry our gas masks wherever we went and all windows had to be covered with blackout material, making sure that no chink of light could be seen from outside. It was the ARPs who were mainly responsible for policing the blackout and the shout of "Put that light out" was heard along many a street, along with a suitable riposte from householders who felt that some ARPs took their authority a little too far. The fear was that a chink of light could help an attacking bomber crew, but in reality it is highly unlikely that such a sliver could be seen from 10,000 feet. Nevertheless, the blackout was an essential precaution and was strictly enforced for much of the war.

The weather that autumn was particularly warm and pleasant, and as the anticipated bombing attacks and invasion did not materialise, normality took over and we drifted into the period of what became known as the 'phoney war'. It was apparently the same for the Germans, who called it 'der sitzkrieg', the sitting war, although it wasn't quite so in Scotland. On the night of 14th October, the U-47, commanded by Kapitänleutnant Günther Prien, slipped past the defences of the Royal Navy's supposedly impregnable main anchorage at Scapa Flow in the Orkney Islands and sank the World War I battleship HMS *Royal Oak* with great loss of life. Fortunately, most of our more modern capital ships were out at sea, but nevertheless the sinking of *Royal Oak* inside Scapa Flow was a tremendous propaganda coup for the Germans and was equally embarrassing to the Royal Navy.

Two days later, at lunch time on 16th October, the first bombs of the Second World War to fall on a British target were dropped out of a clear blue sky onto our warships at anchor off South Queensferry, near to the famous Victorian railway bridge, when nine enemy bombers flew across the North Sea and up the Firth of Forth. The first civilian casualty of the war was also in the Orkney Islands and the first bombs to land on British soil were in the Shetlands. It wasn't much of a phoney war in Scotland.

The Military Training Act proved to be wholly insufficient. By October, and more than a month into the war, we were still a long way short of a million men in the Services and so the government introduced conscription for all men between eighteen and forty-one who were not in reserved occupations. Call-up was by age and started with men between twenty and twenty-three. The conscription call-up age was very quickly lowered from twenty to eighteen and this affected Art. Like many of us, he was anxious to join the RAF and he immediately volunteered; had he waited to be called up, he would have had to go into whatever Service he was allocated. Despite having had typhoid, he passed all his fitness and education tests and was accepted for aircrew, destined to become a wireless operator/air gunner with 49 Squadron in Bomber Command. However, just before he left home to join the RAF, mum dropped her own bombshell when she gave birth to Brian, a baby brother for us.

The winter of 1939/40 was bitterly cold and still remains one of the coldest on record. The lovely Indian summer which we had enjoyed that autumn seemed to roll on and November and early December were very mild, but then the temperature began to tumble, bringing hard frosts and fog at night. The days were lovely and clear, but with no warmth in the sun the frost barely lifted. The freezing weather stayed all over Christmas and the New Year and, apart from a very brief spell early in January, we were snow and frost bound until late February, with a biting east wind that went straight through you. It just kept on getting colder each day and that January would become the coldest month in Britain since February 1895. Rhayader in Powys recorded a low of -23.3°C, a record at the time, whilst Newport in Shropshire got down to -20°C. The Thames froze over for eight miles between Teddington and Sunbury, ice covered stretches of the Mersey, the Humber and the Severn, and even the sea froze at Bognor Regis, Folkestone and Southampton.

But there was much worse to come. In the early hours of Friday, 26th January, it started to snow heavily across eastern Britain, and Kettering wasn't spared. It continued all over the weekend without letting up until well into the following Monday. Falling onto the frozen ground, it soon built up and drifted in the strong east wind. I had quite a struggle to get to work on that Friday morning. However, by lunchtime the offices closed and we were sent home, a very rare event in those days. All weekend, the storm continued. I sat in our kitchen by the fire and watched as frantic snowflakes swirled past the windows in a hypnotic frenzy, blown almost horizontal by the strong wind. It was far too cold and the snow too thick to go out unless you had to. We kept the fire burning all the time and it wasn't long before the electricity went off because the power lines had been brought down by the weight of snow and ice on them.

Art was doing his initial training at Blackpool during this terrible weather but managed to get home on leave one weekend, although he had a lot of trouble getting back again because of the deep snow. The conditions were the same all across Europe and this was one reason why the war seemed to have stalled. The British Expeditionary Force (the BEF) over in France waiting for the Germans to attack had a particularly hard time of it living under canvas, trying to keep their equipment ready for action. Later it transpired that the morale of the troops had been badly affected by this long hard winter.

For a week after the storm, Kettering virtually came to a standstill, as did much of Britain, but slowly things began to move and people could return to work, although the lack of electricity was a problem in some factories and offices. It was late February before the thaw really came and the snow and ice melted away, but before then I had enjoyed some very happy hours ice skating on the flooded meadows beside the Ise.

Along with the thaw at the end of that dreadful winter came our Anderson shelter in anticipation of the forthcoming bombing raids. Once the ice had released its grip on the ground in our back garden, I set to and dug the hole, then dad and I put together the corrugated iron sheeting to make the shelter. The next job was for me to heap all the soil which I had dug out of the hole against the sides and on top of the sheeting to a depth of about two feet. The ground around Washington Square was very wet and the water table was close to the surface, consequently it wasn't long before the shelter filled up with water. It was so bad that the Council had to come and line it with concrete so that we could use it, which we did on many occasions, although as the war went on, we used it less and tended to stay in the warmth of our beds when the air-raid sirens sounded.

Friday, 10th May 1940 was the day when Europe exploded. The Germans launched their *Blitzkrieg* attack on the Low Countries, within a week coming around the end of the heavily defended French Maginot Line and into France. That evening, King George VI summoned Winston Churchill to Buckingham Palace and asked him to form a government, replacing Neville Chamberlain as Prime Minister.

On Tuesday 14th the Home Secretary Anthony Eden announced the formation of a new organisation to be known as the Local Defence Volunteer Force, soon to be re-named the Home Guard, and called for all men over sixteen and not eligible for military service for whatever reason, to go to their local police station and volunteer for this force, which would be part of the Home defences. Eden had expected a few thousand men to come forward, but police stations across the country were inundated as within six weeks more than one and a half million men volunteered.

I was seventeen by now and so, with most of my friends, I volunteered straight away and was detailed to 'D' company, which had its headquarters in the changing rooms on the grammar school playing fields alongside Wicksteed Park. We were given a fairly basic training but it included being taught to fire a Ross army rifle on the firing range at Sywell and to use a bayonet. Although I was on duty most nights, like everyone else, I still had my day job for the British Legion at Avenue House, which was the HQ of another of the four companies of the Kettering Home Guard Battalion. Our duties included patrolling the outskirts of Kettering and general duty at Cransley Reservoir in case German paratroopers should land in the area. I remember one night as I was leaving the house to go on duty, my dad said to me, "You do know, boy, don't you, you wouldn't stand a chance if you really did meet a German paratrooper."

"Well, maybe not, but we could shoot one or two as they came down and we know the area like the back of our hand, so we could slip away easily enough." He just smiled knowingly.

I really didn't want to think about what he had said, but he had been through the last war in the trenches of the Western Front and knew what we were up against and just how good our enemy was. Perhaps it was just as well that I had the naivety of youth because, of course, he was right.

Another of our nightly duties was to place a guard on the roads and railway bridges on the outskirts of Kettering. After dark, all vehicles entering the town had to be stopped and the driver was required to produce his identity cards. It would usually be a corporal who would hold his hand up and stop the vehicle whilst I stood in front of it pointing my rifle at the driver. One evening after the blackout time, we saw a van coming down the road with its headlamps on dip beam and shielded. The corporal stepped out into the road, stopped the van and asked the driver for his identity cards. While he was doing this, I slowly walked around the van, all the time pointing my rifle at the driver. After a few moments, the driver shouted out to the corporal who was examining the cards,

"Hey, corporal, I don't mind being stopped but will you tell that young lad not to keep pointing his rifle at me."

"Don't worry, mate, it's not loaded," replied the corporal. "I keep the bullets in my pocket!" I didn't tell dad about the incident, he would only have hurt himself when he fell off his chair laughing.

As the spring gave way to the early summer of 1940, the British Expeditionary Force were pushed back to Dunkirk and then rescued from the beaches by the armada of small boats which went across the English Channel to save them. It was not only the scale of the BEF's defeat that shocked us all but also the speed with which the Germans had achieved it. Within six weeks from 10th May, they had swept through Holland and Belgium, and on into France, taking Paris with ease. The much-vaunted Maginot Line had been a complete failure and the six-million-strong French forces had surrendered; the largest standing army in the world had been swept aside with an ease which filled us with dread.

"What General Weygand called the Battle for France is over; the Battle of Britain is about to begin." The words of Winston Churchill rang in our ears all through the long hot days of the beautiful summer that was 1940 as RAF Fighter Command took the war to the Luftwaffe crews in the skies over southern and eastern England, and with it the freedom of these islands and the British nation.

Not everyone was quite so anxious to 'do their bit', let alone actually get involved in the war or in saving us from invasion. There were plenty of advertisements in the newspapers for a 'quiet country retreat', a 'sanctuary hotel' or some similar description, where people who had money could go and be certain, as far as anything was certain, that they would be untroubled by the German bombers. They were advertisements for funk holes. These were not about conscientious objectors, some of whom served with great courage in non-combatant roles such as stretcher bearers or in bomb-disposal teams; they were hideaways for rich cowards who were generally despised by everyone, whether rich or poor, who was fighting the enemy.

All through that summer and autumn, the bombing of Britain's towns and cities increased and the factories around Kettering were frequent targets for the Luftwaffe. Consequently, I spent many nights huddled with my parents, Doris and little brother Brian in our Anderson shelter listening to the sound of the aircraft passing overhead and waiting for the bombs to start falling.

Despite my dad's efforts to make the shelter as comfortable as possible and the Council lining it with concrete, it was dark, cold, damp and terrifying. There was a bunk down each side on which mum laid out bedding for Doris and Brian; I sat with my parents on the ends of the bunks. Dad always kept a small primus stove and a hurricane lamp together with a couple of candles in the shelter, with fresh matches. Mum brought some bread from the kitchen and whatever else she had put ready. There was a bucket in the corner if anyone was caught short, but mum refused to use it.

Some people would be able to keep books and games in the shelters for their children to play whilst waiting for the All Clear, but our shelter was still too damp to leave anything like that in it. Mind, when the bombs were falling, it was far too frightening to think about reading or playing games. Everyone was the same, you just sat there, helpless, soaked in cold sweat and gripped by terror, praying that each bomb would miss you and that the raid would end soon. I think it was the vulnerability of just sitting there, not being able to fight back, that made it so terrifying. The crews of the ack-ack guns might have been in the open, but at least they were able to shoot back.

Whenever a bomb landed close to us, the ground would shake with the explosion and the shelter filled with a booming sound. It wasn't too bad when the bombs fell some distance away, but when they were very close I couldn't help thinking that maybe the next one would fall on us and we would all be killed. After several hours in the damp stuffy shelter, the air became stale and dad would blow the light out in the hurricane lamp and open the door for a little while, but in the winter the air that rushed in was freezing cold and occasionally filled with the smell of cordite or smoke drifting on the wind from a building on fire.

By and large, Kettering escaped fairly lightly. A few bombs fell around the Blandford Road area and also close to Rockingham Road and the Kettering Furnaces, but I don't remember being told that anyone was killed, although they might well have been. Wellingborough was targeted quite a lot more and one day a school in Rushden was hit, killing a number of young children who were in their classes at the time. Understandably, the parents were devastated that their children should have been killed like that and angry that a school was hit in broad daylight, as these were very often low-level hit-and-run raids by just one or two aircraft, so the crews would be able to clearly see what they had hit.

Meanwhile, Bomber Command, flying mainly Vickers Wellingtons, Armstrong Whitworth Whitleys and Handley Page Hampdens, were attacking targets in Germany, but with little success. Unlike the Luftwaffe, which was using airfields in the Low Countries and France, our crews had much further to go and come back and, in 1940, without proper navigational aids, often didn't drop their bombs within five miles of the target.

I knew that as soon as I was old enough I was going to join the RAF, like Art had, but in the autumn of that year I had my first very graphic introduction to the dangers of flying and the likely consequences of a crash, which I have never forgotten. For whatever reason, one of our Blenheim bombers crashed on some open scrub ground between Cranford and Grafton Underwood, killing the three crewmen. Once the RAF had taken the remains of the aircraft and the crew away, together with a couple of friends, I visited the crash site in search of souvenirs. There was a great gash in the field close to a small pond where the Blenheim had hit the ground and burst into flames, burning the grass and nearby bushes. I stood looking at this patch of scorched earth for some time, beginning to realise the forces that had been involved to cause it.

After a while I started to look around and saw the remnants of various pieces of flying clothing hanging from the branches of the small trees several yards away. Thinking once more of souvenirs, I wandered over to the tree that seemed to have the most clothing wedged in it, but after collecting two or three pieces I was stunned by what I was looking at. In the clothing that I was holding were small pieces of human flesh and bone, parts of the young man who had pulled that jacket on just a few hours earlier. Just then I saw some young boys shooting air rifles at a small object floating in the pond. Looking for some relief from my shock, I went over to see what the interest was. I couldn't make out the object at first, but then as it floated closer to the bank, to my horror, I realised that it was a human eyeball.

I couldn't speak; I was so shocked by the obvious violence of the crash and the realisation that the bodies of these three young men had literally been smashed up and scattered across the field at the moment the aircraft hit the ground. It was probably just as well that as I stood there that day, I had no idea that before I turned twenty-one, I would come so very close to meeting the same fate.

I didn't have long to wait before my next crash site visit, only this time it was an enemy Heinkel He111; and I was prepared for what I might see. It had been shot down by one of our Hurricanes and had crashed into a field beside the A6 near Rothwell. Four of the crew had managed to bail out before the aircraft hit the ground and had been captured by the Home Guard, but the other two had been killed, whether by the .303 bullets from the Hurricane or in the crash, I didn't know. I had taken a small seaside spade with me and began digging for souvenirs around the remains of the Heinkel. I found several items of interest, but the most useful of all were the navigator's dividers which, although a little bent, were typically very well engineered; they had been made in Cologne.

"Reg after 12 months Home Guard service"

"Reg's little brother Brian in 1944"

"Kettering Home Guard 'D' Coy. Reg is back row left"

*"Kettering Home Guard on parade. Reg looking at the camera, is
third back in the left column"*

Chapter Four

"I slept and dreamed that life was Beauty:
I woke and found that life was Duty:
Was then the dream a shadowy lie?
Toil on, sad heart, courageously,
And thou shalt find thy dream to be
A noonday light and truth to thee."

- *'Duty'*; Ellen S Hooper

In 1936, the RAF had been organised into separate Commands; Bomber, Fighter, Coastal, Control and Training. During the war, Army Co-operation, Transport, Maintenance and Balloon Commands were added. Each of these Commands were divided up into Groups and within the Groups the individual squadrons were allocated. Conscription applied to the RAF as it did to everything else, with the exception of aircrew; the young men who flew against the enemy, whether in bombers, fighters or sea-planes were all volunteers.

My time was coming and the Royal Air Force beckoned. I wanted to be aircrew like Art, but it was not that easy. Firstly, all aircrew were volunteers and the RAF were very choosey about who they accepted because, as I later learned, you were part of a team and had to have the right aptitude in many different respects. There were many hurdles to get over before I became part of a bomber crew, but I was determined not to get called up into the Army, so my friend Dennis and I went along to the RAF Recruiting Office in the town to offer our services and start the long process.

It was late 1940, and by now I was seventeen and a half. I filled in all the necessary forms giving my name, address, age and so on. A few days later, both Dennis and I were called for the first of several interviews and were told to report to the RAF Recruitment Centre at Dover Hall in Northampton. I was given time off work to attend and my manager wished me luck. There was never any problem with getting time off work for these sorts of interviews because everybody was doing something for the war and they knew that sooner or later I would leave to join one of the Services.

The RAF interview process was divided into four parts. The first was a medical examination, which was at best fairly superficial. Next came a series of written tests including general knowledge and intelligence. The intelligence test was very simple to start with, but gradually became more difficult as the paper progressed. Then they gave us a Morse code aptitude test, which I found very easy as I had been practising Morse for some time. Lastly, we were each interviewed by a serving RAF officer. All of these tests were to determine which particular job in the aircraft each one of us would be most suited to, if any at all. At the end of the interview with the officer, he told me that my education fell short of the likelihood of me becoming a pilot or navigator, but that my skills were best suited to being a wireless operator or air gunner. I was very pleased with that since I had wanted to be a wireless operator like Art, which was why I had been working on the Morse code.

I was about to get up from my seat when the officer said, "Just before you go, Payne, I want you to realise that you will not just be flying in an aircraft, you will be fighting in one, too; and the enemy will be doing his best to kill you. Are you sure that you still want to volunteer for aircrew."

Having it spelt out so boldly made me stop and think for a moment. I could still picture the wreckage of that Blenheim and the fate of its crew but I had made up my mind, I wanted to join the RAF.
"Yes, sir, I do. My brother is in the RAF and I want join too."
"Well done. You will be given more tests when you go to Cardington. Good luck, lad."
"Thank you, sir." And with that, I was over the first hurdle.

The interview had lasted nearly all day and by the time they were finished with us it was dark outside. Dennis had been selected to go forward too and we carefully made our way back to the railway station in the blackout. Despite having reasonable night vision, in the total darkness of the streets we still bumped into a few people on our way but we were both in high spirits.

The following Saturday evening, as was usual by then, I put on my best suit and went into town to the Angel Hotel and, although not yet eighteen, joined my friends for half a pint of ale, then went to the Empire cinema where we had reserved our seats for the second house to see the latest film. I really felt that I was on my way to joining the RAF and being able to fly as part of a bomber crew.

One night in November, the Home Guard held a dance at the George Hotel in Kettering. I had certainly enjoyed myself and it was quite late when, together with some friends, I tumbled out of the hotel. As soon as we were outside we could hear the sound of German bombers passing overhead in a steady stream flying west. In the distance I could see the shell bursts from our anti-aircraft guns and a great orange glow beginning to fill the horizon. All the way home I could hear the aircraft droning their way overhead, sometimes just a small group together, then a much larger group would come along. Even in the half an hour that it took me to walk home, that orange stain had spread higher and wider into the night sky, and for the attacking bombers it must have been visible from well out over the North Sea.

I said goodnight to my friends and walked round to our house in Washington Square, and all the time the bombers were passing overhead; even in the house as I got into bed and drifted off to sleep, I could still hear the steady rhythmic beat of their engines.

The next morning was Friday, 15th November 1940, and the news began to filter through; the constant drone of bombers that I had heard the previous night had been the sound of them making their way to Coventry. That morning the city, together with its magnificent fourteenth-century cathedral, lay in smouldering ruins, razed. The utter devastation that the

Nazis had visited upon Warsaw, Belgrade and Rotterdam had come to Coventry. Two days later, the King visited the city, as did Winston Churchill; the nation was in shock at this blatant attack upon the civilian population, the death toll of which ran to around 568. The exact figure has never been known because no-one really knew how many people were in Coventry that night.

Five nights after Coventry, West Bromwich was once more a target in a raid which resulted in ARP Dispatch Rider Charity Bick becoming the youngest person ever to receive the George Medal. Born in 1925, at fourteen and having only just left school, Charity lied about her age, presumably with the knowledge of her parents, and volunteered for the ARP as a Dispatch Rider, where she joined the team at the Brickworks office near her home in Maud Road. Sixteen was the minimum age for the Service. One of the first casualties of any bombing raid was the telephone system and so the ARP had young dispatch riders on bicycles to ride between posts taking urgent messages to other posts and the emergency services. On the evening of Tuesday, 19th November 1940, the all too familiar sound of the air-raid sirens wailed across the town, closely followed by the drone of German bombers. The air vibrated to the roar of the defending anti-aircraft guns while the searchlight beams weaved across the sky scanning the dark for their attackers. Within moments, the first bombs exploded and fires quickly sprang up from the hundreds of incendiaries that rained down upon the streets.

Charity's father was an ARP Warden and together they rushed up to the roof of a building which had been hit by several incendiaries and, fully exposed to the continuing waves of falling bombs, they urgently but with great care tipped sand over each glowing magnesium core until all were extinguished and the building saved. But the old roof had been mortally damaged and as Charity and her father were about to leave, it collapsed and they plummeted to the floor beneath amongst the broken timbers and plaster. Largely uninjured, Charity picked herself up, helped her father to his feet and they ran down the staircase; he returned to his post and she jumped on her bicycle to collect her first message in what was to be a long night.

During the next few hours of the air raid, Charity cycled many miles to deliver vital messages through dangerous streets where bombs were still falling, where fires raged and buildings were collapsing. Several times she was blown off her bicycle by the blast from bombs exploding so close to her as she cycled along. At other times she jumped off her bicycle to put out incendiary bombs or to throw them into the cut or elsewhere out of harm's way; bombs which at any moment could have burned her alive in seconds.

On 10th September 1941, King George VI bestowed the George Medal upon sixteen-year-old Charity Bick for her outstanding courage during that raid. The minimum age to receive the George Medal is sixteen, but on that November night Charity had been only fifteen, although because she had lied about her age, it was thought that she was seventeen. She is likely to remain the youngest-ever recipient.

Without television to haemorrhage away the hours each day, there was so much more time to fit in everything that I wanted to do. In addition to my Home Guard duties, I still attended the shorthand and typing classes which I had started not long after going to work at the British Legion, and I was also working hard at practising my Morse code.

Every day the skies were full of aircraft flying over the town, mostly RAF but sometimes during the day and certainly at night we were often visited by the Luftwaffe. Making models of these aircraft became an irresistible pastime. Together with a few friends, I carved scale models of the different types of aircraft which we saw flying over Kettering from a solid piece of balsa wood, then painted them in the correct colours according to whether they were RAF or Luftwaffe. This hobby paid dividends for me later on as it gave me a head start with my aircraft recognition when I began my training.

In these closing days of 1940, my friends and I were on the cusp of adulthood. Like the Roman god Janus, we were young men looking both ways at the same time: to the future and the war that beckoned us, and to the past, to a childhood that was disappearing into the mists of memory along with a way of life. Nothing would be the same in Britain after the war; the world in which I had grown up was being destroyed along with its values, both good and bad.

My alarm clock rattled out its persistent clatter on the table beside my bed until I pressed down on the button at the top of the dial. Six o'clock. Time to get up for work, but just for a few minutes I lay there reflecting upon the significance of this particular morning. The blackout curtains at my window kept the light out as well as in and I had no idea whether it was bright or dull, wet or dry, but it didn't matter because today was a special day for me. Today was Tuesday, 11th March 1941, my eighteenth birthday; I was now old enough for military service.

When I looked, it was a lovely bright early-spring day. I washed, shaved and did my usual jobs for mum around the house then cycled to work on my Humber bicycle in the warming sunshine. They all knew that I was eighteen that day and wished me a happy birthday. They also knew that I would soon be leaving to join the RAF.

A few days later, the letter that I had awaited for so long dropped through the letterbox and lay on the door mat. Bending down, I picked up the official brown envelope marked 'ON HIS MAJESTY'S SERVICE' and held it for several seconds before daring to open it. This innocent-looking envelope held the key to my future in this war, and indeed whether I would have a future; but there was no going back now, the die was cast. I carefully sliced open the flap and read the contents. I was to report to RAF Cardington in Bedfordshire the following week for three days of final tests before being confirmed as fit for aircrew duties. A travel warrant was enclosed, and so, on Sunday afternoon, carrying my small suitcase containing a change of underwear, socks and pyjamas, together with my shaving kit and hairbrush, I set off to walk to the railway station.

Cardington was a very large initial training centre where so many who entered the RAF during the war years spent at least some time, even if it was only a day or two. For the three days that I was there I was subjected to a great number of tests, most of which were different forms of medical examination. My eyes were tested for vision and colour blindness, my head was tested for dizziness, my teeth were tested for holes and my urine was tested for goodness knows what. At the end of it all I was told that I was fit for aircrew duties. However, I needed to see a local dentist to have a number of my teeth filled as otherwise they would cause me considerable pain and trouble when flying at 20,000 feet, and I was duly given a warrant to cover the costs of the dental work.

Before we left Cardington, along with the others who had passed, I was given my RAF identification cards containing my photograph, personal details and Service number, 1435510, a number I shall never forget. I was also told to attend the Air Training courses for Morse, aircraft recognition and some advanced mathematics. I returned home, but with shorthand, typing, Home Guard duties and now the Air Training courses my social life took a severe battering.

In June, I was invited to join the Air Training Corps, the ATC, for their summer camp at RAF Wittering, near to the beautiful medieval town of Stamford. With a recorded history which dates back for more than a thousand years, Stamford remains a unique jewel amongst the finest of English market towns. Located on the Great North Road, its early wealth in the Middle Ages came from wool and then later from the stage coach traffic between London, York and Edinburgh. The legacy of this wealth is the many fine buildings made from a wonderful golden local stone, and having been largely bypassed by the post-war modern world, it has retained its great charm.

In 1941, Stamford was even more beautiful than it is today and a great fear was that German bombing would destroy it. Fortunately, though, there was no heavy industry nearby, but there was RAF Wittering, and only a few weeks before I arrived for the summer camp, on 14th March, it had been attacked again and this time the bombers had hit the main hangar, destroying all the aircraft inside and killing seventeen ground crew. In all, the airfield was bombed five times during the war.

The station had started life in 1916 as RFC Stamford, becoming RAF Wittering in 1924. From 1926, it was the home of the Central Flying School until that moved to RAF Upavon in 1935. During the Battle of Britain, Wittering was home to Hawker Hurricanes of No.12 Group but by the summer of 1941 the focus was on 151 Squadron and their Boulton Paul Mk1 Defiant night fighters. The enemy's nightly bombing of British towns and cities was causing huge disruption, damage and loss of life and so night fighter aircraft and tactics were developed to combat this threat, which is where the Defiant came in. It's strange how things come round; when I was looking at these fighters I thought what a good show it was that we were able to shoot down the German bombers before they got to their targets. Two years later when I was part of a Lancaster bomber crew flying over Germany, I hated the night fighters and lived in great fear of being attacked by one. It's just as well that I couldn't see into the future.

For the week that we were on the base, we slept in bell tents, ate all our meals with the operational crews and ground staff, which was very interesting, and were drilled by RAF instructors, but best of all was getting close to the aircraft. One night, after we had turned in and were falling asleep, the airfield defence guns started firing. I thought that we were going to be bombed again, but the sirens didn't sound and the firing soon stopped. I think that the gunners were a little twitchy after the serious attack in March; I just hope that I wasn't one of ours that they were firing at!

In early October the letter arrived; my call-up papers. I was instructed to report to RAF Padgate, a recruitment centre in Manchester. The timing of this letter couldn't have been better for me. Later that same week, I attended my shorthand and typing classes as usual on Friday evening where Miss Taylor, my tutor, informed me that, certain of my success, she had put me in for the exam, a prospect that I had been dreading despite her confidence in me. Somewhat gleefully, I was able to tell her that I was very sorry but I would have to decline because by that particular date I would be at His Majesty's service in the Royal Air Force. She said that she would be very sorry to lose me from her classes. She wished me good luck and I breathed a sigh of relief.

The British Legion too knew that I was leaving, and when my final day at work arrived, all the staff came to wish me luck and presented me with a leather writing case and pen, a kind and thoughtful gift which I put to very good use throughout my service.

I had already visited the barber's to have a short back and sides haircut, having been tipped off by Art and others already in that if I didn't, the RAF would do it for me and that was to be avoided if possible. I packed my pyjamas, shaving kit, and toiletries once more into a small bag, together with the sandwiches which mum had made for me to eat on the train; now there was nothing left to do but walk to the railway station. I said goodbye to mum, who I knew was choking back the tears, pulled my mackintosh a little more tightly around my neck and stepped out into the pouring rain. I was going to war.

The rain cascaded out of its leaden sky in unrelenting stair rods. The wind blew it into my face and down my neck; the pavements were awash and the water soaked through my shoes until my feet squelched inside them with every step. It was the most miserable day for weeks and I hurried along Montague Street towards the shelter of the station. In an agonising moment, my RAF career nearly ended before it had begun. In her rush to get out of the rain, a woman pushed past me and as she did one of the spokes of her umbrella struck my face and stabbed my eye. I felt the searing pain and realised I couldn't open it.

Standing in the entrance to the station, I tried in vain to open my eye, but it was too painful. With the train due I had to manage with one eye, much to the obvious consternation of the ticket collector at the platform gate when he saw my travel warrant and closed, bruised eye. Feeling dejected and convinced that I would be sent home again from Padgate, I boarded the crowded train, luckily found a seat and settled down for the journey. However, by the time we got to Derbyshire I was able to open my eye again and, most importantly, see. I have given umbrellas a wide berth ever since.

The nearer to Manchester that we travelled, the harder the rain seemed to be coming down. There was nothing to be seen out of the windows of the compartment as the rain and mist merged to crash against the glass before being whipped away by the wind to join the trail of smoke and steam from the engine. I closed my eyes for much of the journey and dozed until I was awoken by a jolt as the train began to slow, and the blurred shadows of the houses along the trackside took shape; we were arriving in Manchester.

Hundreds of fresh-faced young men tumbled out of the compartments of that train only to be left standing in the incessant rain whilst waiting for the Service buses to take us to Padgate. Even though I was wearing my mackintosh, the rain had driven through it leaving me soaked and cold. I idly read the advertising posters on the walls of the station whilst the rain continued to splatter against my face, run down my neck and out through the bottom of my trousers. Cadbury's were anxious to assure me that its milk chocolate was as good as ever even though milk, cocoa and sugar were all on ration, whilst in the next frame it exhorted me to leave their chocolate for the children anyway, just in case I had been tempted by the first message. Other posters carried various government information messages; Fougasse reminded me that 'careless talk costs lives', another one told me to 'be like Dad, keep Mum', or if I had money to spare, which I didn't, I should help the war effort by buying some war bonds. At the end of this line of gripping information was a rather shabby, pre-war poster telling me that the London Midland & Scottish Railway Company would take me to the golden sands of sunny Blackpool where I would have the time of my life. I wished that whoever thought that one up was here now in the cold driving rain and I could tell him that if Blackpool was anything like Manchester he was wrong, I wasn't.

Finally the buses arrived and drove us to Padgate, where once more we were left standing around in the pouring rain as we slowly made our way from one department to another, filling in forms and receiving further medicals to ensure that we were all still FFI [Free From Infection]. Welcome to the RAF. At long last, we were allocated a bed, taken to the mess hall for a meal and told that the next day we would be issued with our uniforms.

Next morning I was up early, washed, shaved and ready for breakfast. My clothes were still soaking wet. Not that it mattered as it was still raining and we had more forms to fill in as we trudged from one office to another. Finally it was uniform issue time. A civilian worker took my rough measurements, called across the counter to a store man, who quickly selected a uniform more or less the right size and I moved down the line and changed into the RAF jacket and trousers. Next I was measured properly, removed the jacket and trousers and waited. Within ten minutes, one of the army of women seamstresses had miraculously made the alterations and the uniform fitted well.

Most of the rest of my kit was then issued, along with a large sheet of brown paper and a length of string. I wrapped up my civilian clothes and addressed the parcel to my mother, making sure that it was well secured with the string. Later mum told me that my wet clothes had soaked through the paper and it was only the copious amount of string which had held it together.

On the third day came my kit-bag, webbing, gas mask, tin helmet and PT kit. That evening I packed my kit-bag and the following day it was back to the railway station for the short journey to PDC Blackpool, the Personnel Dispersal Centre. On the way, the train went around the outskirts of Liverpool and I had a vivid insight into the widespread destruction of the houses and streets in the residential areas by the German bombing.

Together with some other chaps, I was billeted in a house in King Street for the first week, where the landlady made us very welcome. She also showed us how to bull our boots until the toecaps gleamed like glass. The first day on parade, the corporal told me to get my hair cut, which was a surprise to me since I had already had a short back and sides at home before I left. Nevertheless, at lunchtime I duly went to the barber's and had another haircut. On the afternoon parade he looked at my hair and said that he had told me to get a haircut. I told him I had, but later that day he marched me with three others to the barber's where we were virtually shaved. The corporal was good, though, because he showed us a small workshop in a backstreet where, for a few pence, they would buff your uniform buttons on a machine, making them very smooth and so easy to clean each morning.

The week at PDC passed quickly and taught us the basics of RAF life; how to salute an officer, the RAF structure, how to answer on parade and so on. At the end of the week, I packed my kit again, bade farewell to my landlady, thanked her for her help and joined the waiting group of recruits in the street outside, whereupon we marched a few hundred yards to Charnley Road. Here, the corporal halted us whilst he visited a number of boarding houses in the road. Presently, I was allocated to occupy No. 4, the home of Mr and Mrs Clegg, and my billet for the period of my signals course.

Whilst we were standing out in the cold of Charnley Road, another young lad came over to me and asked if I also came from Kettering. His name was Ron Boydon and, before joining up, he had been a junior reporter on the *Kettering*

Evening Telegraph. Inside No. 4, I shared a bedroom with Ron and another lad from our area named Arthur Bromich.

Mr and Mrs Clegg ran a typical Blackpool boarding house of the time and I don't think that the war made a lot of difference to them, except that they were now full all year round, payment was guaranteed by the government, and their rules were even stricter than in peacetime. There were twelve of us in their house and we had a roster for daily washing-up duties; no food was to be taken into the rooms, not that there was any food to spare; boots were to be taken off in the hallway; the electricity was turned off between 21.30 and 07.00; the front door was locked at 22.00; any trouble would result in being moved to another boarding house and, of course, the most heinous crime of all was strictly forbidden - there were to be no women in the bedrooms.

It would be generous to describe our accommodation as spartan. There was no hot water to wash and shave in and there was only one lavatory for the use of the twelve recruits; we did, though, have a small chest of drawers in each bedroom, affording us the great luxury of one drawer apiece. However, Mrs Clegg's was no worse than most billets in Blackpool and was better than some.

Our training corporal was a decent chap who looked after us, helping whenever he could. We marched everywhere, had rifle drill, daily physical training and learned to drill in the Tower Ballroom, having changed our boots for P/T shoes. However, most of the time was taken up learning Morse code. For four hours each day, we sat in the perishing cold of the unheated South Shore tram sheds wrapped in our greatcoats and gloves as former Merchant Navy wireless operators taught us Morse. These sessions were split up as two hours in the morning and two hours in the afternoon. In between we had to march back to our billet for the midday meal and then perhaps to the Tower for a two-hour lecture.

In the first week at Blackpool, we were given all the various injections and inoculations which we needed, so by the end of a fortnight, we were all sporting a nice scab covered with sticking plaster. In these days of en suites and homes with multiple bathrooms, it may seem inconceivable that our billet did not have a proper bathroom, but this was the norm rather than the exception. Consequently, so that we could maintain cleanliness, we were allowed to go to the Derby Baths to have a shower followed by half an hour swimming. Inevitably, all this exposure to water brought the sticking plasters and scabs away and left them floating on the surface of the water until the attendant, armed with a shrimp net on a long pole, could scoop them up.

The RAF laundry allowed one piece of each item of clothing to be sent for washing each week. That is one shirt, one set of underwear, one pair of socks. When it came to laundry parade, despite everyone having their name and number in each item of clothing it was a complete lottery what you were thrown when your name was called out. With over 5,000 airmen in Blackpool, it was hopeless trying to find who had my kit, so I started to send my washing home. I wrapped it in brown paper, tied it with string and wrote my return address on the inside so my mother could use the same sheet of paper by just turning it over. This definitely had a fringe benefit because when my washing came back to me, there was always some of mum's home baking inside.

Examinations were held at the end of each week of the course. A fail would put you back a week; three consecutive fails would put you back on the train to be re-mustered for other duties. As Christmas 1941 approached, there was no home leave but Mrs Clegg offered to give us some chicken and a small bottle of beer for our Christmas dinner, in exchange for 2/6d each.

Just after the start of 1942, our four months training at Blackpool came to an end. Thanks to my time in the ATC, I had no trouble passing the final examination and looked forward to going home for a week's leave. On that final morning, Ron, Arthur and I said goodbye to Mr and Mrs Clegg, slung our kitbags and gas masks on our shoulders, and headed for the railway station and home. On the journey we chatted about the course we had just completed and some of the friends we had made, in particular Keith Kenway from Bridport, George Plank from Liverpool and Tubby Melhuish.

At last, the train pulled into Kettering station and, after making arrangements to meet up during our leave, Ron and I made our way through the cold evening air. I was so pleased to be home again, to see Mum and Dad, eat mum's cooking and sleep in my own bed. Whilst I had been away, mum had bought a couple of chickens which she kept in the pen dad had made in the back garden; that was how she managed to give me a real treat for my breakfast the next morning, a fresh egg.

"Blackpool 1941. The white flash on the forage cap denotes trainee aircrew"

"No.4 Charnley Road, Blackpool"

"Wireless operators course at Blackpool. Reg is seated front row 4th from the right"

Chapter Five

"Say not the struggle nought availeth,
The labour and the wounds are vain,
The enemy faints not, nor faileth,
And as things have been, things remain."
- From '*Say Not the Struggle Nought Availeth*';
Arthur Hugh Clough

I met up with Ron a couple of times during my leave and went over to his house. His mother was a lovely person who was devoted to looking after her son, and she made me very welcome. She lived on her own now that Ron had joined the RAF. I'm not sure whether she was widowed or if Ron's father had left her soon after he was born but neither of them ever spoke of his father and I didn't ask. The week went by far too quickly and in no time at all I was packing again and getting ready for my next posting, this time to the radio school at RAF Yatesbury.

I had arranged to meet Ron at the station but in order to be in Wiltshire at the stipulated time, we had to catch the four o'clock early milk train to London. Mum made me a good breakfast, including another fresh egg, and then at three-thirty in the dark of the morning, I said goodbye to her, slung my kit-bag over one shoulder and my gas mask over the other, and stepped out into the gently falling snow for the long walk to the station. By the time I reached Gold Street there was a good three inches on the ground and I was looking forward to getting under the cover of the platform and boarding the train.

Even though the blackout was in full force and the streets would normally be as black as pitch, the falling snow gave them a hint of ghostly grey light, which was just enough for me to see a few yards ahead. I had turned my collar up against the snow and, with my head down, peered through the curtain of white flakes as they drifted silently to earth. Lost in thought about mum and dad and what it must be like for them with both Art and me away in the RAF, I plodded through the deserted streets with only the crunch of my own footsteps on the fresh snow for company, when suddenly, from a darkened doorway, a police constable stepped out in front of me.

"And where are you off to at this time of the morning, lad?"

He shone his torch into my face and asked to see my identity card and leave pass; I could really have done without this but I suppose he was only doing his job, as it was very early for me to be out and I could have been a deserter. I lowered my kit-bag onto the snow-covered pavement and started to undo my greatcoat buttons to get the documents out of the top pocket of my battledress tunic.

"RAF Yatesbury in Wiltshire. I'm catching the four o'clock milk train to London," I replied, handing him my ID card and pass.

He directed the masked beam of his torch over the documents and, satisfied with the details, folded the leave pass, slipping it back into my ID card as he closed it and handed them back to me.

"That's all in order. On you go." I put them back into my tunic pocket, buttoned my greatcoat again, hoisted the heavy kit-bag onto my shoulder and wished him good morning.

"Safe journey, and good luck, lad," he replied with a faint smile, before once more stepping back into the darkness of the doorway and out of the snow.

Instead of a coat, the constable was wearing his heavy cape with the high-neck collar, and with his helmet pulled right down, it was difficult to tell in the gloom, but I am sure that I recognised him as one of the policemen that I used to look out for when riding two on a bike whilst helping my friend with his paper round ten years earlier. That seemed such a long time ago now; halcyon days from a different world.

I arrived at the railway station a few minutes before the train pulled in; Ron was waiting for me.

"Sleep in, Reg?" he asked with a grin.

"No, I was checked in Gold Street by a bobby."

"Bad luck. It always happens when you've got a train or a bus to catch."

We stood in the barely cast glow from one of the dim, shaded gas lights on the walls of the station; I pulled my greatcoat a little more tightly around my neck against the wind that always seems to blow through railway stations and watched as the train drew alongside the platform, coming to rest with a noisy chorus of hissing steam, squealing brakes and clanking couplings.

"Kettering, Kettering this stop," the porter called out as he walked along the platform just beyond the reach of half a dozen heavy compartment doors as they swung open to reveal the mostly uniformed occupants, a handful of whom stumbled out, complete with kit-bags, glad to be home for a few days' leave before moving on to some other part of the war.

Ron and I made our way through the steam rising from beneath the carriages and joined the others waiting to board the train, finally sinking into a couple of seats in a compartment occupied by the sleeping figures of two sailors and an army corporal, none of whom stirred when I slid the door closed and shut out the cold air in the corridor from the slightly less cold air in the compartment.

The two of us exchanged a few sentences about the last days of our leave since we had seen each other for a drink and then settled down to the peace of the journey, with only the hypnotically rhythmic sound of the clickity-clack as the wheels passed over the joints in the track to mark our progress southwards as we slipped through fields and villages and towns in the darkened countryside beyond the windows.

At Yatesbury we learned all about radio sets, Ohm's Law, electrons, valves and their functions, lead acid batteries, the receivers and transmitters used by the RAF and radio procedure. We also had to increase our Morse efficiency to eighteen words per minute and then learn semaphore, although I didn't ever use this again.

Exercise and general fitness were increased here through PT and various sporting activities. I enjoyed the cross-country runs because the scenery was so lovely, even in winter time, and once the snow had melted, I remember seeing the famous White Horse carved in the chalk hillside, although the white chalk had been painted khaki to blend into the hillside and not provide a navigational landmark for the German bomber crews.

Lectures were either theory or practical, and for the theory we had to take notes then swot up on them in the evenings. Ron and I were in the same hut and he proved a great asset to everyone in there because, having been a reporter in Civvy Street, he could do shorthand. I remembered some of my shorthand from my Friday night classes with Miss Taylor, but nothing like Ron's speed. Consequently, he had a more or less verbatim account of each lecture and shared all the extra information with us, so when we came to our final exams we had a lot more information than we would have had otherwise.

The finals were in three parts, written, practical and oral. Those of us who passed were allowed to wear the 'Sparks' badge on our arm to show that we were wireless operators. Success in the exams was followed by two very different rewards. The first was to have a flight in a de Havilland Dominie training aircraft, one that we would spend a lot of time in during the coming months. The other was to go to the local farm and help the farmer plant out a field of potatoes. The farmer had a tractor, and as he ploughed up and down leaving the deep furrows, we would follow behind and place the potatoes at a given distance apart. The field seemed immense when we started the job, but divided up between so many of us, we managed to complete the planting before it got dark; and then we received our reward. Leaving the field, we went into the great barn, where the farmer's wife had laid on mugs of local ale and hunks of homemade bread and cheese. It was one of the best meals that I have ever eaten and after being in the classroom for so many months, the fresh air and the uncomplicated job had been a welcome relief; it had also given me a raging appetite.

The end of my course at Yatesbury was followed by another, unexpected week's leave. By now it was the end of May 1942 and Art was stationed at nearby Cottesmore, which meant that he could come home when not flying. This was a great comfort to mum and when he got home whilst I was on leave, it was the first time that mum had had us both home at the same time since Art had left to join the RAF.

In the evenings, we would put our best suits on and go into town to one or more of the local pubs, sometimes meeting up with Ron. It made a nice change to be out of uniform, but it was essential to carry ID cards and leave passes because it was quite unusual now to see anyone out of uniform and the Kettering or Military police regularly stopped men in civvies to check their papers.

This would very often happen in pubs, when the police would come in through the front and back doors at the same time, looking for deserters. It became quite entertaining for us to stand at the bar watching the mayhem as the young girls made a dash for the side doors or the ladies' lavatories to scramble out through the windows so as not to get caught for underage drinking, as the licensing laws were much stricter during the war.

Once more my seven days' leave was over all too soon and it was time to go again. Poor little Brian, every time he got used to me being at home, I would disappear for months at a time and leave him to mum, dad and Doris. This time I was posted to North Coates, near Grimsby and right on the coast of the North Sea. It wasn't really part of my training but there was a bit of a backlog with wireless operator training, which was why I had been given the seven days' unexpected leave and was now being posted to North Coates to fill time. The base was home to the Canadians of 415 Squadron Coastal Command equipped with Hampdens, although there were other squadrons passing through at the time with Beaufighters and Hudsons.

My duties here had nothing to do with my training but because I was a wireless operator I was part of the listening team, that is we would give round-the-clock listening cover for our aircraft and other Coastal Command aircraft which were out on patrol. We didn't reply to anything that we heard, just wrote it down and then passed it on to be de-coded and acted upon as necessary. I spent many boring hours listening to nothing, so it was always a relief when something came in. In my off-duty time I would go clay pigeon shooting or up to the rifle range, which was good practice for the air gunnery part of the course. At other times I would walk along the coast to Cleethorpes or sit on the sea wall overlooking the Humber estuary and watch the Luftwaffe trying to bomb the ships sailing into the harbour. There would always be a group of people at these times and we would give a great cheer when the Spitfires and Hurricanes of Fighter Command arrived and chased away the enemy, sometimes even shooting one down before they could escape.

One night, as I was just booking in at the guardroom after returning from a 48-hour leave, there was a full-scale raid taking place very close by over Hull, which was the most heavily bombed of all Britain's cities during the war, with over 70% of the buildings destroyed. The raid had spread to Grimsby on our side of the Humber and the nearby searchlights were sweeping the sky in a criss-cross pattern whilst the anti-aircraft guns were all blasting away into the darkness. Suddenly one of the searchlights picked out a German bomber and then several others locked on to it. Caught in the cone of light, the pilot twisted and weaved the bomber through the air as the anti-aircraft gunners turned their fire to it. I could see the shells exploding on every side of that aircraft, but the gunners just couldn't hit it; it seemed incredible that it was going to escape. Standing on the ground, as yet unaware of the gripping terror the crew were feeling, I watched this struggle for life play out, hoping that the gunners would prevail and bring the Dornier crashing out of the sky. However, the only thing that came crashing out of the sky was a large piece of one of those ack-ack shells, which buried itself into the gravel road just a few feet away. It was enough to end my sightseeing and, together with the others who had gathered, I made a dash for the cover of the guard room.

I seemed to follow in the wake of attacks on airfields because, just like RAF Wittering when I was at ATC camp the previous summer, just before I was posted to North Coates it had been attacked by a group of Luftwaffe bombers one night. The Waafery had taken a direct hit, killing several WAAFs; airfields were dangerous places.

By mid September I was on the move again, this time to RAF South Kensington to continue with my advanced wireless operator training. I was glad to be continuing with my training and also to be able to meet up again with my pals from the two courses. I knew, too, that I was getting ever nearer to my flying training because before I left North Coates, I was issued with all my flying kit, which I now also had to carry everywhere I went.

I arrived at South Kensington underground station in the afternoon and joined the thronging mass of airmen waiting there. Presently we were called to order and marched off in various directions to our billets. At any other time this would have been described as a most cultural trip to London: I was billeted in a block of flats at the rear of the Albert Hall, where we congregated for large briefings. Classrooms were in the Science Museum and all our meals were provided across the road in the Victoria and Albert Museum. However, although all the exhibit information was still on the walls, the exhibits themselves had long since been removed for safe keeping to, as it later transpired, a disused slate mine in North Wales. What was on offer to us in 1942 was up-to-date radio equipment and much more detailed valve and radio theory.

Our working day finished at 17.00 and, after our evening meal in the V&A, we would walk back along Exhibition Road to our billet in Albert Court, where we would get ready to go out into London for the evening. None of us had very much money as most of us were still sending fourteen shillings each week from our pay back to our parents to help them out, and in any event, we had to be back in the billet by 22.00; nevertheless, we had a lot of fun, including going to the Ice Rink in Bayswater. Another regular haunt was Speakers' Corner at Marble Arch. There was always something going on there, even in the blackout. After the speakers had finished we would have a good sing-along with songs like '*Road to Morocco*' and '*Don't sit under the Apple Tree*'.

There were always plenty of girls among the crowd and we would link arms as we sang along. In the blackout, I couldn't see what any of these girls looked like until one of them lit up a cigarette, or maybe later on if I walked one of them back to the underground station. In the light, they very rarely looked anything like I had imagined they would, although some of them were regulars at these gatherings and I would see them again from time to time. At 21.30, though, whatever was going on, we had to leave and walk briskly across Hyde Park back to Albert Court before the doors were locked. The RAF police were on duty at the main doors; we had to book out and back in again, so they always knew if anyone was late back.

From time to time there were still bombing raids on London and so we had to take turns in doing fire-watch duty in the Science Museum. Although many of the most valuable exhibits had been moved out of London for safety, there were still a large number of significant items stored in the basement, surprisingly including Louis Bleriot's aircraft in which he flew across the English Channel from Calais to Dover on 25th July 1909, becoming the first person to do so. It was too good an opportunity to miss and we gleefully took it in turns to sit in the cockpit seat of this historic little aircraft.

It seemed to me to be fairly clear that the residents of South Kensington, and this part in particular, were not very happy about their bit of London being taken over by the RAF as a training area. They were quite content with us flying over the city shooting down German aircraft and protecting their homes, but didn't want us cluttering up their streets whilst we were being trained to do so. As a result of complaints from these residents, we were only allowed to walk along the V&A side of Exhibition Road, the Science Museum side being reserved for residents, as they objected to us walking in groups on both sides of the road. It was an attitude which was to resonate again at the end of the war and for a long time afterwards, when the job was done and peace had returned.

Our training progressed steadily and included installing and operating the entire radio equipment in a Wellington bomber. A number of fuselages were set up in a large building near to the Science Museum and, working in conjunction with another wireless operator, I had to install the radio equipment in my aircraft and then contact the other wireless operator in his Wellington. He would then return the contact to make sure that I was receiving as well as transmitting.

The course ended just before Christmas 1942 and we were given seven days' leave. So, with my leave pass and travel warrants to home and then to my next posting at RAF Madeley in Herefordshire where my flying training would begin, I joined Ron at South Kensington underground from where we made our way to St Pancras station for the train to Kettering. In war-torn 1942, the journey to Kettering by steam train took fifty-nine minutes. On 28th June 2012, I made the same journey by electric train and, despite all of today's modern railway technology, it still took fifty-nine minutes. Britain is simply not big enough for meaningful times to be clipped from train journeys and very often, the over-dependence upon electricity causes delays and cancellations that simply did not occur in the past.

Mum and dad were really pleased to see me home again and especially for Christmas this year because Art was home as well, his training having been held up, so he was on a seven-day leave pass, too. Mum was thrilled to have the whole family together for Christmas dinner; it was a treat that she had not expected. On Christmas Day, Art and I went into town to meet up with some of our friends at the Woolpack and have a few drinks. Mum told us that dinner would be ready at one o'clock and that we were not to be late.

When we got to the pub, there was a good crowd already there, including a number of girls who made us promise that we would go to the party which they had arranged for that evening. The beer flowed freely, mainly bought for us by the older customers, who were always happy to buy a drink for young lads in uniform. All too soon, it was nearing one o'clock and the two of us collected Christmas kisses from the girls and set off for home feeling very good, if somewhat unsteady. Our path took us past the Trades Club in Mill Road, where a couple of soldiers were just going in. They put their arms around us and ushered us in to have a drink with them, which led to another and another. It was three o'clock when we eventually stumbled home. Mum was furious with us; we may have been old enough to go to war but she was still our mother and she made us go upstairs to sleep it off. When we woke up and came downstairs again, it was nearly seven o'clock and we knew better than to suggest that we were thinking of going out to the party the girls had arranged.

RAF Madeley was not so much a camp but more a collection of huts and classrooms spread around two or three villages, and a grass runway from which the de Havilland Dominie and Proctor training aircraft operated. Since this was January, it was dark when we started in the morning and dark when we finished at night, so whatever flying the weather permitted was done during the middle part of the day.

The initial aircraft training was in a Dominie. A pilot, wireless instructor and six pupils would squeeze into the little trainer and off we would go. During a succession of circuits lasting about an hour, each pupil would take turns in setting the dials and contacting base by wireless and then again on the Morse key using the correct call signs.

It certainly wasn't all plain sailing because most of us had never flown before. As we got into the aircraft each time, we were given a brown paper bag to be sick into. On my first flight I think I was the only one of the six who was not sick, although I did feel dreadful for the whole flight; I just couldn't bear to lose my dinner. After a few flights, we became more accustomed to the movement and the smell of fuel and oil in the aircraft, although for some air sickness remained an occupational blight.

Once having mastered the techniques, we graduated to the Proctor. In this aircraft it was just the pilot and the pupil wireless operator. The route which the pilots took was generally over the Black Mountains of Wales to test our skills. However, these young pilots soon became bored with flying the same course day after day and just to add some interest would come down very low over the mountains and fly along the valleys. Whilst it may have added some interest for them, it was very irritating for us, because it invariably meant that we lost the signal and the contact with whichever station we had linked up with.

In all, I made twenty flights whilst at Madeley, the last one taking place on 20th March, just after my twentieth birthday, and then at the beginning of April I was on the move again, this time to RAF Stormy Down in South Wales for a two-week air gunnery course. There was no official flying for wireless operators at Stormy Down and no time off. It was fourteen days of study, the actual shooting in the air part to be given on our next posting. We were taught all about the .303 Browning machine gun, how it worked, how it was put together and how it came apart. We had to practise taking it apart and putting it back together over and over again until we could do it in the dark, which is exactly what we might have to do in combat.

We were also instructed on the Fraser Nash turret which was being fitted to the new Lancaster bomber that was to become the main heavy bomber of the RAF. A number of these turrets were set up along the sand dunes and then a model aircraft was run along a rail in and out of the dunes on the firing range and it was our job to try to shoot it up.

Air gunners were also being trained at Stormy Down, but their course was much longer and included air firing training. Since the April days were now lengthening, once our training had finished for the day, we would try to get a ride in the old Armstrong Whitworth Whitley bombers which were being used by the air gunners for their training. In this way, I managed to get a couple of trips in these aircraft which I had so often seen flying over Kettering during 1939 and 1940.

In the early years of the war, these Whitleys were one of the RAF's front-line bombers and it was for his airmanship in Whitley 5005 VP-N on the night of $12^{th}/13^{th}$ November 1940 whilst serving with 102 Squadron at RAF Driffield that Pilot Officer Geoffrey Leonard Cheshire was awarded the Distinguished Service Order when he brought his aircraft and crew home safely from Cologne, even though his Whitley had a gaping hole in its side and had been on fire. He would go on to become the RAF's most highly decorated airman, receiving the Victoria Cross, two bars to his DSO, the DFC and being Mentioned in Dispatches. In 1943 he was promoted to the rank of Group Captain; at only twenty-five he was the youngest in the Service. He survived a unique total of one hundred missions in Bomber Command including time as a Master Bomber with the Pathfinder Force, an incredible achievement when the average number of missions survived was seven! His hundred and first mission was as the British observer to the dropping of the atomic bomb on Hiroshima, an experience which left an indelible impression upon him.

I passed out at the end of the course with an above average assessment of 80%. More importantly, I was promoted to the rank of sergeant, sewed three stripes and the air gunner's brevet to my tunic and received nine shillings a day, which increased my pay by a substantial £1-15s-0d a week.

Another week's welcome leave followed before my next posting to No.1 (O)AFU RAF Wigtown, the Advanced Flying Unit near the old county town of the former Wigtownshire in south-west Scotland. Once more, Ron Boydon and I travelled up together. We had to change trains at Leicester station and had a long wait for our connection to Crewe. Whilst we were waiting, two girls came on to the platform to get some cigarettes from one of the machines that we were standing beside and started to chat to us. They wanted to know what we did in the RAF and where we were going. Of course we couldn't give them any detailed information, but nor did we think that they were German spies; we did shoot a line, though. We were sergeants now and had more of what today would be called 'street cred'. At last our train arrived and as we gathered up our kit, the two girls scribbled their names and addresses down on the backs of empty cigarette packets, asking us to write to them when we got to Wigtown; most girls wanted to have a boyfriend who was in the Services.

As she pressed the little piece of cardboard into my hand, one of the girls said with innocent excitement, "You will write to me, won't you, Reg, please." Feeling very flattered, I told her I would and followed Ron and my kit onto the train as the guard walked down the platform noisily closing the carriage doors in time-honoured fashion.

The train wasn't very busy and we easily found seats in the same compartment. We talked about the two girls for a little while and how the RAF uniform had made it so much easier to meet them. Sitting opposite to me was a nice-looking middle-aged woman, and as Ron and I were talking I noticed her smiling once or twice in a rather knowing way, perhaps thinking back to her own younger days during the Great War twenty years earlier. In Crewe we changed trains once more and then again at Carlisle, after which the train crossed the border into Scotland, turned westwards at Gretna Green towards Dumfries, where the great Scottish poet Robert Burns died and is buried, and where we had to change for the fourth time on our long and increasingly tedious journey. Here we joined an assorted mix of passengers on the small local stopping train.

In addition to RAF aircrew heading for one or other of the many bases in south-west Scotland, there were two WAAFs also for Wigtown, some Royal Navy types going to Stranraer and a handful of soldiers who seemed to be making their way home on leave. The rest were local civilians returning home from a day in Dumfries, some of whom had been to the market, because behind the three passenger coaches were two cattle wagons. There was also a woman with some chickens in a basket, a man with a dog and two children who didn't seem to be with anybody but who most of the civilian passengers and the ticket inspector obviously knew. As we travelled through the countryside I was struck by how remote it seemed and by the strange cattle; the Highlands with their long shaggy coats and massive horns and the local Belted Galloways, all black apart from a broad white band around their middle, which gave them their name, were all like nothing I had ever seen before. Having made a couple of unscheduled stops along the way to let the woman with the chickens and then the two children get off in what seemed to be the middle of nowhere, the little steam engine eventually pulled in to Newton Stewart in the late afternoon. Some of the lads from the course were already at the station, as was our transport ready to take us and the two WAAFs to the base, which was not far out of Wigtown.

We flew in Avro Ansons here and much of our work was associated with navigation, including learning how to use the astro-sextant, obtain radio bearings and get radio fixes. Most of our flights were cross-country, including trips out over the Irish Sea. We were now well into May and the weather was lovely, which afforded a wonderful view of the beautiful Galloway and Borders countryside below. Occasionally we would also fly further south, over the Lake District mountains and across the Pennines. On one of these trips, on Tuesday, 11th May, my pilot was an officer staff pilot, and as we approached a large operational bomber base in Yorkshire, he told me that we were going to land there because he wanted one of the engines checked before we started the two-hundred-mile return trip home. We landed and taxied around the perimeter track. When we came to a standstill, the pilot told me to go to the Sergeants' Mess and get some lunch. I was given the best meal I had had since joining the RAF, and an hour or so later we took off on the return leg.

As I clambered out of the Anson back at Wigtown, the young officer turned to me and explained with a satisfied smile, "I hope you enjoyed your lunch. There wasn't anything the matter with the engine. I was stationed at that base until I came up here and just wanted to catch up with the chaps again. Thanks a lot." And with that, he left me to carry on.

The following Monday morning, the whole station was buzzing with the news that the night before, Bomber Command's 617 Squadron Lancasters had flown to Germany at tree-top height and had destroyed the Möhne and Eder dams, flooding the Ruhr valley. The raid was undoubtedly a great strategic success and an even greater propaganda coup. It was also a testament to the very high level of skill and courage which the crews of Bomber Command demonstrated, but after the excitement died down, we began to realise the terrible cost in lives and aircraft. Of the nineteen Lancasters that took off from RAF Scampton for the raid that May night, eight were lost, and of the fifty-six young men in them, only three survived as prisoners of war.

Perhaps of all those who failed to return, the contribution of Squadron Leader 'Dinghy' Young, DFC* to the success of the night has largely been overlooked. As one of Gibson's two flight commanders, he was largely responsible for the preparation of the crews, not just his own, and perhaps more significantly, it was Young's mine which fatally weakened the structure, allowing Flight Lieutenant David Maltby's Upkeep to blow the Möhne dam apart.

By this stage of our training, I already knew nearly everyone on the course because, as we moved through the various stages from one course to the next, the numbers of familiar faces slowly reduced by a few each time; some had failed altogether, others were held back to repeat a section, but whatever the reasons, there were significantly fewer of us now than there had been at Blackpool. RAF Wigtown was also where we did the flying part of our air-gunnery course, this time in the Blackburn Botha, an aircraft with an unenviable reliability record.

Whilst there, I had been writing to Joan, one of the two girls whom Ron and I had met on Leicester station and I looked forward to her replies. There wasn't a great deal of free time and what there was tended to be on Sunday evenings. The town had little to offer by way of entertainment except a couple of pubs and the hotel where we met up with the WAAFs for the evening. The older locals did not approve of women going into the pub or hotel bar to drink, especially on a Sunday. The old women, wrinkled before their time, grey hair tied back in a tight bun, would stand in their doorways, pulling hand-knitted shawls more tightly around their shoulders, scowling at us, tut-tutting and muttering words of disapproval as we walked by laughing and talking. This cultural attitude towards women and pubs in Scotland has only fairly recently been broken down, but in 1943 it was considered disgraceful, and on a Sunday even sinful, made all the more so because we were so openly enjoying ourselves.

The final part of our training at Wigtown was to experience the joys of night flying. The whole of the British mainland and all its many islands were in total darkness because of the black-out. There was not a glimmer of light to be seen anywhere and therefore it was impossible to have any idea where you were by looking down for landmarks. If any were there, they certainly could not be seen from the air; it was like flying with a blindfold on. Although we always had an experienced navigator and wireless operator with us in case of emergencies, it was for me to guide the pilot back to base and it gave me a glimpse of the responsibilities I would carry later on when part of an operational crew.

Ron also completed all these stages of the course and at the end of May we returned to Kettering for a further seven days' leave. Whilst on leave I would go out most nights to have a few drinks with various friends. One night I met up with a pal who was also on leave from the RAF and he, Ron and I made a very good night of it. It was one of those nights when the beer slipped down very easily and it wasn't long before I had lost count of how much I had drunk, so much so that I don't remember getting home. The next evening at teatime, a friend of my mother's called around to ask how I was. It appears that I had drunk so much that I had passed out in a doorway and that fortunately this woman and her friend had found me and, in the beam of her torch in the blackout had recognised the drunken airman sprawled at her feet as Mrs Payne's son, Reg. She and her friend had managed to get me home before the police arrived. It was even more embarrassing that I didn't remember anything after I left the last pub, least of all my rescue, but I did thank her for saving me from a night in a police cell.

At the end of my leave, I was to report to my next base, RAF Cottesmore No.14 Operational Training Unit. I caught an early train to Oakham from where the transport took me to the base. It was also at this point that the group of friends who had started out together at Blackpool eighteen months earlier became split up between the different training centres around Britain. Ron and I were the only two from our little band to be posted to Cottesmore and it was here in June 1943 that I was to meet up with most of my future crew.

"At RAF Yatesbury. l-r back row: Reg Payne, Keith Kenway, Robbie Robertson, front row: Ron Boydon, George Plank, Eric 'Tubby' Melhuish'

"RAF Wigtown AFU Scotland. Reg is standing 3rd from the right. Photo taken by Ron Boydon, which is why he isn't in it"

"Vickers Wellington bomber"

Chapter Six

*"So good luck came, and on my roof did light
Like noiseless snow, or as the dew of night;
Not all at once, but gently, as the trees
Are by the sunbeams tickled by degrees."*
- '*The Coming of Good Luck*'; Robert Herrick

April 1940 saw No.14 OTU formed from 185 Squadron, which was stationed at Cottesmore and flying Handley Page Hampdens. It had been realised that there was a great deal more to training up an increased bomber force than simply producing more aircraft, particularly so when the heavy four-engine bombers, the Stirling, followed a month later by the Halifax and then the Lancaster, came on stream. Each of the crew members had a specialised function and to get the best out of the men and their machines, the crews had to be crafted into a team that worked together as a single unit and could cover for each other in an emergency. That was the job of the Operational Training Units.

RAF Cottesmore was a pre-war airfield with brick-built modern buildings and four large hangars. The accommodation contrast with earlier stations couldn't have been greater; the Sergeants' Mess was like a hotel and we were billeted in the former married quarters with only three beds to a room. There were about fifteen each of wireless operators, gunners, pilots, navigators, and bomb aimers all coming together here to form up into crews. In the early days of the war, the RAF allocated airmen to specific crews, but because the success and survival of a crew so often depended upon the right chemistry between the individuals, it was soon left for the crews to sort themselves out and choose who they wanted.

During the first few days on the station, each trade was given the details of their specific part on the course and shown around the Vickers Wellington aircraft that we were to fly for this stage of our training. Then, all the trades were brought together in one of the large hangars and told to sort themselves out into crews of five. I wasn't really sure what I was supposed to do, and since there were quite a number of officers amongst the seventy-five or eighty men, I didn't feel able to approach any of them to see if they needed a wireless operator. As I was slowly walking around the hangar watching others shaking hands and teaming up, I saw two officers walking purposefully towards me; one was a pilot, the other a navigator.

"Are you fixed up in anyone's crew yet?" asked the young pilot.

"No, sir" I replied.

"Jolly good. Would you like to join our crew?" he invited me with a smile.

"Yes please, sir," I answered eagerly, put at ease by his quiet and confident manner.

I had no idea what the future held for me; none of us did. Yet that pilot's quiet invitation to join his crew settled my destiny in the war, because the young officer who had asked me was Pilot Officer Michael Beetham, who one day, long after the war was over, would become Chief of the Air Staff and then Marshal of the Royal Air Force, although on that day in the hangar he could never have imagined the immense achievements that awaited him.

I felt rather surprised but also very honoured to have been asked by two officers to join their crew. Up until then I had rarely spoken to an officer and now these two pleasant men had asked me if I would like to join them. We shook hands and I joined Michael and PO Frank Swinyard, the navigator, to find the other two members of the crew, bomb aimer Sgt Les Bartlett and rear gunner Sgt Fred Ball, who I actually thought was an unusually big man to have to squeeze into the cramped confines of the rear turret.

The crew had come about in the way that so many did, through compatible personalities. In the first few days Michael had got to know Frank in the Officers' Mess, Frank knew a sergeant bomb aimer, who knew a wireless operator, who knew a gunner. It was as simple as that.

Michael was the youngest member of the crew, having just celebrated his twentieth birthday on 17th May. He had been educated at St. Marylebone School and had decided to join the RAF as soon as he was old enough, having watched the Hurricanes and Spitfires of Fighter Command in dogfights with the Luftwaffe over the south coast during the Battle of Britain. Although his father had served as an infantry officer during the Great War and had been called up again in 1939 to run a training battalion near Portsmouth, it was to the siren of flying that the young Michael Beetham had been inexorably drawn, a decision that would define the rest of his life.

Fred Ball was twenty-two, the youngest son from a large Catholic family. Fred had worked in Birmingham's jewellery quarter before the war and he brought his two main interests into the RAF with him, cards and cigarettes.

Born on 17th September 1917, Les Bartlett was twenty-five when he joined the crew. His early years had been spent in Gloucestershire before moving to the North East where he had been educated at the Stockton-on-Tees Secondary School for Boys. He qualified as a chemist and became a member of the Pharmaceutical Society. Although in a reserved occupation, he had become an ARP and then in 1941 had volunteered for aircrew when the rules surrounding reserved occupations had been relaxed.

The second commissioned officer in the crew was the oldest member. Frank Swinyard had been born in the middle of the Great War on 1st April 1916 at the Manor House, Finsbury Park, in London. Later he moved with his family to Luton, where he went to the local Modern School. Always a keen sportsman, he had worked as the assistant to the Company Secretary of High Duty Alloys Ltd in Slough before volunteering for the RAF.

I had turned twenty barely two months before Michael and was thus the next youngest in the aircraft.

There were still two more members of our final crew yet to join us, a mid-upper gunner and a flight engineer, but that would not be until we moved onto four-engine aircraft; for now our crew was complete. With characteristic leadership, Michael suggested that it might be a good idea for us all to go into Oakham that night to have a meal together and get to know each other a little better. He booked a table at the George Hotel and we enjoyed a very pleasant meal, which cost us five shillings each. This was the first time that I had ever had a meal in a large hotel where I was waited upon at the table, and although 5/- was more than half a day's pay to me, it was well worth it, both for the experience and to get to know the rest of the crew before we started flying together and trusting our lives to each other.

At Cottesmore, once again, I had all my teeth filled. We also had a head-and-shoulders photograph taken wearing civilian clothes, which we then sewed into our battledress tunics. The same photograph was put into our passports. Should we be shot down over friendly territory, the photograph would be cross-checked with the passport which was held at our operational base and so identify us as genuine RAF personnel and not German spies.

I spent the first week back in the classroom learning all about the equipment that was in the Wellington; the wireless set, oxygen bottles, flares, fire extinguishers, exit points should I have to bail out, the dinghy and deployment procedure, and so on. Then at last it was time to fly. We were moved to nearby RAF Saltby, which was a flying training airfield. Cottesmore had come to the end of its time as an OTU and the unit was scheduled to move to a new base, also in Leicestershire at Market Harborough, but it wasn't yet ready to receive us, hence the temporary move to Saltby. Here, during July we flew thirteen sorties together, eight by day and five at night, which were a combination of circuits and bumps, bombing practice and cross-country navigation exercises.

After our training each day, there was usually the chance to go off the base, and so Les Bartlett and I would often go into Melton Mowbray for the evening. I was still writing to Joan, the girl I had met on Leicester station. I enjoyed receiving her letters and especially the little gifts which she managed to send to me, such as razor blades, toothpaste and such things, which were all in short supply. Because Saltby was fairly near to Leicester, I arranged to meet her when I had a leave pass and she took me home to meet her family, who always made me very welcome, probably more so because her brother was also away training for aircrew.

On one of these trips, Les and Fred Ball came with me. The arrangement was that I would go to see Joan whilst they went into the town for a few drinks, after which we would all meet at the bus station in time to catch the ten o'clock bus back to Saltby, as we would be flying at 08.00 the following day. I spent a lovely evening with Joan and her parents at the local social club before going back to their house, where Joan's mother made up sandwiches for Les, Fred and me to eat on the bus back to Saltby.

Joan and I set off to the bus station but by the time we got there, the bus had already gone. It always left on time, so we must have taken longer to walk to the station than I had realised, because I know that we left in plenty of time. There was nothing to be done but to return to her house where her parents let me sleep in her brother's room. At four o'clock the next morning I once more said my goodbyes and set off for Saltby, this time riding Joan's brother's bicycle.

Although it was by now getting light, I had to stop and ask the way several times because there were no signposts; they had all long since been removed in case of invasion. After cycling some thirty miles, I arrived back at Saltby just in time to see the rest of my crew going in to breakfast; we were not flying that day after all.

Bicycles were a great asset on an airfield to cover the substantial distances between the various parts of the camp, especially to where the aircraft were dispersed. At Saltby, we had to cross the airfield several times, depending upon which type of aircraft we happened to be flying in. Consequently, when I turned up on a bicycle, its future became a topic of conversation. I already had a bicycle to use around the base, but Fred didn't, so later that day despite my protests, Les took it and gave it to Fred. However, I was determined that it should be returned to Joan's parents, who had been kind enough to lend it to me in the first place.

Three days later, the wireless operators finished classroom work early, so I seized the opportunity, jumped on the bicycle whilst Fred was still in his class and rode it to Oakham railway station, where I tied a label to it, paid the fee and sent it back to Joan's parents. It was delivered the next day. The railway companies provided that kind of service in those days, but not any more. Les and Fred called me all the names under the sun but I didn't care, the bike belonged to Joan's brother and he would want it when he was posted to his own station when he started operations.

The early training at Saltby was with an instructor pilot but once he was satisfied that Mike was competent, we were on our own. All the time that we were in the air, I was given tasks on the radio equipment, sending and receiving messages. We also had to practise single-engine landings and stalls over and over again.

All this lasted for about a month, each step moving us closer to an operational posting. Now before our flights, we were required to attend a briefing, then it was out to practise over the bombing range, then cross-country flights and gunnery practice over the Wash.

Whenever we had some spare time, our pilot would gather us all together as a crew at the aircraft and we would practise our bail-out procedure and dinghy drill. This was typical of the leadership shown by Michael, and whilst I knew it was important to practise these procedures, I really did not imagine that one day in the not too distant future it would save my life and I would thank him for making me practise bailing out.

Airsickness, like seasickness, is an appalling affliction, because there is no escape until the aircraft lands again, which might not be for hours. Almost everyone in wartime aircrews suffered from airsickness at one time or another, usually early on in their training, but then as they became used to the motion of the aircraft, for most people it would wear off. During training, and sometimes on operations too, the rear gunners suffered worst when the pilot had to go through the corkscrew manoeuvre to avoid enemy fighters. The rear turret was the most uncomfortable seat in the aircraft at the best of times, but during evasion manoeuvres, with the aircraft pitching, twisting, turning, rising and falling, it was dreadful. The centre of the aircraft was a relatively more stable position.

It was, then, a matter of some surprise and concern when our navigator Frank began to feel increasingly airsick as our cross-country flights started to extend beyond a couple of hours, especially in the Wellington. As the trips lengthened, he couldn't control it and started vomiting into his oxygen mask. Frank sat very close to my position in the aircraft and I could see the terrible distress that he was in, but there was nothing that I could do to prevent it. However, as it got worse I did start to take a spare oxygen mask, microphone and some old newspapers with us so that I could give him a fresh mask whilst I cleaned out the other one for him ready for when he needed another change after the next bout of sickness.

We were moving relentlessly through the training programme by now and part of that entailed much longer flights. As a consequence, Frank's airsickness increased exponentially in intensity and regularity. Sometimes, particularly if the weather was not very good, he would be repeatedly sick and became so exhausted with the continual vomiting that he would lay his head on the navigator's table, close his eyes and try to escape through sleep. When this happened, Michael's voice would come over the intercom asking me to give him his repeated courses to get us safely back to base, something which by this stage of our training I was able to do with confidence.

However, Frank's future in the crew was looking increasingly uncertain and our pilot was faced with an awful dilemma; should he report the matter now and replace Frank quickly or wait to see if his navigator could overcome the sickness? An exhausted navigator with chronic airsickness would be of no use to us on an eight-hour operation over Germany when trying to escape the night fighters and flak batteries to find our way home in total darkness. For the time being, however, we persevered with Frank. I continued to keep a spare oxygen mask and microphone in my kit and cleaned up after each of his many bouts of vomiting; after all, we were a crew.

Progress through our training brought an increased awareness of our skills and proficiency, and although we knew that we still had much to learn, we also knew that a large part of that could only come from operational experience. With this increased awareness and the realisation of the imminence of a posting to an operational squadron, came a more intense social life. The cinema showed every evening, the station dance band played at evening mealtimes and there was a dance in the Officers' Mess or the Sergeants' Mess most weekends.

At Cottesmore, there was a stunningly attractive WAAF driver with lovely dark brown hair and sparkling eyes who worked in the MT section and who would drive the crews out to their aircraft whenever flying was on. Rita was a 'chop girl' if ever there was. She would smile, flash her eyes and the other chaps fell over themselves to get into the front of the truck with her. I let them get on with it, I could talk to her any time I wanted to. We had grown up together, gone to school together, played those wonderful games as children in a world far away from wartime, in a land called childhood where her father was our chimney sweep and knew my parents. When the others found out that we knew each other so well, they were very envious; such are the little pleasures in life. After a few days, we arranged to meet and stepped out together to Oakham for the evening. Not long afterwards, she asked me if I would take her to the next station dance which was being held in the Sergeants' Mess that weekend.

The night of the dance arrived and I was delighted to take such a good looking woman with me, but we were hardly through the door when she excused herself, walked over to the bar and started chatting to a number of young officers who were drinking there. I didn't see her again that night. I wasn't surprised, I knew Rita too well. She really was a beautiful girl and understandably very popular on the base. Nor did it particularly concern me because it left me free to talk and drink with Les, Fred and Ron Boydon, who, together with his crew came over and joined us. As the drinks flowed, I forgot all about Rita, but before we left I do remember that the Mess was in a terrible state, with chairs knocked over, glasses broken and beer all over the floor.

RAF Market Harborough wasn't quite ready for us yet and so we were all given seven days' leave, which was extended by a further seven days, but in early August our training resumed. On our first day at the new station, we were told two things. First that our training was now behind schedule and we would have to work hard to catch up, and the other was to follow a three-ton truck around the perimeter track of the airfield and pick up all the brick ends and pieces of timber that the builders had left behind and throw them into the back of the truck; the propeller wash from an aircraft would whip up this debris and rip the fabric of the fuselage.

During the next two weeks, we flew almost every day and most nights to complete our training but also to get us accustomed to night flying, as that was when most of our operations were going to be. All too soon, we had finished at Market Harborough, and on 14th September we moved to No.1654 Heavy Conversion Unit at RAF Wigsley in Nottinghamshire to start our training on four-engine aircraft. We were getting very close now, brought home to us by the large number of heavy bombers flying around in the skies over the county.

It was also at Wigsley that the remaining two members of our crew were allocated to us. We were given a young flight engineer and a much older mid-upper gunner named Arthur, who was nearly forty years of age and had been ground crew before re-mustering as aircrew. Our course here was to last about six weeks and on 20th September I had my very first flight in a heavy bomber, Halifax D287. This was a dual familiarisation flight and it was to be my first and only trip in a Halifax. The instructor pilot that day was New Zealander PO Bernard Gumbley, DFM, who had just completed his first tour with 49 Squadron, the same squadron that my brother Art was with. Later in the war, Bernard Gumbley returned to ops with 617 Squadron. On 21st March 1945 he was the pilot of a specially modified Lancaster carrying one of Barnes Wallis's 22,000lb Grand Slam bombs in a daylight raid by twenty aircraft from the squadron on the Arbergen railway bridge just outside Bremen. Two of the bridge piers were destroyed but, six weeks before the end of the war in Europe, so was Bernard's aircraft, the only squadron loss that day. It was hit by flak and crashed in flames, killing all of the crew.

After the Wellington, the Halifax seemed immense, and indeed it was. The main fuselage was much deeper than not only the Wellington, but the Lancaster too, because the crew positions were situated in a double-deck configuration, so that the pilot and flight engineer sat on a platform above the wireless operator and navigator, who sat in tandem below them.

Then, on 24th September 1943, I had my first trip in an Avro Lancaster Mk I, serial number R5910. Developed from the Manchester, with its notoriously unreliable engines, the Lancaster was powered by four Rolls Royce Merlin XX engines. With a wingspan of over 100 feet and a fuselage of more than 70 feet in length, it weighed 65,000lbs at take-off when fully loaded, had a ceiling of more than 24,000 feet and an operational range of 1,600 miles. It was quite simply the finest bomber to take to the skies during World War Two.

Of the 7,377 Lancasters built, mostly during the war, around 3,946 survived the hostilities and yet it seems incomprehensible now, and is an illustration of the disdain for Bomber Command amongst the immediate post-war establishment, that there are today only two flying Lancasters anywhere in the world, PA474 of the Battle of Britain Memorial Flight at Coningsby, Lincolnshire and VRA in Canada. There is a third one; NX611 is privately owned by Fred and Harold Panton at the Lincolnshire Aviation Museum. It does not fly but carries out taxi runs on a very regular basis throughout most of the year. The government even sold off for scrap the celebrated Halifax 'Friday the Thirteenth', which had completed 128 missions, an incredible record for any bomber, but especially a Halifax, and which had been on a public display tour of Britain after the war.

The power of the Lancaster was staggering and the noise was overwhelming; I have never forgotten that first trip. Unlike the Halifax, the wireless operator and navigator sat next to each other and behind the pilot. Consequently, Frank and I could easily talk to each other without using the microphone system, which helped to free it up for the important communications between the gunners, the bomb aimer and the pilot.

It soon became clear that our young flight engineer was not going to fit in with the rest of us. The relationship between the pilot and the flight engineer was particularly important because part of the FE's job was to help the pilot during take-off and landing which, apart from flak and enemy fighters, were the most dangerous parts of any trip. The open microphone gave privy to the rest of the crew of the difficulty that Michael was having with the FE. The pilot was the captain of the aircraft; it, and we, were his responsibility, but the FE kept insisting upon doing things his way which was different from the way that Michael wanted them done.

One day, after a particularly acrimonious exchange between the two of them, Michael called the rest of the crew together and asked us what we thought about the flight engineer. The whole crew agreed with Michael that we were very unhappy about going on operations with this FE; we didn't see him again. On our next trip we were joined by Don Moore, who was as different as chalk from cheese. Don fitted in very well and we thought that we now had a full crew. Don was a Londoner in his late twenties, married with a young daughter but, more importantly, had worked as an RAF engine fitter before volunteering for aircrew. Even for a flight engineer, he knew a great deal about aircraft engines and we were very lucky to have him on the crew.

Although our crew, like most bomber crews at the time, was made up of a mix of NCOs and officers, the relationship between us was one of friendship, irrespective of rank, and we mixed and socialised together as a crew when off the base. Sometimes when sitting out on the grass in the warm summer sunshine waiting around for the Chief Flying Instructor to tell us what to do next, Michael, who was only a couple of months younger than me, would indulge in horse play by jumping on my back and wrestling me to the ground. Of course, I had to let him win because he was the officer. However, once in the aircraft there was no horse play; everyone knew the job they had to do and also that Michael was the captain of the aircraft and in charge. It was the relationship that was to keep us alive. The young FE hadn't accepted that and so he had to go.

During our first few days at Wigsley, we were introduced to the station Medical Officer, a young Flight Lieutenant. Amongst other information, he gave us a short pep talk about STDs in straightforward language. "It's as simple as this," he explained, "when you go into Nottingham at night, you'll find plenty of girls who are happy to share their pleasures with you. However, about one in every twelve of them has venereal disease of one sort or another. If you must indulge and then regret it afterwards, come and see me straight away. I would rather you came to the sick bay, pulled out the offending part, plonked it on the table and asked me to fix it than be like the young airman who left it very late and then told me that his rash was caused by frost. He tried to convince me that whilst peeing in a bramble hedge one frosty night on the way back from the pub it been so cold that the frost had got it. As I told him at the time, the only frosts around here are whore frosts!"

There was plenty for me to familiarise myself with in this new aircraft. Although the ARI 5033 radio receiver and transmitter set with the aerial located on top of the main canopy was the same on the Lancaster as in the Wellington, there was also the DF equipment [direction finding] with the loop aerial, also on top of the main canopy, and the IFF [Identification Friend or Foe] equipment, which sent out a signal showing that we were not the enemy. The fuse board was much larger and more complex than in the Wellington and since I was also an air gunner, I had to familiarise myself with the guns and the turrets should I need to use them if either of our gunners were injured.

The wireless operator in a Lancaster sat on the port side at the back of the main cockpit compartment next to the leading edge of the wing spar. I also had the astro-dome close to my seat and a side window that I could look out along the wing from; a detail that in a few months would help to save my life. Part of my role in the crew was to be responsible for checking and looking after the safety equipment on board because most of it was stowed close to where my seat was. The dinghy survival packs, should we have to ditch in the sea, the First Aid cabinets, the fire extinguishers, the 'dead man's rope', the axe and the signal pistol were just some of the aircraft's survival and safety equipment that I had to look after. In the event of a ditching, it was also my job to pull the release lever for the Type J dinghy once we were in the water. The dinghy was stowed in the root of the starboard wing and would deploy automatically after the lever was pulled so that the crew could climb into it from the wing without getting wet before the aircraft sank.

That was the theory, anyway, and so we continually practised new dinghy and parachute drills. The Lancaster was a much larger aircraft than the earlier bombers which the RAF had used, but despite the greater space inside the fuselage, in the event of ditching or, even worse, of fire and an aircraft out of control, there would only be a few seconds for escape before the G-forces or incoming sea water trapped the crew inside.

By now, we were fully familiar with our aircraft and there was little that we didn't know about it and how to operate it. Consequently, our training became more focused upon attacking the enemy and fighter avoidance techniques, all of which came under the general heading of Combat Manoeuvres. Our cross-country flights became longer and we spent more time at the bombing range on the Isle of Man using 25lb practice bombs from various heights between 16,000 feet and 20,000 feet, which would be our typical bombing heights when on operations.

We also practised searchlight avoidance and night fighter interception techniques over and over again. Corkscrewing, a diving, turning, climbing, turning and diving movement, was the bombers main defence against the fighters. It was known as corkscrewing because when looked at from above the movement resembled the shape of a corkscrew. This manoeuvre generally prevented the pilot of the incoming fighter, who would invariably attack from the rear of the aircraft, from being able to line up the bomber in his gun sights. We didn't know it at the time, but to overcome the corkscrew the Luftwaffe had already developed a technique called *Schräge Musik*, translated literally as jazz music. By fitting a 20mm cannon in an almost vertical upward firing position, the night fighter pilots were able to slip underneath our aircraft, all too often undetected against the pitch black background of the earth far beneath them, and fire up into the wings of the bombers. It was a devastatingly effective method of attack and one that we would come to fear greatly.

One afternoon when we were not flying, as Les and I were cycling back across the airfield to our billet, we were caught in a torrential thunderstorm. By the time we reached the shelter of our room, our uniforms were soaked through and we were wet to the skin. I decided that the only way to get them dry was to light the stove in the room, so I went out to collect some dry wood from under the hedges near to our billet. I soon had the fire going and our clothes hung up to dry. We had just finished changing when the door opened and a pal asked if either of us would like to make up a four in a card game. Les enjoyed his cards and so said he would gladly do so. Not long afterwards, the door burst opened again, only this time it was the Station Warrant Officer.

"Who gave you permission to light that fire?"

"No-one, but we were caught in the thunderstorm and..." I tried to explain.

"Don't you know that it's against RAF Regulations to light a fire in the stove before 30th September?"

"But our clothes were soaking wet," I persevered, "and there was no other way to dry them. We have only used wood which I collected from the hedge bottom. There's no RAF fuel on the fire."

"Three evenings on NCOs' Parade starting tonight." And with that, he left the room as abruptly as he had come in.

This parade was a form of punishment given to NCOs for minor infringements of the regulations and consisted of drill and marching for an hour or so each evening at the far end of the airfield. With typical military mentality it was a double punishment because we all had to walk the two miles or so to the outer reaches of the airfield; bicycles were not allowed. Then afterwards, we had to walk back again, by which time it was too late to go out anywhere. I did feel a bit put out as I thought the SWO had been very unreasonable, but Les and I devised a way round this.

Each evening, Les would slowly ride his bike along the road outside the camp whilst holding onto mine and hide behind the hedge where we were drilling. After the parade finished and the discipline sergeant had set off to pedal back to the Mess, Les would emerge with the two bikes, whereupon we would cycle off to one of the local pubs for the rest of the evening.

On the second night, as we were about to leave, we saw a Lancaster racing down the runway gathering speed and preparing to take off. The more I watched it, the more fascinated I became. It looked as if one of its six-foot-high wheels had become detached and was simply rolling along underneath the wing at 70mph. To my horror, I realised that it really had come off and was slowly moving away from under the aircraft. Finally, the tyre left the runway and began to bound over the grass in ever increasing leaps towards the perimeter fence, just like one of the Dambusters' bouncing bombs. Meanwhile, the Lancaster was still racing along the runway on its one remaining wheel, the pilot desperately fighting with the controls to keep the unsupported wing from ploughing into the ground. Then, almost imperceptibly at first, but with growing certainty, the stricken aircraft began to curve away as if trying to chase the disappearing tyre across the grass, finally careering on through the adjoining fields, over the hill and out of sight in the gathering gloom of dusk.

Les and I stood in the silence that followed, staring in disbelief towards the hillside and the track of destruction ploughed up by the Lancaster as it had chewed everything in its path during those few final frenetic moments. The thundering explosion and the orange glow of fire encased in a black plume of petroleum smoke climbing into the evening sky shook us from our stupor. Pedalling as hard as we could, we headed for the scene of the disaster, dreading what we would find but driven by a need to help if we could. As we arrived, the aircraft was already burning fiercely, its ammunition exploding in a series of popping sounds. We tried to get to the crew but were forced back by the intense heat and the .303 bullets which were now whizzing over our heads and past our ears. We both dived behind a nearby log, helplessly listening as successive explosions followed and the furnace fire consumed the aircraft and the young crew inside her.

Any hope for the crew was quickly gone, but after about twenty minutes the ammunition was spent and we heard the voices of a recovery team on the other side of the crash site. Clambering out from behind our protective log, we ventured down to the remains of the Lancaster, now little more than a shell of twisted, tortured, and broken metal surrounding the white-hot glowing heat within.

"We saw the wheel come off on the runway. I suppose all the crew are dead?" I hesitatingly asked one of the RAF firemen who was damping down some of the smouldering remains spread around the hillside with foam.

"Dead? Not them, mate. When it stopped they would have been out of there in double-quick time." Then he added with a laugh, "They'll all be down the Sergeants' Mess by now drinking their health." Which is exactly where we should have been!

It was a happy end to what could have been a terrible tragedy, and Les and I slowly pedalled to the pub, still unable to fully believe what we had witnessed. It did, though, serve as a reminder to us that not all the danger was in the skies over Germany. There was many an instructor who light-heartedly maintained that training crews was more dangerous than operations. Perhaps not entirely true, but nevertheless 5,327 airmen were killed and 3,113 injured in training accidents. We had undoubtedly witnessed a remarkable escape for one crew.

Our last flight at Wigsley, which lasted for five and three-quarter hours, was a cross-country time-and-distance run, culminating in us dropping six 25lb bombs from 20,000 feet. On our return, Michael brought the Lancaster down onto the runway back at Wigsley and we taxied round to the dispersal pan. As we climbed down the ladder and out into the fresh air, I turned to Frank, our navigator.

"Have you realised, Frank, that since we moved onto Lancasters, you haven't been airsick once."

"I know, Reg. I didn't want to tempt fate by saying anything to you, but you're right. I haven't felt sick either, even with the fighter affiliation; strange, isn't it? It must simply have been something to do with the Wimpey."

Michael had been right to persevere with Frank because now we had a first class navigator in the crew.

One afternoon in the middle of October towards the end of our time at Wigsley, having finished early, Frank, Les, Fred and I decided to catch the train into Nottingham for the evening. When we got to Wigsley station, the ticket office was closed, so we hopped onto the train without tickets. It was a small local train with only two coaches, a couple of cattle trucks and a guard's van behind, so there was no clippie. Fred and Les, always ready for a way to save money, suggested that when we got to Nottingham we should tell the ticket collector at the barrier that we had got on the train two stops back down the line and so wouldn't have to pay as much as from Wigsley.

The little train gently chattered into Nottingham station and we jumped down with its few other passengers, joining the throng of troops and civilians who were milling about the platforms. Les was first to the ticket collector at the barrier, full of confidence,

"It's the four of us, chum, we just got on two stops back but the ticket office was closed."

The railwayman looked at our RAF uniforms with disdain. "Oh yes, and where is your aerodrome two stops down the line? There isn't one. You chaps are from the Lincoln area."

With that, he closed the barrier and rang for an RAF policeman, who appeared moments later. The ticket collector told him what had happened. In front of all the other people waiting to go through the barrier, the policeman called us to attention and marched us out of the station, shouting orders at us very loudly. I felt terrible, but I knew that it was even worse for Frank because he was a commissioned officer and could lose his rank. We marched out into the late afternoon sunshine and around the corner of the station building until we were well away from the entrance. It came as a surprise then, when we heard the policeman say quietly,

"Squad, halt." Wondering at the change in volume, we came to a stop, and then quietly again he said, "Okay, you lot, bugger off quick and don't get caught again."

Unable to quite believe our luck, we thanked him and left the area very smartly. Perhaps he had served on an operational station at some time and knew better than us what was waiting for us; whatever the reason, we didn't try that trick again.

"Sgt Reg Payne posted to No50 Squadron at RAF Skellingthorpe"

"ATS Lance Corporal Ena Goodrich as Reg first met her"

Chapter Seven

"Think no more, lad; laugh, be jolly:
Why should men make haste to die?
Empty heads and tongues a-talking
Make the rough road easy walking,
And the feather pate of folly
Bears the falling sky."
        - From '*A Shropshire Lad*'; AE Housman

Apart from a ten-day survival course, we were now at the top of our training and with the knowledge that after two years we were soon to be on operations, we were inevitably in high spirits. The Sergeants' Mess at Wigsley had no furniture in it, just a carpet on the floor, because the parties were so riotous that the tables and chairs always got broken and so in the end the RAF refused to provide any more. During the day, if you wanted to sit and read a newspaper, you sat on the floor and either leaned against the wall or sat back to back with another chap. When I first arrived at Wigsley, I thought that this was a bit much but after I had been to a couple of the parties I understood better!

We were young and full of a life that could be cut short at any moment. We had started to live every day as our last. The final party there before we left was wild even by Wigsley standards. Most of the officers from the various crews were in the Mess with us, the beer flowed all night and we all drank far too much. Ron Boydon had somehow managed to relieve the bass drum from the dance-band drummer and he marched around the Mess with it strapped to his chest, beating out the time with two beer mugs as everyone cheered and sang along. Finally, the party ended and we all stumbled back to our billets. Les and I shared a room and we were just getting ready to fall into our beds when the door flew open, two officers rushed in and, with much laughter and whooping, sprayed us both with foam from the fire extinguishers. Very pleased with their efforts, they bade us goodnight and disappeared. I still have a good idea who they were.

Then it was time to move on again. At Moreton Hall, we were taught survival in the event of being shot down over occupied Europe. Sleeping rough, living off the land, using water cleansing tablets to produce drinking water, and a great deal of cross-country running and fitness exercises; we had got out of condition whilst concentrating on flying training. The end of this course was the last tick in the box, the last hurdle to jump, the last step of the way; our training was over, the RAF could give us no more help. From now on it was on-the-job training and we were given our squadron postings. We knew that it would be a Lancaster squadron, but which one? For the Beetham crew it was to be 50 Squadron based at RAF Skellingthorpe, just outside Lincoln, in No.5 Group.

Ron Boydon and his crew were posted to 207 Squadron at the newly opened station of Spilsby, a satellite of RAF East Kirkby, and on that last morning I said cheerio and wished good luck to a valued friend that I had spent the last two years training with.

I packed up my kit and, as with every other posting, went through all the clearance procedures from each department on the base, clothing stores, Sergeants' Mess, library, dentist, even FFI, all the time knowing that as soon as I arrived at Skellingthorpe, just a few miles away, I would have to go through it all over again, just as I had done on every posting.

It was late afternoon on Tuesday, 26th October 1943 when the truck pulled up at the gates of RAF Skellingthorpe and we reported to the Orderly Room where our names and other details were recorded, including next of kin. The two officers were then taken to their quarters and the rest of us to ours, a cold ten-bed Nissen hut which we shared with another new crew, close to a small wood on the far side of the Skellingthorpe Road, the lane from Lincoln that ran past the airfield to the village two miles away which gave its name to the base.

The station was a relatively new satellite airfield of RAF Waddington and had three concrete runways, the main one of nearly two thousand yards running north-east to south-west, which gave us a spectacular and sometimes worryingly close view of Lincoln cathedral standing high on the hill above the city when we took off in that direction. Building work on the cathedral started in 1088 and continued in stages throughout the medieval period until its final completion in 1311, at which time it was, at 525 feet high, the tallest building in the world and remained so until 1549 when the central tower was destroyed in a storm. There were times when we had to take off north-eastwards that we were rather pleased that it was no longer so high, because it was certainly high enough to lift up and over with a fully laden Lancaster bomber; but what a beautiful sight it was rising up out of the morning mist when we were returning home after a raid.

Knowing that this was a relatively new station, we were rather surprised and disappointed to find that our quarters were somewhat spartan. There were lavatories but no washing facilities; these were located in the common wash-house at the rear of the Sergeants' Mess, some ten minutes' walk away. Rather disconsolately, having had great expectations of an operational station, we unpacked our kit, made up our beds and, since it was now getting dark, decided to cycle over to the Mess to have something to eat. There weren't many airmen in the Mess at all and the few who were there took no notice of us. After a look around the different rooms and having discovered that there was not even a NAAFI on site, we returned to the cold uninviting room that was our billet.

Fred, Les, Don and I were sitting on our beds feeling sorrowful and forlorn when an airman, who had been concerned to see the lights on, came into the hut.
"Who are you lads?" he asked cheerfully.
"We're a new crew. We've just arrived at this dump. Where is everyone?"
The airman laughed. "They're in Lincoln. This is no dump, it's a marvellous posting. The whole city of Lincoln is just fifteen minutes' bike ride down the road. All the pubs and

girls you could wish for, and plenty to spare. No-one stays on the base unless they have to."

Fred and I looked at each other, picked up our greatcoats and gloves, put on forage caps and, after getting directions from the airman, set off on our bikes for Lincoln. Les and Don were both married so decided to stay in the hut and write home. It was late October and cold outside by now. As we cycled along in the pitch dark of the moonless night I could feel my breath condensing on my face. It wasn't long before we came into the outskirts of the city but in the total dark of the blackout it was difficult to see which of the buildings were pubs and which were shops. As we coasted along, we saw a group of airmen going down a passageway. As they opened the door at the far end, a shaft of light lit the entrance and from inside the sound of laughter and chinking glasses spilled out into the frosty night air. That would do nicely.

The cosy warmth and smoky atmosphere in the Unity contrasted with the darkness and gathering frost of the clear crisp air we had left outside. The pub wasn't too crowded so Fred and I ordered a glass of brown ale each and then found a seat away from the main group in there, who obviously all knew each other. At the far end of the room were two ATS girls sitting quietly chatting and sipping their drinks. We didn't take a great deal of notice of them other than to comment that we thought they were both very attractive and that they had looked our way a few times. If this was an indication of the girls in Lincoln, then indeed it was a very good posting.

A little before ten o'clock, the two girls got up, pulled on their coats and caps and headed for the doorway. As they passed our table we started to chat to them, telling them that we had just been posted here. They told us that they had been in Lincoln for some time and were with the Royal Army Service Corps, the RASC. They were billeted at the top of the hill near to the cathedral and had to be in by ten. We offered to walk them back to their billet and so, leaving our bikes where they were, we accompanied them up the aptly named Steep

Hill, arriving outside their quarters just before the cathedral clock struck the hour. Arranging to see Ena and Joan the following night in the same pub if we weren't on night flying, we made the much easier descent of Steep Hill to find our bikes and try to get some idea of where the Unity was in Lincoln before cycling back to the aerodrome.

The next morning, each of our crew had to report to their individual section officers, so I made my way across to the Signals Office. I didn't know any of these chaps and there was no-one from the many courses I had been through. After being introduced to everyone, I met the section Warrant Officer, an Australian with an interesting past. His aircraft had been shot down over France but he had managed to evade capture and made his escape to Spain, only to be thrown into a Spanish prison. There, perhaps because he was Australian, he was given as much wine to drink as he could manage in the hope that he would drink himself to death. He told me that he had certainly made a good attempt at it, but just in time the British Consul heard about him, and because he was by then so desperately ill, he was repatriated to England on medical grounds. Nevertheless he did recover, but his flying days were over. Not surprisingly, he never wanted to see another glass of wine, especially Spanish wine, ever again.

He took me across to one of the Lancasters and showed me some of the up-to-date operational equipment which had not found its way onto the training curriculum. There was the new radar GEE and MONICA, which enabled us to detect an aircraft flying close by, especially one coming in from the rear, as an attacking fighter would do, and a jamming device called MANDREL. He also explained another jamming expedient which entailed putting a microphone into one of the aircraft engines and the wireless operator then transmitting the deafening noise through his transmitter; this was all new to me.

For reasons best known to the RAF, our mid-upper didn't go with us to Moreton Hall for survival instruction but had instead been sent here to Skellingthorpe on an advanced gunnery course. The Gunnery Flight operated Wellingtons from the far corner of the airfield and at lunch that Wednesday we learned that Arthur would not be coming back to us. A few days before our arrival he had been in a Wellington which had crashed and, although he survived, he was badly burned and would not return to active service; instead he was on his way to East Grinstead and the ground-breaking burns care unit of Dr Archibald McIndoe. I thought back to the intensity of the fire a few weeks earlier in the Lancaster that had lost its wheel and shuddered at what Arthur must have experienced; but at least he was alive.

Ian Higgins was assigned to our crew as the new mid-upper. Single, Ian was a good-looking Glaswegian who was very popular with the WAAFs, in fact with all the girls. As the only Scot on the crew, he was inevitably known as Jock. He was a very pleasant lad, who, despite the difficulty of coming into an established crew, fitted in well with us and stayed. He also brought with him a considerable bonus; he was blessed with exceptionally good night vision, a considerable asset for an air gunner at that stage of the war. Again, we were lucky with our replacement crew member and now at last we were a complete crew and ready to go to war.

After lunch, we met the Squadron CO, Wing Commander Edward Pullen, who brought our eagerness to get on with the job down to earth somewhat by telling us that we were certainly not ready yet and needed a lot more training before he would send us out on operations. Then it was over to the stores to draw our electrically heated flying suits, gloves, socks and flying boots. These were the latest 'escape' boot design and had a knife in a small inside pocket. In the event of being shot down, the knife could be used to cut away the lambswool sides, leaving a pair of ordinary-looking boots. Wing Commander Pullen would be killed seven weeks later on the night of 20th/21st December in Lancaster DV234 VN-M in a raid on Frankfurt whilst taking FO Peter Boyle on his 'second-dickie' trip.

That evening, Fred and I went into Lincoln again to the Unity pub to see if the two ATS girls would show up. We hadn't been there very long when they arrived and came over to where we were sitting. This time we had been able to have a wash, shave, and put on a clean collar before seeing them, which was a great improvement from the previous evening's impromptu meeting.

In these first few days at Skellingthorpe, I also managed to go out for a drink with my brother Art. He was with 49 Squadron at nearby RAF Fiskerton. Art had already been on a number of operations over Germany, including three trips to Hamburg and told me something of what to expect. I was soon to learn that he had spared me a great deal of what it was really like and how terrifying it could be.

Two days after our arrival, we were allocated our aircraft, JA961 VN-A for Able which we would take over when Flight Lieutenant Ian Bolton and crew finished their tour, so we went to look her over. What a difference to the dirty, scruffy aircraft we had been training in. The ground crew had this machine clean and shining. It was packed with all the latest equipment, neatly stored away and in full working order, filling us with confidence in the aircraft as well as ourselves.

On Saturday, 30th October, our pilot Mike Beetham, by now promoted to Flying Officer, was told that he would be flying on his second-dickie trip in VN-A with Flt Lt Bolton. This second-dickie trip was for new pilots, who would fly with an experienced crew to get a taste and feel of what operations were really like and so be better prepared when taking their own aircraft on a raid. However, at six o'clock that evening, the operation was cancelled due to bad weather over the target. There was nothing else to do that night so the whole crew went to the pub.

Four nights later, the 3rd November, Mike's second-dickie trip was on again; the target was to be Düsseldorf in the Ruhr Valley, or Happy Valley as it was known to bomber crews. Once more, he was scheduled to fly with Flt Lt Bolton in VN-

A. The crews were due back from the raid around midnight, and so after we had watched them take off, we waited up to see Mike following the debrief with the Intelligence Officer. Full of encouragement and confidence, he told us that so long as we stayed alert we would be all right; a masterful piece of understatement.

As well as being the raid on which Mike Beetham flew his first operation, the raid also resulted in the award of a Victoria Cross to Flight Lieutenant Bill Reid. The son of a blacksmith, Bill was from Glasgow and on this particular night was the captain of a Lancaster of 61 Squadron, then stationed at Syerston in Nottinghamshire but soon to join us at Skellingthorpe for the rest of the war.

The citation in the London Gazette read as follows:

> *Wounded in two attacks, without oxygen, suffering severely from cold, his navigator dead, his wireless operator fatally wounded, his aircraft crippled and defenceless, Flight Lieutenant Reid showed superb courage and leadership in penetrating a further 200 miles into enemy territory to attack one of the most strongly defended targets in Germany, every additional mile increasing the hazards of the long and perilous journey home. His tenacity and devotion to duty were beyond praise.*

For me, however, the raid heralded considerably less joyous news. After lunch the following day, I found a telegram waiting for me in the Sergeants' Mess. It was from my mother, saying that Art had been posted as missing from the raid. His had been one of eleven Lancasters lost over the Ruhr. She wanted me to go home to see her, so I contacted the CO and showed him the telegram.

"I'm sorry about your brother, sergeant, but I don't want to grant you permission to go home."

"It would just be for one night, sir, so that I can reassure her that my brother will be ok," I pleaded.

"I know what will happen; your mother will make you promise not to fly any more and I don't want your crew being broken up at this stage. You are all almost ready for ops."

I took a chance and tried once more. "I promise you, sir, that I will be back here tomorrow ready to fly. I won't let her talk me out of it."

Wing Commander Pullen gazed out of the window across the airfield and I could see that he was thinking very hard about this; I understood his dilemma. All aircrew were volunteers and could refuse to fly at any time. A court martial would follow such a refusal, but that wasn't what he was concerned about. He knew Mike Beetham had just done his second-dickie trip and that we were almost ready to go; he didn't want to lose the wireless operator from the crew at this late stage.

Presently, he turned back to me. "All right, sergeant, you can have a twenty-four-hour pass, but don't let me down. Be back here tomorrow afternoon ready to fly."

"I will, sir, and thank you very much."

With that, I collected my shaving kit, travel warrant and leave pass, and cycled down to Skellingthorpe station to catch the train into Lincoln and then on to Kettering. My parents were very pleased to see me when I arrived that evening. I tried to reassure them that Art would be fine and that if anyone would get out of the aircraft it would be Art. I wasn't so sure and just hoped that he had managed to parachute to safety. Fortunately, my mother didn't say anything to me about not flying, she just told me to take great care and to come back to see her whenever I could. The following morning I was at Skellingthorpe as I had promised and the crew were very pleased to see me back; I had no intention of letting them down.

On Friday 19th, the crew were called to the flight offices and briefed to carry out a search in the North Sea close to the German/Dutch coast for the crew of a Lancaster that had ditched the night before whilst returning from Ludwigshafen and who were thought to be in a dinghy in bad weather. Well it wasn't quite ops but it was at least something positive. We donned all our flying kit, drew parachutes, harnesses and so on and at 3 o'clock in the afternoon thundered down the Skellingthorpe runway in Lancaster DV217.

The weather in the area was atrocious; the cloud cover was down to 500 feet and a huge sea was running. With the driving rain, the wind and the heavy seas, Mike had a really difficult job to turn the Lancaster at the end of each sweep; each turn potentially bringing disaster for us too. Although it was barely possible to see anything below us, we stuck at it for over four hours until the light began to fade, and with it our hopes of finding the crew. Everyone was thinking the same as I was; that it could so easily be us down there one day and we would want someone to come and find us too before the sea took us. It was with heavy hearts that we turned for the last time and headed back towards the Wash and home.

The area that we had been searching in was very close to the enemy coast, especially Sylt in the North Frisian Islands where the Luftwaffe seaplane base at Hornum was located. The following day we were informed that since our search had lasted so long and in such appalling weather conditions close to the enemy coast, we were to be credited with the first operation of our tour. It wasn't quite what we had expected, but now there were only another twenty-nine to go.

By now, 61 Squadron had joined us from RAF Syerston and, apart from a few weeks between February and April 1944, would stay with us at Skellingthorpe until the end of the war. During the first three weeks of November, we had carried out several cross-country flights, air/sea firing exercises and bombing practice, all part of our final preparations for ops. After breakfast on 22nd November, once more I looked down the Battle Order list in the Sergeants' Mess; Flying Officer Beetham and crew were on operations that night. My stomach tightened as I stared at the entry. So this was it; all that training, all that waiting, all behind me; tonight I would meet the reality of what I had volunteered for, of what it really meant to be aircrew in Bomber Command.

The morning unfolded in a mixture of excitement, anticipation, and nervousness. What would be the target? What would it be like over there? Would I come back? I thought of Art and that we still had no news of him. The tension around the airfield was palpable, and the closer to take off, the greater it seemed. I was excited at the prospect, but also had a growing nervousness, made worse by the strain of waiting, the expectancy of the unknown. It was something that I would get used to, but not overcome.

I knew that generally new crews were given what was considered to be an easier target for their first mission; none were easy, of course, but some were seen as less dangerous than others. On 11th November the squadron had been part of an attack on the railway yards at Modane, part of the German supply route to Italy. Not only did we not lose any crews that night, but Bomber Command suffered no losses at all; all 342 aircraft that took off for the raid returned safely. I was surprised we hadn't gone on the raid if it was that trouble free, so I was looking forward to a similar target tonight.

In the late morning, we took off to do our NFT [night flying test] in VN-D, the aircraft we had been assigned for the raid, after which it was time for the wireless operators' briefing. We gathered together in one of the briefing rooms and the Wireless Operator Leader gave us all the information that we would need for the sortie; our bomber codes, call signs, the times for us to listen in to broadcasts, identification charts for when we were challenged by the wireless/telegraph [W/T] stations, colours of the period, distress sections to be used in the event of an emergency, Wireless Operators' logs, and finally the frequency bands for us to use when searching for the German operators who would be directing their night fighters onto us. We were told everything except the target.

Following the section meetings, all the crews gathered for the main briefing where the target would be revealed, shown on the large map of the North Sea, Germany and northern Europe which hung on the wall. As I went into the room, I glanced towards the wall at the far end where a curtain hung over the map, concealing the target until the last moment. Once we were all in, the doors were locked and the SPs, the RAF Service Police, guarded them to make sure that no-one left before the end. As the CO entered the room to address us, we all stood up.

"Thank you, gentlemen, sit down please." He stepped up to the curtain and pulled it across the map. "The target for tonight is Berlin. It's the Big City again."

A single piece of red tape stretched from Lincoln, over the North Sea and all the way to Berlin. I felt my stomach turn over and my chest tighten. Not Berlin, surely not for our first op. An audible hum went around the room; it had been only four nights since the squadron had last been to the German capital.

After the CO's briefing, it was the turn of the Meteorologist, then the Navigation Officer, the Intelligence Officer, the Bombing Leader, the Wireless Operator Leader, and the Gunnery Leader. Between them, they gave us take-off times, turning points, engine revs and boosts, bombing time and height over the city, the different colours of the various marker flares, which wave we were in and our height in the stream. When all the briefings were finished, the CO would pick on anyone at random and ask them to repeat all that we had been told. If the CO wasn't satisfied that the airman had a sufficient grasp of what had been said, he would be taken off the operation and someone else detailed to fill in. Finally, the Padre would say a few prayers for us all. I don't think I have ever said 'Amen' with so much feeling before or since those days.

With the briefing finished, the SPs unlocked the doors and it was over to the Mess for the traditional operations tea of bacon and the treat of a real egg. Before every operation, the assembled airmen ate that pre-flight meal very differently; some with great relish, seemingly oblivious to what awaited them over the next few hours, others with great diffidence, knowing exactly what awaited them, perhaps accompanied by the dread that maybe this time it was to be the last meal they would ever eat; most, however, just ate it engrossed in their own thoughts. On this particular afternoon, I was still largely unaware of the terror that I would face and so concentrated on what Michael had said to us after his dickie trip and upon the details of the briefing. It would be ok; we'd be all right.

In order to maintain security, when the squadron was on ops no-one was allowed to leave the camp, and so when the meal was over, the crew locker room was the next stop. It was getting very close now. I pulled on my wool and silk long johns and long-sleeved vest, then my white polo-neck woollen sweater and battle dress, followed by the kapok flying suit. On top of that I put on my Mae West life jacket, parachute harness, flying boots and helmet. The wireless operator's position was the warmest in the aircraft, but just in case I needed to man one of the gun turrets, I also took my Irvine flying jacket with me. Then the Medical Officer gave out our methamphetamine tablets, universally known as 'wakey-wakey' pills, to help us stay awake and alert on long trips. The golden rule, though, was not to take them until you were sure the operation was on or you'd never sleep. They've messed around with it a bit since the war, labelled it a designer drug and called it crystal meth, but it's still just wakey-wakey and we were given it for nothing.

I drew my flying ration of sweets, chocolate, flasks of coffee, escape currency which was French, Dutch or Belgian money, depending on the target and route, emergency rations and, most important of all, my parachute. Finally, I went through the flying helmet check to ensure that the intercom and oxygen mask were working all right.

There had been quite a bit of chatter in the crew room to start with, but gradually it faded away until it was all but gone; the imminence of take-off and the mission ahead of us concentrating all our minds. I bent down and picked up my bag into which I had put my gloves, torch, goggles, rations and escape kit, and joined the others outside getting into the transport truck. The WAAF driver gave us a cheery smile, put the truck into gear and set off round the perimeter track towards the aircraft dispersals; it was about an hour to take-off.

The WAAF made her way inexorably from one dispersal pan to the next; at each one my stomach turned and tightened a little more. As she drew her vehicle up in front of each aircraft its crew struggled out of the truck with their kit and mumbled "Thanks a lot" to the girl behind the wheel, who acknowledged their thanks with a wan smile; and then it was our turn. VN-D stood valiantly on the concrete in the fading light, the ground crew still busily fussing around their aircraft. I clambered up the ladder at the rear of the Lancaster and followed Frank over the wing spar. This was no easy job with all our kit on, but at last I put my bag and parachute down at my wireless table as Les went past me on his way to the bomb aimer's position in the nose bubble.

Although all the equipment had been checked that morning on the NFT, we checked it all again; I felt better now that I had something to do. I heard our pilot still talking to the ground crew as he signed to take over the aircraft whilst I went back down the ladder to check that all the aerials were in place. Then I checked the other equipment, particularly the Very pistol in its holder in the roof close to my position, and made sure that there was a full range of colour cartridges either in clips on the side of the fuselage or in the drawer of my table. Next I checked that the massive 24 volt batteries were reading 27 volts on the meter, if not we couldn't go. I switched on the intercom to make sure that it was working and then tested my wireless receiver, but not my transmitter as that could be picked up by the enemy across the North Sea. We were part of a force of 764 aircraft going out that night and if all the wireless operators checked their transmitters at the same time, the Germans would know that a raid was about to take off.

Then I checked the fire extinguishers, emergency portable oxygen bottles and escape hatches. All along the floor between my position and Frank's were bundles of 'window', thin metal strips which were thrown out during the sortie to confuse the enemy radar controllers. When I was satisfied that everything was in order, I clambered down the ladder once more and stood outside with the others to wait. An eerie quiet had fallen across the airfield. From the hedge behind me, came the blackbird's evocative evening melody as it serenaded the fading light of day. In contrast to the serenity of its song, my insides were in turmoil again, a mixture of anticipation, excitement and fear. We were all frightened of what might happen; it was to be a constant companion on ops.

Our bomb load that night was a fairly typical 4,000lb high explosive 'cookie' with the rest made up of incendiaries and smaller high explosives. Then the waiting was over and it was time to go. Once more we all heaved ourselves up the ladder through the rear door and into the aircraft. Fred slipped over the tail spar and into his rear turret, whilst I stowed his parachute in the rack on the fuselage. It was such a tight fit for him with all his clothes on that I would push him in with my feet and then close the doors behind him. By now the rest of the crew were in their positions, except Michael, who was always last on board. Once in the pilot's seat, Michael would call us all up on the intercom to check that everything worked then he and our flight engineer Don Moore would go through the start-up procedure with the ground crew.

Across Skellingthorpe aerodrome mighty Rolls Royce Merlin engines roared into life and our own joined the cacophony, their power vibrating through the aircraft. Then "chocks away" from Michael and as the large wooden blocks were pulled aside, I felt the Lancaster start to move forward onto the perimeter track. Through the small window beside my seat I looked out over the port wing and was surprised to see quite a crowd of people standing beside the runway. The CO, station commander and some of the ground crew were there to see us off, together with a collection of WAAFs, frantically waving to their boyfriends, their anxiety all too evident. Then we had the green on the Aldis lamp from the Controller, radio silence, and we turned onto the main runway. The revs of the

Merlins started to build up to a deafening crescendo, I could feel the aircraft straining against the brakes, then Michael's voice came over the intercom, "All right everybody, here we go". He released the brakes and we started to roll, 65,000lb of bomber, full of petrol, ammunition, high explosives, incendiaries, and the lives of seven young men who were beginning their first bombing sortie against the enemy: it was 16.45 hours.

VN-D headed down the runway; Don held the throttles wide open and the engines roared loader than I had ever heard. Frank read out our speed, 70, 75, 80; not fast enough yet, but the runway was disappearing behind us rapidly and I could still hear the tyres on the concrete. I looked out of my side window again and saw the streaks of orange flame from the port inner engine exhaust licking up over the leading edge of the wing and stretching back across its surface. The Merlins were on full power now and straining against gravity to take to the air. Frank continued to call out the speed, 95, 100, 105; the runway was almost all behind us now, we didn't have much left. And then the tyres went quiet and I heard Michael say, "Wheels up, Engineer," and Don's reply, "Wheels going up, Skipper," followed by the reassuring clunk as the undercarriage locked into place. We were up.

The flames from the exhausts eased a little as Don reduced the revs, but only by two or three thousand, as we would be climbing for the next hour until we reached our cruising height in the stream at 20,000 feet. Once over the Lincolnshire coast, I let out the two hundred feet of trailing aerial, which was used for distress frequencies. We soon ran into cloud as we climbed away from Lincoln, but then at about 9,000 feet it was clear sky for a short time.

Still climbing, we ran into the cloud again and then passed over the Dutch coast where we got our first taste of flak, but it was predicted because of the cloud and they burst well below us. We pressed on and then the engine notes changed; we levelled out at 20,000 feet and Don trimmed back the revs to cruising speed at about 180mph. In the very nose of the aircraft, I could hear our bomb aimer tell Michael the colour of the various track markers which we passed, laid down by the Pathfinder Force [PFF] to mark the route. Near Hanover, we ran into more flak, with searchlights roaming the sky for us, but the cloud cover was too thick for them to penetrate. The defenders threw up all they could, but Frank had given us a course well away from the range of the flak batteries and we passed safely by, the steady drone of the Merlins unchecked, the rhythm of the Lancaster unbroken.

The route to Berlin was more or less straight, but there were turning points, and with a stream of 764 aircraft converging on these points, the risk of collision was very great, so as we approached them Michael would tell all the crew except Frank and me to watch out for other bombers. Suddenly, our Lancaster started to lurch, caught up in the wash from another aircraft's propellers just in front of us. It was something that we would get used to, but unsettling all the same. Then the gunners began to report one or two aircraft going down in flames, almost certainly victims of night fighters. It kept us alert, reminded us of the deadly danger that lurked out there in the dark: fighters, the scourge of night ops. Frank dutifully recorded these losses with times and locations on his charts for later reporting to the Intelligence Officer when we got back – if we got back.

All this time, I was searching the wave-band given to me for the sound of German voices so that I could start jamming that particular wave-length. I also had to listen for the half-hour broadcasts from Group, which would send us any updated information, such as course changes, wind strengths or raid instructions. After a while, I became curious to see what was happening so I turned out my light and stood up in the astrodome. It was very dark out there, but I could see the mid-upper turret moving round as Jock Higgins kept a wary lookout for fighters or any of our own aircraft straying too close to us; collision in the stream was a constant risk.

At my table once more, I began searching the wave-band again before I heard Frank say that we would be over the target in fifteen minutes. At last, we were nearly there. Les said that he could see the searchlights ahead of us illuminating the cloud base, and back up in the astrodome, I could see the first of the PFF sky markers come into view before drifting down into the clouds below. Then, as if in slow motion, the strings of red and green 'sausages' of flak came rising up through the clouds and burst around and just below, but nothing close enough to worry us. Looking down, I could see the black shapes of other Lancasters and Halifaxes crawling over the tops of the clouds, silhouetted by the glow of the defending searchlights.

The intercom crackled again as Les, having selected the correct target indicators [TIs], prepared to release our own load into Dante's Inferno that was Berlin that night.

"Ok, everyone, we're starting our bombing run. Bomb doors open." The cold rush of November night air that sucked around my ankles from the bomb bay accompanied Michael's orders.

"Left, left, steady, steady; bombs gone." Les's voice rang through the intercom as he pressed the 'tit' and the aircraft gave a fifty-foot lift the instant that the cookie slipped out and then a series of jolts whilst the remaining bombs tumbled away. I couldn't help wondering where they would land. We held our course and height steady for some thirty seconds or so until the aiming-point photograph was taken, then he shouted, "Ok, camera operated, bomb doors closed." Then Les came back and shone his torch through the small hatchway to check that there were no hang-ups.

The city's flak defences were throwing everything that they could up at us, but they must have been getting overwhelmed by now, for it was all falling short. I was transfixed by the scene below me. Although we had been in the fifth wave, aircraft were still coming through the target area. In the clouds below, I could see the dull stain of fire from the incendiaries seeping like blood through a calico cloth spreading across the city, and every few seconds immense yellow flashes as each 4,000lb blockbuster cookie pounded the capital of the Third Reich and erupted like pus spurting poison from the wound that we had opened. It was what we had come to do.

But now the focus was upon running the gauntlet of fighters and flak. All the way to Berlin we had had a tail wind helping to push us along but now we had turned into that wind and would have to struggle against it for six hundred miles, four hours' flying time, if we were to get home. We headed out into the cover of darkness, away from the burning city, but to where the night fighters waited. The red Very signals they use to attract one another were dotted all around our course, so to help reduce the chance of an attack, Michael steadily weaved VN-D for five minutes or so, giving our gunners a good view of the sky around and, critically, below us.

Frankfurt and then Aachen came and went for us, but for a handful of crews who had strayed off-course the defences opened up and punished them. Over the intercom came the periodic report from our gunners that a bomber was in flames, shot down, and whether any parachutes could be seen. Then Michael reported the same, and then Don the flight engineer added another one. Frank and I just looked at each other without saying a word; we were both thinking the same and I felt my stomach tighten a little more, felt the cold sweat trickle down my back. Now I knew what fear felt like.

I made sure that I received the half-hour broadcasts, one of which told us not to switch on our navigation lights over the sea, which meant that there were intruders in the area, German fighters waiting to infiltrate the returning bomber stream and attack when we were least expecting it. At last, I heard Frank ask Les to look out for the Dutch coast through the cloud and almost immediately the navigator's GEE set started working again, so we must have already been over the sea. Time to reel out my trailing aerial again. The roar of the engines started to quieten down and we began to lose height, and I had to swallow a few times to let my ears pop. At 13,000ft I took my oxygen mask off and could breathe the air again; more importantly, I could have a cup of coffee and take one to each of the gunners.

It wasn't long before we crossed the English coast and, still losing height, we were cleared to switch on our navigation lights. All around us there were twinkling sets of lights, aircraft that had been there all the time but we just hadn't been able to see them. Presently they began to peel off for their various aerodromes and I brought the trailing aerial back in and started to tidy up. The forecast was clear for landing at Skellingthorpe and soon enough we saw the airfield Pundit flashing ··· –·–, spelling SK in Morse code. Michael called up the airfield, "Hello, Black Swan, this is Pilgrim D-Dog."

We were given a number and, gradually descending 500 feet with each circuit, were soon on our approach to land. We touched down at just turned midnight, after seven and a quarter hours of flying. It was a wonderful sensation to feel the wheels on the concrete as we raced along the runway, home at last, safe. The relief washed over me, replacing the tension with excitement; we had made it, done our job. The perimeter track was pitch dark and so to help Michael taxi back to our own dispersal, Les shone the Aldis lamp through the bomb aimer's Perspex until we swung into the pan and turned around. The engines were cut and I removed my helmet; the quiet welcome after so many hours with the heavy throbbing roar of the Merlins for company.

Our ground crew, Jock, Fred, Mac and Allan, were there to greet us; friendly voices and helping hands opened the door and put up the ladder then helped us out with our kit. Whilst our two gunners and Les wandered off a little way to have a cigarette, Michael chatted to the chief mechanic for a while about how the engines had performed, and then the crew bus was waiting for us. Tired, weary, but thankful to be home, we clambered into the bus with all our gear to join another crew as the WAAF driver headed back to the operations block and the debriefing room.

When I went in, I handed my Wireless Ops log, codes and so on to the duty signals officer and then took a very welcome mug of steaming hot, sweet tea from one of the WAAFs who had volunteered to stay up and wait for the crews to come back. As soon as a table with a debriefing officer was free, we sat down and started to answer the questions which would in time become so familiar to us. What time did you bomb? Which coloured markers did you aim at? Did you see any aircraft shot down? Did you see any fighters? Did you shoot any down? Did you see any large explosions on the ground? When did your GEE pack up? What was the weather like over the target? On and on they went, until finally we could answer no more.

After going to the crew locker room and putting all our flying kit away, handing in all the foreign money and any of the rations that we had left, it was off to the Sergeants' Mess for a meal and then to the washroom to get the grime and rubber marks off my face. The wireless operator's position in the Lancaster is the warmest place of all in the aircraft, and after the warmth of my little office, at one o'clock in the morning our quarters seemed cold, damp and unwelcoming with no fire in the stove. We talked about the raid for a while and then collapsed into bed. The adrenalin had gone and I was suddenly very tired but sleep wouldn't come. For quite some time, the reality of what I had just done and experienced over the last few hours tumbled through my head. I thought about Art and wondered if he was alive, and it was with a lot of trepidation that I reflected there were still another twenty-eight to go.

*"Flight lieutenant Michael Beetham DFC, 1944
[Sir Michael Beetham]"*

Chapter Eight

"Beyond this place of wrath and tears
Looms but the Horror of the shade,
And yet the menace of the years
Finds and shall find me unafraid"
                    - '*Invictus*'; William Ernest Henley

Up until the raid on 22nd November, I had been seeing quite a lot of Ena and our relationship was developing from friendship to something stronger. I was pleased about this because I needed Ena to understand that once I started on ops, I would not be able to see her as often and I might not even be able to let her know that I couldn't keep a date. When ops were on, we were not allowed to communicate with anyone outside the base. However, I usually did manage to slip out and telephone her to say that I would not be able to see her that night but would see her the following night. She knew not to ask any questions. I had to use the public telephone kiosk about a mile away, because all outside lines from the base were closed when operations were on; if I had been caught letting Ena know I would have been in terrible trouble as it was a flagrant breach of security.

The morning after the Berlin raid, I went over to the Sergeants' Mess for breakfast. As I passed the noticeboard, I had a look at the Battle Order; Flying Officer Beetham and crew were listed. So ops again tonight; I wondered where it would be. After breakfast I cycled out to our aircraft and removed the two heavy LT batteries which were connected to the intercom system. I took them to the accumulator room near to the Watch Office, collected two fully charged replacements, returned to the aircraft, tested the intercom and signed the confirmation on Form 700.

The procedure prior to the raid was the same as the day before, although when we got to the main briefing and found that the target was to be Berlin again, there was a definite groan in the room. We were to be part of a much smaller raid of 383 aircraft that night, but there was no doubt that the Battle of Berlin was well and truly under way.

At 17.05 we were once more heading down the runway at Skellingthorpe, taking off into the gathering darkness. The route was the same as the previous night and the German controllers quickly identified Berlin as the target; the fighters were waiting for us. Cloud once more obscured the city, but we could still see the glow of the fires from the previous evening burning beneath them, acting as markers for us. The Mosquitoes put down spoof marker flares which distracted the enemy pilots and helped us to get in and away again.

Vigilant all the way, we came back to Skellingthorpe without meeting any serious flak or fighters, but as we flew on the downwind leg of the circuit before our final approach we ran into trouble. Michael had called for ten degrees of flap to slow us down a little; nothing happened, the flaps wouldn't move. After several attempts he radioed the Watch Tower to say what our problem was. The runway at Skellingthorpe wasn't long enough for a Lancaster to land without flaps and the Controller didn't want us pranging on his runway while two squadrons of aircraft were still waiting to land, some of them low on fuel. So we were diverted to nearby RAF Wittering, which, although not a bomber base, had a three-mile runway attached to it at Colley Weston. With no flaps to slow us down, we were going to need every yard of it.

As we circled Wittering aerodrome, Michael told the Controller that we had no flaps. Ambulances and fire tenders were quickly scrambled and awaited our arrival. The news of our predicament travelled quickly; a collection of expectant onlookers eagerly gathered at available windows and doorways, not wanting but waiting to see us crash. We came in fast; the Lancaster struck the runway at 130mph and, like a bat out of hell, we hammered down the concrete strip, eating up the yards at a frightening rate. Gradually, though, we slowed enough for the brakes to come on and the tail to drop. To the relief, but probably a little disappointment too, of the assembled crowd, Michael had made a brilliant landing and we had not crashed. A little way short of the three miles, he brought JA899 VN-D to a walking pace and taxied back along the perimeter track, parking up near the Great North Road which ran alongside the airfield.

It was turned one o'clock in the morning by the time we tumbled out and left the aircraft to the duty ground crew, who were not greatly impressed at being got up at this hour to deal with our Lancaster. However after the debriefing, news soon got around that we had just returned from a raid on Berlin. After that, nothing was too much trouble. As guests of the Mess, we were given a really good meal, cigarettes for those who smoked, and someone even broke open a bottle of whisky. Accommodation was found for us and after the food and whisky, I slept like a log. Twenty-seven to go.

The next morning, I was awakened by a naval rating, who informed me that a bath had been run for me and was ready whenever I was. Was this luxury or not? I couldn't believe it, but I enjoyed it all the same. Later in the day we were told that our Lancaster was fine now; the flaps had frozen up on the way back from Berlin and the cold November air in Lincolnshire had slowed the thawing process. The ground crew had checked them over and we were ready to go. We thanked our hosts for their hospitality and took our leave, arriving back at Skellingthorpe just in time for our evening meal, during which we learned that W/O John Saxton's crew had been shot down over Berlin, one of twenty Lancasters which had failed to return.

The next day there were no ops for No.5 Group, which gave us all a bit of a rest and gave me the chance to see Ena. I cycled into Lincoln and met her when she finished work, taking her for a meal at Boots, which had a very popular restaurant upstairs in a building near the Stone Bow on the corner of Silver Street, where a pretty decent meal could be bought at a reasonable cost. I had not intended to get involved with anyone whilst on ops, but fate doesn't work like that. I had stopped seeing Joan a few weeks before I met Ena following a rather unhappy incident at her house involving too much to drink, Les Bartlett and Joan's mother's prize marrow.

Ena's mother, Mildred Goodrich, had been called up for essential war work in the NAAFI and, having been given the choice of where to work, since her husband was serving in the Navy, had left her home in Greenwich and moved to Lincoln where Ena was stationed. Rather than live in the NAAFI quarters, she had found lodgings close by in Winn Street with Mrs Fatchett, which was convenient for Ena to be able to call and see her mother fairly often. It was on one of these occasions that she took me with her and introduced her mother to the young airman who was courting her daughter. After that we were regular visitors, the Fatchetts always making us very welcome.

By 26th November we were down on the Battle Order again, and at the briefing the red tape once more stretched across to Berlin. This time there was a gasp of disbelief in the room that we should be sent there for the third time in five nights. Take-off was 17.20 hours so there had not been time to do an NFT; however, we had spent much of the mid morning carefully checking over our aircraft, which that night was to be VN-F.

Cloud covered the ground for most of the way, but as we approached Frankfurt it broke up and the massed banks of searchlights had a clear view of the sky. There was nothing to be done but to hope for the best and fly through the flak barrage, which we managed to do unscathed. We turned on the last leg in, and as we approached Berlin yet again, the first wave had already set the city burning so intensely that it was possible to pick out streets and buildings amongst the flames, even from four miles high. We made our run-in without any trouble, but the same could not be said for everybody for, looking out of the astrodome, I could see two aircraft twisting and turning, trying to escape the searchlights until finally one of them was hit by flak and started a slow spin to earth, gradually falling away out of my line of vision.

With our bombs gone and photograph taken, VN-F climbed high into the darkness, taking us back home. All was going well until Fred radioed from the rear turret that we were leaving four bright condensation trails in the night sky, a perfidious stream of vapour that would draw in the night fighters like bees to a honey pot; we had to lose height quickly into warmer air. Then, ahead, as we approached Hamburg, lay a wall of searchlights over fifty miles long that we had to pass through, there was no way round. Mike put the nose of the old Lancaster down and we went in, but almost immediately they caught us.

The cockpit lit up in the full glare, brighter than sunlight. Instantly, we went into a long steep dive to port followed by a sharp climbing turn to starboard as the radar-controlled flak came up at us. At the same time there was a tremendous crash and clatter close to my seat and the intercom went dead; the HT batteries had been ripped out of their housing by the G-forces of the first dive, but we were out of the grip of the searchlights. With the passing of the immediate danger and the aircraft back on an even keel, Mike got the emergency intercom working and I retrieved the batteries. Only then did I have time to think about how close we had come to being shot down, but now we were racing home. On through the clear night sky we charged, the Merlins throbbing, the gunners alert. The Dutch coast came and went, the heavy flak falling below and behind. On still we flew, homeward bound, safety beckoning with every passing minute.

Over the sea, cloud engulfed us, a thick solid mass, and then came the message to divert to RAF Pocklington in Yorkshire; Lincolnshire was fog-bound. It was a race against time now, we were nearly out of fuel. There would be a lot of aircraft making for Pocklington and the circuit would be very busy. I passed the message to Frank and to Michael. To save time and precious fuel Frank asked the aerodrome for a QDM, which is a direct course to fly; a little later I asked for another one as the fog was getting thicker by the minute. Almost there, we contacted the tower for permission to land and were astonished to be refused, even though Michael could see the flare path below; we were to divert to nearby RAF Melbourne. What were they thinking of? Our fuel was draining away and our chances of a safe landing with it. Then the Melbourne flare path appeared in front of us, the lights glowing dimly through the gloom, a beacon of rescue. We were given permission to land with caution when we were ready. If anything, the fog was thicker here but we were right in line with the main runway, so with wheels and flaps down we came straight in, our fuel tanks almost dry. At the far end of the runway a van was waiting to take us to a parking area.

We had been the first of the squadron to arrive and as we taxied around the perimeter track I heard two more aircraft calling up saying that they must land now as they were out of fuel. Permission to land was refused, instead came the instruction to the crews, "Head your aircraft out to sea and bail out. I repeat, head your aircraft out to sea and bail out." Those poor blighters, I just hope that they survived. After that, things just went from bad to worse. VN-A, flown by P/O Toovey, landed just behind us, ran off the concrete and got stuck in the mud. Behind Toovey came P/O Weatherstone's VN-X, which missed the runway altogether, careered across the airfield, ran straight over a Standard 8 van, killing the driver, and then ploughed into VN-A just as her crew were getting out. The little remaining fuel in the two aircraft exploded, along with the ammunition, the flames lighting up that corner of the aerodrome with a fluorescent orange glow, through which the .303 ammunition whizzed. It reminded me again of the one-wheeled Lancaster at Wigsley.

Once we had parked up, we got out of VN-F as fast as possible and got as far away from the runway as we could. In the distance we heard an explosion and knew that it could only be another crew meeting disaster. Unable to find the runway in the dense, swirling fog, F/Sgt John Thompson's VN-K had finally run out of fuel and crashed onto a farmhouse, killing both the occupants together with all of the crew except for the two gunners, Sgt Wyllie and Sgt Corbett.

It was past 01.00 again and we were all exhausted, not helped by the events of the last hour. Grateful for the hot mugs of tea thrust into our hands by a friendly WAAF, we sank forlornly into the seats at the Intelligence Officer's table ready to begin the debrief when, to our astonishment, Toovey and Weatherstone, together with their entire crews from VN-A and VN-X, walked in as large as life and without a scratch between them. It cheered us all up no end. After a hot meal, we were found beds for the night and I was never more pleased to close my eyes and let that blissful sleep wrap around me. Twenty-six to go.

The fog persisted all day; there was no prospect of us returning to Skellingthorpe until there was a significant improvement. Bomber Command had lost twenty-eight aircraft the night before and a further fourteen had crashed in the fog on their return to England. We were there until the fog cleared, but with no money, no shaving kit, only our flying clothes and sharing the station with about a hundred other stranded airmen, we were not able to be treated to the comfortable surroundings that we had enjoyed at Wittering. Nevertheless, on that Saturday evening, after scrounging a few shillings from the regular chaps on the station, we caught the base bus that ran into York and were dropped near to the King's Arms. The pub was on the quayside of the River Ouse and was a haunt of the army. We just about had enough money to buy a pint of beer each and, still dressed in all our flying kit, we stood in a small huddle in one corner. It wasn't long before a couple of Army lads, not realising that Michael and Frank were officers, wanted to know why we were in flying kit and where the hell had the RAF been during the evacuation of Dunkirk.

Whilst the Navy and many civilian volunteers had been rescuing more than 338,000 British and Free French troops from the beaches and port of Dunkirk, the Luftwaffe had attacked the little boats near the shore, bombed the ships further out and strafed the men on the beaches. Understandably, the troops had expected Fighter Command to be there in large numbers shooting down their German attackers. The apparent freedom that the Luftwaffe enjoyed over the beaches had led to some ill feeling between the two Services. In point of fact, Fighter Command had been there and in many other places as well, but as one senior Luftwaffe commander was to encourage his pilots a few weeks later in the Battle of Britain, "*Even a Spitfire cannot be in two places at the same time.*"

Fighter Command's strategy was to attack Luftwaffe airfields in the early morning and destroy their aircraft on the ground, but there was an inevitable limit to how successful this could be and most fighters remained free to attack the beaches. There were two other major problems facing the Command. Firstly, Air Chief Marshal Dowding rightly anticipated the fall of France and the need to conserve his fighters for the imminent defence of Britain, and secondly, RAF pilots were stuck with the same reality that their opponents would experience a few weeks later, the lack of fuel. The Luftwaffe were fighting very close to their bases and therefore had maximum time in the air before needing to refuel, whereas our pilots had to use up most of their fuel crossing the Channel both ways, so severely restricting their time in the battle area.

However, huddled in our little group at the King's Arms that evening, we didn't have to explain any of that because as soon as Frank told the Army lads that we had been diverted to RAF Melbourne on our way home from bombing Berlin the night before, the news spread like wildfire around the pub and for the rest of the evening plentiful beer was provided for us by the lads in khaki and the civilian locals. In 1943 everyone loved Bomber Command.

It was Sunday afternoon before the fog cleared enough for us to return to Skellingthorpe and the following night there was a squadron 'stand-down', so I was able to get into Lincoln and see Ena. I had been able to telephone her from York, so she had at least known that we were back safely. If there were no ops on, the RAF still tried to keep us occupied and so our afternoons were spent playing football, dinghy drill in

Hartsholme Park Lake, which was always cold and smelly as well as wet, or escape and parachute practice at the aircraft. On the 30th November, ops were on again but then called off just as we were going out to our aircraft. Amid loud cheers, we all got out of our flying kit and into Lincoln as quickly as possible, having had the bonus of a bacon-and-egg tea!

Two days later we were on the Battle Order again, down to fly in a replacement VN-A. We did the NFT in the morning, but when we got to the briefing we found that we had been taken off the mission. Mr LL Bennett was an American war correspondent who wanted to fly on a bombing mission to Berlin. He had been directed to Skellingthorpe and it was decided that he would fly with one of 50 Squadron's most experienced crews, that of Flt Lt Ian Bolton, with whom our pilot, Mike Beetham, had done his second-dickie trip. The crew were at the end of their tour and this would be their last trip. VN-A was really their Lancaster and so they took it back from us for the op. The next morning, their table in the Mess was empty. There but for the Grace of God.

Much later we found out that VN-A had been shot down over Berlin and five of the crew and Mr Bennett had parachuted to safety and were taken prisoner. The navigator, PO AM Watson, and the mid-upper, Sgt RF Moody, didn't make it. With the loss of VN-A, we had no aircraft, so the next afternoon we were taken, along with our flying kit, parachutes, harnesses, escape kits and so on, by crew bus to nearby RAF Waddington, where we would be briefed, given an aircraft and on our return from the mission bring it back to Skellingthorpe.

During these long winter nights, the targets were always far away, deep into Germany, involving around eight hours or more flying time. Nevertheless, at the briefing that afternoon it was something of a relief to discover that the target was to be Leipzig and not Berlin. The route was to be straight to the capital and then turn south to Leipzig at the last moment, whilst fast-flying Mosquito fighter bombers would carry out a diversionary raid on Berlin. The idea was that the enemy would think that the target was Berlin once more and send their fighters there to defend the city whilst the main bomber stream flew on to the real target. The plan more or less worked, except that the fighters intercepted us much sooner than had been anticipated before the diversionary raid drew them off, although we did lose quite a few aircraft on the return leg to the Frankfurt defences.

It was 00.23 by the time we took off from Waddington in VN-F for Freddie, heavily laden with bombs and fuel for the long journey in a finely balanced ratio. We knew that the fighters would be out to get us tonight, and so once we got into their area Mike started to weave Freddie so that our two gunners could get a good look at the sky below us as well as above and behind.

Freddie was fitted with MONICA, a radar device which detected aircraft approaching from behind and acted rather like sonar on a ship, bouncing back a signal in the form of a loud pinging sound; the closer the aircraft, the more rapid and louder the ping sounded. The trouble was that MONICA couldn't distinguish between our own aircraft and the enemy's so in the bomber stream it was pinging away all the time, driving the rest of the crew round the bend. "Reg, can't you turn that damned thing off?" became a regular plea, so from time to time I did.

About fifty miles from Berlin, I was intent upon this pinging sound and also scanning the German wavelengths when suddenly our mid-upper, Jock Higgins, spotted an Me110 fighter trying to get underneath our wing to attack us. His words were like an electric shock, stretching taut nerves even tighter, knowing that at any moment cannon shells could come blasting through the side of the fuselage or turn our wing into a flaming torch and rip us out of the sky. Michael violently weaved the Lancaster, the German pilot knew he had been seen, banked away and we survived, then we turned for Leipzig. Vigilance was everything.

At last, the target was in front of us, but the flak was light, which meant their fighters were in the stream with us. Just as we started our bombing run, Mike and Les both picked out another Me110 waiting for our run-in. Even though we were approaching the target, Mike managed a fierce sideslip to out-manoeuvre the fighter and give Les a chance to release the bombs and get the aiming-point photograph. I could feel the sweat running down my face and down my back; it felt cold against my skin. This was our worst trip yet. I knew that everyone felt the same. The voices over the intercom were tense, nerves were stretched tight, concentration was intense. With the bombs gone, we started to weave our way out of the target area and into the blessed darkness beyond, and I focused once more on the MONICA screen. It wasn't long before I picked up a ping that seemed to be getting louder and was sure that whatever it was out there it was getting closer, but I had no way of telling whether it was RAF or Luftwaffe. Then there was no doubt, the pinging was fast and loud.

"Aircraft, port rear, closing!" I shouted into the intercom, and at the same instant I heard Fred Ball from the rear turret bellow, "Down!" Instantly, Michael put the Lancaster into a starboard corkscrew dive, but even as Fred was echoing my warning, I felt the thudding hammer blows as the fighter's burst of cannon shells ripped into the fuel tanks of our port wing close to the engine and too close to where I was sitting. Fred's guns had frozen up but Jock in the mid-upper furiously returned fire as the Ju88 followed us down and then up in a climbing turn, rolling over the top and down once more. Still the fighter followed, despite Jock's bursts of machine-gun fire, and still we corkscrewed, until finally our attacker gave up. Once the gunners were satisfied that we had lost him, Michael levelled out and asked if everyone was all right. Assured that we were, he then called for a damage report. I climbed up into the astrodome and looked out along the port wing, which seemed to be leaving a trail of smoke. Don Moore came and had a look, too, and decided that it wasn't smoke but petrol.

We had been unbelievably lucky that the tank had not caught fire, but now we were in danger of not having enough fuel for the long return leg home. Whilst I helped Frank retrieve his charts and navigation instruments, which had been thrown off his table by the sudden dive, Don set about running all four engines from the holed tank until it ran dry, by which time he had switched the engines back to the other tanks. To add to our problems, the port engine was now running decidedly rough, the flaps on that wing had been damaged in the attack, we had no idea whether the tyre had been punctured, and Frankfurt still lay ahead of us.

Michael and Don decided that with damaged flaps we should make straight for the long runway at Wittering rather than risk trying to get to Skellingthorpe. To save us time and especially fuel, I obtained a QDM for a direct course and then fifteen minutes later, another one. In the meantime, we jettisoned everything that we could in the aircraft to lighten the load, eventually including the guns and ammunition. We were defenceless and completely at the mercy of any night fighter that found us, but we were still flying, heading for England and riding our luck.

With engine revs trimmed to their most economical and the port inner still firing, we sped across the black canvas of occupied Europe that lay stretched out beneath us. High above those oppressed peoples the heartbeat of VN-F throbbed, supporting our faith and raising our spirits as each minute ticked by, as each mile slipped behind, as England drew nearer. On over the Dutch coast we flew, then out across the North Sea, cold, dark, foreboding, the waves beckoning to us. Still we flew on, limping home, daring to hope. Then the east coast came up; we had almost made it, but we weren't down yet and the tanks were nearly dry. It was coming up to 08.00 by now, though still dark, and we needed the runway lights to be switched on quickly; we didn't have many minutes to spare.

Undercarriage down early to be sure that it worked and praying that the port wheel had not been damaged in the attack, Michael called up the Watch Office asking for permission to land immediately as we were almost out of fuel. Nothing. He called again; still nothing. Then, after what seemed an eternity, a rather tired-sounding Controller told him that the lights would be switched on shortly. Sooner rather than later would be very useful, I thought. We went round once more and repeated the call for the lights to be switched on, our fuel now almost gone. I had put on my parachute and was standing by the back door of the aircraft together with our two gunners ready to go should the engines start to splutter and the pilot give us the order to jump. Then the runway lights came on. "Thank God," said someone.

We had just enough fuel for one attempt and we came straight in, holding our breath in case the port wheel collapsed. Our luck held and we arrived at Wittering for the second time in three operations. We taxied into the first available space, came to rest and, with a great sigh of relief, switched off the engines that had brought us back home again. Last out of VN-F was Frank, our navigator, who came and joined the rest of us standing out on the concrete gathered around inspecting the damage in the gloom of the approaching daylight. There were cannon holes right across the wing alongside the port inner engine. Some of the exhaust stubs had been shot away, there were cannon holes in the propeller blades and the main spar had been shot-up so badly it could have collapsed at any moment. We had just missed disaster once more.

"Reg, did you see my dividers when we were gathering the stuff off the floor?" asked Frank as we walked across to where we were going to be debriefed.
"No, I didn't, sorry, but they must be in there somewhere," I replied.
"I can't find them anywhere. The kite's going to have to stay here when we leave so I'll need to get another pair before the next op."
"I've got a pair in my kit. I always carry them but don't use them. They're German, made in Cologne. I'll show them to you after debrief."
"Where on earth did you get a pair of German dividers from, Reg," he asked in astonishment, and I told him about the Heinkel 111 that had been shot down by a Hurricane over Kettering just before I joined the RAF and how I had found the navigator's dividers.

On our way to get some breakfast after the usual debrief and our account of the fighter attack, we passed through the ante-room of the Officers' Mess and from the state of the place it was obvious why there had been a delay with the runway lights. At each end of the room, the furniture had been piled high to form barricades behind which the officers had taken cover during a running battle of firing Very flares at each other. They had certainly had a lot of fun because the floor was littered with empty cartridges which had burned and melted the lino where they lay. The walls were pock-marked with scorches and burns where the flares had struck before falling to the floor and burning the skirting boards. The whole room resembled a battle zone, and goodness knows how it had not gone on fire; that was certainly some party that they had had last night. However, when we arrived literally out of the blue, they were all sleeping it off; we were lucky to have got down at all.

There was no hot bath for me this morning as we didn't stay long at Wittering. By the time we had finished breakfast, PO Smith was on his way over from Skellingthorpe in Lancaster JA899 to collect us, but whilst we were waiting for him, I showed my souvenir dividers to Frank, who looked at them with great interest, even though they were a little bent.

"My word, Reg, these are beauties. They are much better than my RAF ones. I can soon get these straightened out. You've got to hand it to the Jerries, they really are first-class engineers. "

"If they're any good to you, Frank, use them until you get some more."

"Thanks, Reg, I will," he replied, smiling, and then he added solemnly, "Let's hope they bring us better luck than their last owner had."

Well, they did, but I didn't see them again. Many years afterwards, I asked Frank what had become of them, but he didn't know, which was a great shame; they were a real keepsake from the early days of the war and my time in the Home Guard. By late morning we were back at Skellingthorpe and were greeted by the news that we had been granted seven days' leave. Our passes and travel warrants were waiting for us, so none of us wasted any time with sleep. Twenty-five to go.

Chapter Nine

"'Peace upon Earth!' was said. We sing it,
And pay a million priests to bring it.
After two thousand years of mass
We've got as far as poison-gas."
- 'Christmas: 1924'; Thomas Hardy

Lord Nuffield, the motor manufacturer and owner of Morris Motors, had great concern for British servicemen and women and wanted them to enjoy the best whilst on leave without breaking the bank in the process, particularly when staying in London. He had been so impressed by the willingness of men and women to volunteer for active service that when the war came he set aside one million Morris Motors Ordinary shares, at that time worth £1,650,000, to form the Trust for the Forces of the Crown. He also made additional gifts of £100,000 to cover the first year's running expenses. It was from this trust that a small amount of money was paid to, amongst many others, all operational aircrew to take with them on leave wherever they went, and it certainly helped. Alternatively, aircrew could take their leave in a number of hotels across Britain without any charge for their food and accommodation, and if accompanied by their wife there was similarly no charge for her either, but she did have to be the airman's own wife. The trust still exists today.

When war broke out, and particularly when the London blitz started, the clubs, cinemas and theatres in the capital were ordered to close, although most stayed open. There was one notable exception to this order: the Café de Paris on Coventry Street. It was the most glamorous of all London's nightclubs, considered to be the safest as it was situated four floors below Leicester Square and was officially permitted to remain open. Royalty, the famous and the well-heeled all gathered here to put some glitz into the blitz, to dine and dance the night away to some of the best-known bands of the day, almost oblivious to the bombing going on above their heads. Inevitably, it became a frequent haunt of servicemen and women.

The lavish interior of the nightclub was reminiscent of the ballroom on the Titanic, but on the evening of 8th March 1941 it came to a similarly ill-fated end when, during the air raid that night, two bombs fell straight down the club's ventilation shaft. They exploded in a blinding blue flash in the centre of the dance floor. Somewhere between thirty-four and eighty people died in the club that night, including band leader Ken 'Snakehips' Johnson, along with most of his musicians. Lord Nuffield's trust had acquired a building literally around the corner in Wardour Street, the Nuffield Centre, to make provision for British Forces below the rank of commissioned officer to call in, have something to eat and be entertained. Underground, the Centre adjoined the Café de Paris, and after the destruction of the club, one of the remaining interior walls was taken down and the two premises became one. Thus the Café de Paris was reborn and became a Forces Club.

In March 1942 the first American servicemen began to arrive in Britain and, just as in the Great War, there was a huge gap between the pay of British military personnel and our American cousins. As a rough guide, an American private soldier, a GI, was paid about the same as a British Army Lieutenant, a Royal Air Force Flying Officer or Royal Navy Sub-lieutenant. On 11th November 1942 the American Red Cross Club was established at Rainbow Corner, 23 Shaftsbury Avenue, near Piccadilly Circus, along much the same lines as the Nuffield Centre. Its doors remained open twenty-four hours a day until 9th January 1946. It was a very respectable club, run as a home from home for non-commissioned Americans, and as well as thousands of GIs, it played host to some very well-known people including General Eisenhower, Captain James Stewart, the song writer Irving Berlin and actor George Raft. Glenn Miller made his Eagle Broadcasts from there and on one very special occasion Artie Shaw's Navy Band played the club. Fred Astaire's sister, Lady Charles Cavendish, also helped out at the Club throughout the war and the little girl who entertained the troops at Rainbow Corner on several occasions would grow up to be one of our biggest international singing stars of the 1950s, 60s and 70s; she was Petula Clark.

I telephoned Ena to let her know that I had been given seven days' leave and that I was going home to see my mother and father. I caught the train into Lincoln at Skellingthorpe village station and then the connection that would take me south to Kettering. I soon found a seat and as I settled back, I suddenly realised just how tired I was. I asked the sailor in the next seat to wake me when we got to Nottingham as I needed to change trains there, and then I closed my eyes and slept. It seemed only a few seconds later that he was shaking me as the train slowed for Nottingham station.

Slowly I pulled myself together, thanked him and got off the train. The wait for my connection wasn't too long and then I was on the final stage of my journey home. This time I shared a compartment with a woman who had two children with her. It was Saturday and they were going to Kettering to see their grandparents. The boy, who was about ten, recognised my uniform and signaller's brevet and wanted to know what I did in the RAF. I told him that I was part of a bomber crew and that just last night I was in a Lancaster over Germany. He wanted to know a lot more but I wasn't allowed to tell him anything else. His mother saw how tired I was and put an end to his questioning, saying that she would wake me up at the station, and so once again I drifted off to sleep.

True to her word, the woman woke me at Kettering and I lifted my kit down from the rack, bade them farewell at the ticket barrier and stepped out into the familiar streets of the town. When I opened the back door of the house, my mother was standing in the kitchen. I thought that she would never stop crying and then she told me the wonderful news: she had heard from the Red Cross that Arthur had survived after all and was a prisoner of war. His aircraft had exploded, but he had been blown out through the roof and, although injured, was alive. And to round it off, I had turned up. Our house was certainly a happy place during my leave. We knew we were blessed because many of the lads that I had gone to school with were killed.

I enjoyed my leave and the rest that it gave me, but without my friend Ron Boydon, the evenings in the pub weren't such good fun and I was missing Ena. I telephoned her during the week and told her the good news about Art and arranged to see her on the last day of my leave if she could get some time off. When it came time to go back, mum packed me some sandwiches for the journey and gave me a big hug, telling me to be very careful. She had no idea of the terrible conditions that Art was going to have to live in for the next eighteen months and the hardship that he would have to face, but I don't think she really cared. So far as she was concerned, he was safe and would come back to her one day; now she just had me to worry about. I caught the first train of the day up to Lincoln and managed to spend some time with Ena before going back to the airfield. I was getting very keen on her and it was good to see her again.

Back on the squadron, there was time to catch up with the rest of the crew. It had been a fairly quiet period with mainly routine duties but we were no longer the sprog crew, and after going to Berlin three times and having been shot-up on our last trip, we were seen as fully paid up members. I noticed that a number of the chaps in other crews were wearing a long white silk scarf when flying. The scarves were certainly warm but the thing to do was to write or embroider the name of each city or target as a memento of the operation. Consequently, I obtained a silk scarf to wear on ops and after each one would proudly write the name of the target on it. As our tour progressed, I was very proud of the list of places that we had been to. In due course, however, the RAF put a stop to crews wearing these scarves on ops. News had got back that many airmen who had been shot down and were found to be wearing such a scarf by the civilian population they had just bombed were treated very badly. In a great number of cases, these airmen had been hanged and the scarf had been the noose around their necks. That made us all the more determined to continue adding the names to the scarves, but we didn't wear them on ops any more.

Our next operation came on Monday, 20th December. We found that we had been allocated ED588 VN-G, affectionately known by the crews as 'Lucky G for George', and psychologically it gave us a good start to the day. This would be ED588's fifty-first operational sortie and she would go on to become one of only thirty-four aircraft from more than 7,000 to return from a hundred operations or more. ED588's final tally would be 125 operations before her luck ran out on the night of 29th/30th August 1944, when she was one of fifteen aircraft which failed to return from a raid on Königsberg.

Now in the very depths of winter, with the nights at their longest, take-off times had been brought forward to the late afternoon around teatime so that we could be back home before midnight from all but the longest trips, which meant we got to bed much earlier and so were less tired throughout the mission. All that morning we did the usual checks on the aircraft and then at the briefing in the afternoon there was great relief to find that the target was Frankfurt rather than the long haul to Berlin. We took off just before 17.30 and, true to form for George, we were back just after 23.05 without having experienced any trouble. However, the German radar had picked up the bomber stream soon after we left the English coast and plotted us all the way to the target, bringing in the fighters long before we got to Frankfurt. Both Les and our two gunners reported seeing aircraft going down in flames, victims of the fighters and it is quite likely that two of the Lancasters that they saw were 50 Squadron aircraft. That night we lost PO John Heckendorf and our CO, Wing Commander Pullen, who are both buried in Durnbach War Cemetery along with six members of their crews; the other seven crewmen, including W/C Pullen's second-dickie pilot, managed to parachute to safety, were captured, interrogated and became prisoners of war. Twenty-four to go.

During this time, the 'back-room boys' had been working away to try to improve MONICA, make it more efficient and get rid of that infernal pinging; they had come up with visual MONICA. It performed the same function but instead of producing the loud pinging sound, it created a blip on a cathode ray tube screen which would be located on the wireless operator's table. Our friends on 61 Squadron over on the other side of the airfield had already been equipped with it and so, on the following Wednesday, the 22nd of December, I was detailed to go on a night practice bombing flight with one of the 61 Squadron crews to learn how to use the set when it was installed in our own aircraft.

It was a particularly dark night when we left Skellingthorpe in QR-S for Sheila, but in the dim green glow from the MONICA screen at the wireless operator's table I watched as I was shown how to set up the equipment and how to read off the direction and distance of the various aircraft that were being picked up and shown as blips. Presently we arrived at the bombing range and the bomb aimer began to guide the pilot in on the first practice run.

At about the same time, I became aware of some sort of dispute building up between the pilot, who was a Flying Officer, and the rear gunner. With each exchange, the argument became increasingly acrimonious, during which the pilot reminded the gunner that he was the captain of the aircraft and also of a senior rank. It made no difference to the gunner, who persisted with his point of view until the whole thing degenerated into an out-and-out slanging match. We were now over the bombing range and, whilst the rest of the crew stayed completely quiet, from opposite ends of the aircraft the two of them continued to express their disagreement in increasingly rich and descriptive vocabulary, until finally the pilot told the gunner that he was going to come down to the rear turret and knock the hell out of him, to which the gunner replied that he would save him the walk and they could meet in the middle and sort it out there. At that point, the navigator bluntly said that he had had enough, adding that we should return to Skellingthorpe before the whole trip ended in disaster. An hour after we had taken off, much relieved to get out of their aircraft and very grateful that I was not their wireless operator, I climbed down the ladder and into the waiting truck, convinced that this crew were destined to get the chop very soon, never to complete their tour of operations.

But fate was a contrary, unpredictable companion of the crews she accompanied. Not only did this crew go on to complete their tour in April 1944, but they distinguished themselves by being the first crew on 61 Squadron to do so since the previous August and the pilot was very deservedly awarded the Distinguished Flying Cross. Towards the end of their tour, however, the rear gunner suffered frostbite and was replaced by air gunners from elsewhere on the squadron, including on the two missions to Stuttgart and Schweinfurt on the 20th and 24th February by WO Trevor Bowyer, DFC, veteran survivor of two tours, whose fascinating life story is told in the book *Another Dawn Another Dusk*. I have no idea what the argument was about, but sixty years later I met up with that pilot again at one of our 50/61 Squadron reunions and a more pleasant and amiable fellow it would be hard to find; he was Flt Lt Bernard Fitch, DFC.

We weren't on the Battle Order for the following night's raid on Berlin and we hoped that there would be a squadron stand-down over Christmas. The Army had taken over the Lincoln City Council offices and Ena's ATS unit were going to hold their Christmas dance and buffet there during the evening of Christmas Day, to which our whole crew had been invited. However, after breakfast that morning all NCO aircrew were told to report to the flight offices to see what was on for the day. After we had been there for a little while, our Flight Commander came out and told us that there was indeed a squadron stand-down for the day and that we were all invited to the Officers' Mess where drinks were on the house.

This news and invitation were greeted with a resounding cheer, and whilst it was somewhat early to start drinking, the booze was free and it would have been rude to refuse! For the next hour or so we drank steadily, becoming increasingly merry, it was Christmas Day, after all. As lunchtime approached, one of the senior catering officers came in and asked for volunteers to go over to the WAAFs' Mess and wait on their tables for them during lunch. Together with a few others, I volunteered to go, all part of the Christmas spirit, and at noon reported to the Mess. The girls were already there and seated, duly wearing party hats waiting for their meal. Serving the soup was the easy part, but it became more difficult as the meal progressed. Each WAAF had been allowed two bottles of ale to go with their meal, but some of them couldn't drink both bottles. As we went round the table serving the courses, every so often one of the WAAFs would ask me, "Help me out, Sarg, I can't drink all this ale. Would you share it with me, please?"

I couldn't refuse and drank some of the beer out of her bottle and then moved on to serve the next one. As the meal progressed, the requests increased, so that by the time the pudding was due to be served I was having great difficulty in focusing on the table, the WAAFs and where to put each dish. I can't really remember a great deal about my last hour in the WAAFs' Mess, but I do know that by the time we got back to our own Mess they had finished lunch and we had missed Christmas dinner; no-one had thought to put any aside for us.

Fred, Les and I were in a bad way, so, with no food on offer, we staggered back to our billet and crawled into bed to sleep off the morning's drinks. By the time we woke up, it was about six o'clock and pitch dark outside. As we sat on our beds feeling a little better but still rather fragile, one of us remembered that we were supposed to be at the ATS dance at Stamp End by the river in Lincoln. Ena would never have forgiven me if I'd forgotten; this was our first Christmas together. Giving ourselves a shake, we cycled back to the Mess, had a wash, put on a fresh collar and got tidied up. Doubling up on the bikes with Don and Jock, the five of us set out for the ATS.

To say that we were given a frosty reception by the Army lads at the do would be an understatement. The dance had already begun by the time we arrived, but as soon as we walked into the room, a number of ATS girls, including Ena and Joan, left their dancing partners and came straight over to these five young RAF aircrew chaps. We made our excuses for being late and for the rest of the evening we had all the company we could have wished for, which didn't go down at all well with the lads in khaki, but with several officers present, we knew that there wouldn't be any trouble.

I saw Michael and Frank at the bar talking to Ena's CO, Captain Lewis, with whom they stayed for most of the evening. He had been a pilot with the Royal Flying Corps during the Great War and proudly wore his RFC wings. Michael was very impressed by Captain Lewis and invited him to the station to come and have a look over a Lancaster bomber to see how it compared with the aircraft he had flown nearly thirty years earlier. After the dance finished, a few of us went to visit Ena's mum at Mr and Mrs Fatchett's house. They were very pleased to see us, but time slipped away and when I got Ena back to her billet it was after midnight and she had been missed by the Orderly Officer when making her rounds. Ena was given seven days' CB, confined to barracks, so I wouldn't be able to see her for the next week.

Wednesday 29th December and we were on the Battle Order again; the target, well, where else but Berlin? We were to be part of a force of 712 aircraft which attacked the German capital, with diversionary raids by Mosquitoes on Düsseldorf, Leipzig and Magdeburg to confuse the enemy controllers and keep the fighters away from the main stream both there and back.

The air had been growing colder all day, but by the evening it seemed particularly cold out on the dispersal pan as we waited underneath the wings of our new aircraft, LL744 VN-B for Baker, or B for Beetham as she affectionately became known. The lazy wind blew gently enough, but coming across the open expanses of the aerodrome it cut straight through our clothing. This final waiting outside the aircraft, despite the cold, had its purpose as it gave us all, especially the gunners, a last opportunity to take care of the calls of nature in the dark at the side of the dispersal. Once in the air, the gunners could not leave their turrets even for the short time it would take them to relieve themselves. In that moment, disaster in the form of a night fighter could slip in unseen and bring death to us all. For the rest of the crew, we were able to pass a can around and then empty it out as we flew along, but the gunners either had to hold it or, as was more often the case, just let everything go in their flying suits and then get washed and cleaned up once back at base.

On one of our early trips Don saw flashing lights, sparks and smoke coming from somewhere along the fuselage and I was asked to investigate the cause. When I got to the area around the mid turret, there was only some smoke but no sparks or flashing lights and all seemed well. It wasn't until years later when Jock and I were chatting about our tour of ops that the subject came up again and Jock admitted that he was the culprit. Unable to hold on any longer, he had wet himself so much that the urine had run down into some of the electrics around his turret. It was his first time and he was rather embarrassed, but he got used to it, as did Fred in the rear turret, for whom this was a fairly regular event on these long cold trips deep into Germany.

Eventually it was time to fire up the engines, and with some relief we climbed the short ladder into the Lancaster and out of the wind. At 17.07 we took off and joined the bomber stream heading for Berlin. The heating system for the Lancaster came off the port inner engine and the hot air blew into the fuselage beside my seat with a knob to control the air flow, so wireless operators were always warm, at least as long as this engine kept working. When the heat was on, the air was so hot it would quickly melt my bar of chocolate on the table if I forgot to move it. The next warmest seat was the navigator's, which was just forward of mine. Frank would ask me to turn the heat down as he was too hot and having trouble concentrating, but life was a lot less comfortable for the mid-upper gunner and the bomb aimer who were the first to feel the loss of heat and were quick to call for me to turn it back up. The rear gunner was always cold. On a night like this one, in Fred's turret the temperature would be lower than

- 40°C at 20,000 feet. It had been freezing at ground level when we took off and the air temperature drops at a rate of two degrees for every 1,000 feet of altitude.

Even allowing for the customary cold of their positions, not long after we had taken off and whilst we were still climbing, both gunners came on the intercom to say how cold it was. Our pilot asked me to go and investigate to see whether we had a problem with the aircraft. I disconnected my oxygen tube and, taking a portable oxygen bottle and a torch, slipped over the main spar and headed for the rear of the aircraft. As I passed Jock in the mid-upper I soon saw that we did indeed have a problem, the rear door was wide open and a 180mph -40-degree icy blast was howling around the inside of the rear fuselage; no wonder they were cold. Try as I might, I just couldn't close the door on my own against the slipstream, and even when Don came to help me, we still couldn't shut it properly. In the end, we tied it as tight as possible with the dead man's rope and went back to our positions. I kept the heat turned up full for the rest of the mission.

The dead man's rope was a length of rope used in the event of a crew member being so severely injured that they would not survive the trip home. The injury would be dressed, usually requiring a tourniquet, a lit torch would be tied to their belt and one end of the rope to their parachute-release handle, the other end to the aircraft. At that point, the injured airman would be pushed out, the rope would pull the parachute-release handle and he would drift down to earth, the theory being that the Germans would see the torchlight floating down, investigate and find the wounded airman, who would then stand a better chance of survival in a German hospital than remaining in the aircraft. As I say, that was the theory, but there were a lot of links in that particular chain and it really was an act of last resort.

When we eventually got over Berlin, the city was covered by cloud but I could see the glow from the fires beneath reaching up to us. Through the intercom I could hear Les guiding Michael onto the target markers and then the Lancaster started to buck as we were caught by the wash of the aircraft in front of us. It was always an uneasy sensation because it meant that we were very close to another aircraft with the risk of collision only feet away. At last, "Bombs gone" came from Les as we rose vertically with the sudden loss of the weight that we had been carrying. Then, "OK, camera operated, bomb doors closed," and we were done, speeding away into the darkness before turning northwards for home.

Just after 00.30 we touched down at Skellingthorpe once more and a sigh of relief passed through the aircraft as we sped along the familiar runway, gradually slowing and taxiing round the perimeter track to our trusted and loyal ground crew waiting for us in the freezing cold at dispersal. One by weary one, we clambered down the short ladder carrying our parachutes and other kit and stood on the solid ground again after seven hours and twenty-five minutes in the air.

Helping us with our kit, the ground crew asked if we had suffered any damage to our new aircraft and we were happy to tell them that we hadn't, but I did mention the rear door and Michael asked them to check the catch. Then it was into the transport, the usual debriefing, followed by bacon and eggs and off to bed in our perishingly cold hut. Twenty-three to go.

The next morning after breakfast, Michael was on his way to the flight when he met Squadron Leader Chadwick, the 'A' Flight Commander.
"Ah, Beetham, just the person I was looking for. Tell me about your damage report after last night's op."
"No damage, sir, we had a trouble-free trip, apart from a slight problem with the rear door blowing open when we were at about 19,000 feet."
"You didn't feel anything on the controls?"
"No, apart from the usual turbulence from the aircraft in front when we were on our run-in."
"Interesting. Come with me."

Chadwick indicated to Michael to get into the little Tilley pick-up as he slipped in behind the steering wheel. They drove around the perimeter track in silence, the tyres crunching on the sharp overnight frost whilst Michael wondered what this was all about, certain that we had not been hit by flak and knowing that no fighters had attacked us. On the dispersal pan, VN-B stood looking forlorn in the grey light of the deep winter morning, silhouetted against the white ground and the distant trees shrouded in their icy cloak. The starboard wing was covered with scaffolding, the ground crew standing deep in contemplation. The two men got out of the Tilley and joined the corporal fitter under the wing, who jokingly asked Michael, "What have you done to our new Lancaster, sir?"

As the Flight Commander pointed up to the wing, Michael was astonished to see a neat four-foot hole where a 30lb incendiary bomb had passed clean through the outer fuel tank. A kaleidoscope of visions flashed through Michael's mind as he stared in disbelief at the hole. Fortunately, by the time we reached Berlin we had used the hundred gallons of fuel the tank held and it had been purged by nitrogen to prevent a fire. More startling, though, was the realisation that this was just one bomb from a full load which had slipped out of a Lancaster flying above us in the dark only a few hours ago. By how much had the remainder of the load missed us, especially the 4,000lb cookie? The cookie was usually released first followed by the smaller high explosives and incendiaries, all of which must have passed so close to us.

Later that morning, Michael told the rest of us about our near miss and we cycled out to see VN-B. As I looked at the hole, I shivered, and felt my blood run cold at the stark evidence of how close we had come to death. Even in the context of life as an operational bomber crew, it made a deep impression upon us all. So many crews had been lost this way and would continue to be so, including 61 Squadron's VC holder, Flt Lt Bill Reid, long after he had left Skellingthorpe and was with 617 Squadron, although fortunately Bill and at least some of his crew did survive the bomb strike.

The following day we flew ED 588 VN-G to Wittering and back, otherwise that was our flying done for 1943. Fred finally managed to secure himself a bicycle for the princely sum of twenty-five shillings, somewhat rusty and battered though it was. The form for selling a bike was for the owner to walk into the Mess holding it shoulder high and anyone there who wanted to bid for it would shout out an offer. This one fell to Fred, so he was now independent and we didn't both have to keep riding on mine or borrowing Les' when we went into Lincoln to see Ena and Joan.

During the first half of the twentieth century we had proper winters with heavy snowfalls and days on end of below-freezing temperatures. The winter of 1943/44 was bitterly cold, almost as bad as 1939/40 at the beginning of the war, and our hut offered us little comfort from the weather. There was an iron stove for which we had a coke ration, but unless it was well stacked with fuel it didn't give off much heat and our ration wasn't that generous. However, the route from the Mess to our hut passed the camp coke store, which was surrounded by a wire fence and only a few yards from the Guard Room and the SPs. Undeterred and under the cover of darkness, Jock would climb over the fence and throw some coke over to Don, Les, Fred and me. Once back in the hut, we would stoke up the fire so that it would at least take the chill off the room whilst we slept.

1944 began in the same way that 1943 had finished, with a raid on Berlin. It was a late briefing, which is probably just as well since it gave us all time to recover from the night before. Take-off was delayed and it was 23.44 before Lancaster ME567 VN-M for Mike finally got into the air. Whilst our own VN-B for Beetham was being repaired, we felt that M for Mike was a good replacement; such lucky omens, mascots or whatever were psychologically very important. We joined the bomber stream and thankfully had a completely uneventful trip, although the route took us the long way round and at eight hours fifteen minutes, was our longest yet. 50 Squadron didn't lose any aircraft on the raid but over on the other side of the aerodrome, 61 Squadron lost two crews with no survivors. The next day I wrote Berlin on my silk scarf for the fifth time. Twenty-two to go.

For the next few days the harsh winter weather prevented any flying, but then on 5th January we were on the Battle Order once more, the target this time, Stettin in modern-day Poland. I had been seeing as much of Ena as I could, but on this occasion I wasn't able to let her know that we were on ops that night. When Fred and I didn't turn up as usual to meet them, she and Joan caught a bus out from Lincoln and enquired about us at the main gate. We were told that they were there and went up to meet them. I suppose because we were young and foolish we took the girls back to our hut, which was over by the woods alongside the Skellingthorpe Road. If we had been caught we would have been court-martialled because of the operation that night. After an hour or so, we took them back to the road to catch a bus to Lincoln and then went to get dressed ready for the op. Thinking back now, I can't believe that we really did that, but, as I say, we were young and foolish. The spectre of a sudden, violent death hung over us all every day, so, when not flying, being sensible wasn't something that aircrew were good at.

Once more it was a late take-off, five minutes past midnight, this time in VN-F. The trip would take us eight hours and forty minutes, even longer than Berlin. It was the last op before the full-moon period, but even so, it was a beautifully clear night as we flew 300 miles out over the North Sea towards the Baltic. When we were close to neutral Sweden, I looked down at the glittering lights in the streets and houses of the towns and villages along the coast. After years of blackout, those scattered twinkling lights looked very pretty, a nostalgic reminder of happier, more peaceful times.

The rest of the trip was uneventful for us, although the enemy was very active around the target area. After we had dropped our bombs, Michael climbed up to 25,000 feet and we headed for home. After a while we ran into thick cloud which gave us no visibility at all. I opened a bar of chocolate and settled down to listen for any messages in the half-hour broadcast.

Suddenly, another Lancaster roared by just a few feet above us, its Rolls Royce engine exhausts spitting flames as the crew pressed on homeward seeking safety but nearly taking Jock and our mid turret with it and making me instinctively duck. Even over the beating throb of our own Merlins, the thunderous roar of this aircraft filled the fuselage. My heart rate doubled instantly, my insides turned over, and I sucked hard for air through my oxygen mask. That had been far too close for comfort, and we were rapidly running out of our nine lives.

Presently, we came out of the cloud and back into the fading moonlight, able to concentrate on seeing the enemy rather than thinking about a collision. Away to the east, the new day began to show itself to us long before those earthbound souls far below. Then, to my astonishment, I saw a Lancaster open fire from its mid-upper turret at another Lanc. The sky was clear and visibility very good, but it may have been a captured aircraft which had entered the stream and was being flown by a German crew, or possibly a collision warning to a tired crew. Whatever the reason, no harm was done.

After that, things settled down and I took the chance to watch the dawn chase us across the North Sea as we sped towards the east coast of Lincolnshire and home. Slowly we began to lose height as the grey light of morning pulled back the covers of darkness from the land beneath. The snow which had fallen during the night prematurely brightened the ground so that I could see the stone walls and hedgerows dividing the fields, and little villages nestling in the hollows between the gentle undulations and rolling hills of the Wolds. At 08.45 that morning we touched down at a cold and windswept Skellingthorpe, tired and hungry, but home with a new name to write on my scarf. Twenty-one to go.

Bad weather kept us on the ground for most of the next ten days, with a single bombing practice flight being our only time in the air. The role of Bomber Command ground crews is so often overlooked and particularly the hard work that they carried out in cold and often hostile conditions; so hostile, in fact, that two aircraft fitters actually froze to death whilst working on an aircraft at East Kirkby. If it snowed when we were away on ops, the ground staff were up all night keeping the runway clear for our return. When crews brought their aircraft home full of holes or with damaged engines, it was the maintenance crews who worked so hard to repair them and bring them back to readiness, with all but the most major of work done out in the open. Even when not damaged, there were daily inspections to be carried out, whatever the weather. In short, without them, we wouldn't have been able to do our job.

Friday 14th January brought a return to operations for the squadron and we were once more on the Battle Order. By now we had our own VN-B back; carefully repaired by the ground crew after the bomb had gone through the wing, we felt comfortable in her. We left Skellingthorpe to attack Brunswick at 17.15 as part of a force of 496 Lancasters and two Halifaxes. The German night fighter force entered the bomber stream as soon as we crossed the enemy coast after a long flight across the North Sea and they stayed with us until we crossed the Dutch coast on the return leg.

On every operation we carried bundles of 'window', small metal strips which were designed to confuse the enemy radar. The window was stored on the floor of the aircraft all the way from the main spar up to the cockpit area. When we were sending it out, I would keep pushing the bundles up to Don, who would break open the larger parcels and pass the smaller packets through to Les, who would push them out through the opening on the right of his bomb aimer's compartment in the nose of the aircraft. With so many fighters in the stream, Les started pushing the bundles out every three minutes until we got near to the city, and from then on, every minute. Each time he pushed a bundle out, he would say "window", because the metal strips immediately showed up on my MONICA screen; that way I would know that it was window behind us and not an aircraft. We returned home safely, but the raid was a failure and Bomber Command lost thirty-eight

Lancasters, 270 highly trained young men gone in the space of a few hours. Twenty to go.

"The original Beetham crew with their ground staff when arriving at RAF Skellingthorpe, 1943"

"Their trusted Avro Lancaster bomber VN-B for Beetham LL744"

Chapter Ten

"They are not long, the days of wine and roses:
Out of a misty dream
Our path emerges for a while, then closes
Within a dream."

- From *"Vitae Summa Brevis Spem Nos Vetat*
Incohare Longam"; - Ernest Dowson

[Life's short span forbids us to
enter on far-reaching hopes]

Bad weather again prevented any ops for the best part of the next week but it gave me chance to go into Lincoln to see Ena, a ride which was much more comfortable now that Fred had his own bike and I didn't have to sit on the crossbar all the way there and back. One of the pubs that we visited a lot was the Brick Makers' Arms and I often met Mr Fatchett, Ena's mother's landlord, in there. However, the landlady of the Brickies, as it was known, rather enjoyed playing dominoes or cribbage with her customers and wouldn't leave the game to serve. Consequently, it was the custom to go behind the bar, pull your own beer and just leave the money on the side.

It was also at this time that Michael was made up to Flight Lieutenant even though he was still not yet twenty years of age, and his promotion gave us another excuse to celebrate; so it was off to Lincoln for the Beetham crew. In those dark winter days in the Battle of Berlin, the only future we could think of was to return from the next mission, which, as we discovered a few days later, was yet again to be the German capital. But for now there was time to relax, to unwind, to get drunk, to see girlfriends and wives, to enjoy life and be the young men that we were. One group of airmen certainly enjoyed their night out so much that on the bus back to their base they decided to have an early firework display. They fired rockets at the front windscreen, used bangers as hand grenades and put jumping jacks under the seats of the other passengers. It was all too much for the driver, who wouldn't go any further until they got off his bus; the company refused to carry any more airmen. But any one or all of those young men could have failed to return the next night; that was the way it was for us, living each day as our last.

I hadn't seen my good friend Ron Boydon for some time. Our home leave hadn't coincided recently and, although he wasn't too far away at RAF Spilsby with 207 Squadron, inevitably I spent most of my off-duty time with Ena. Nevertheless, with this stand-down of operations because of the bad weather, I thought it would be a good chance to meet Ron in Lincoln, have a few beers and catch up with how things were going for him. In the event, I didn't manage to see him and the 20th January brought a break in the weather and a return to operations for the squadron. Once more we were on the Battle Order and once more the target was Berlin. This would be the sixth time that I had been to Berlin; two-thirds of our trips had been to the 'Big City', it was becoming a familiar pattern. This time, however, the route in was via Heligoland and passing to the south of Hamburg. At 16.35, in the dwindling light of the late afternoon, we raced down Skellingthorpe's runway and lifted off with our full load plus a 2,000lb overload.

For a little while we caught up with the setting sun far out in the western sky and watched it go down for a second time that evening. The long route to the north gave the German controllers time to guess where we were going and it wasn't long after we crossed the enemy coast that the fighters appeared and I concentrated hard on my Visual Monica screen, calling out warnings to the gunners and pilot as each contact showed up. Thankfully, most of these turned out to be our own bombers in the stream, but presently Jock and Fred both started to report seeing aircraft on fire. During this period of the war, the Luftwaffe night fighter force was operating at its most efficient and effective, which for us meant at its most deadly.

As we neared the target, I went up into the astrodome. After our close shave with the incendiary bomb through the wing, Michael had asked me in future to stand in the astro whilst we were over the target area to make sure that no other Lancaster was flying above us with its bomb doors wide open. When we got to Berlin, we found that we had arrived over the target amongst the first wave, just behind the Pathfinder Force, but even though the city was again shrouded with cloud, the sky around the attacking aircraft was already lit up with searchlights, flak and the orange glow from the first bombs.

I was watching another Lancaster flying quite close on the port side and a little ahead of us, making sure that it didn't drift across our path, when, to my horror, I saw a FW190 single-engine fighter climbing up underneath it from behind. Jock in the mid-upper saw it too and involuntarily called, "Watch out!" The Luftwaffe pilot had come in very close now; surely the rear gunner must see it. I was transfixed, powerless to do anything to save the crew, waiting to see the tracer cannon shells rip into the Lancaster and send it crashing to the earth in a ball of flame; but there was nothing. Then, as if in slow motion, the fighter banked and fell away amongst the clouds. I couldn't believe how lucky that crew had been, blissfully unaware of how close they had come to death in that moment. I can only imagine that the German's guns had seized, possibly frozen, or else he was out of ammunition. Such was the fragile thread of luck by which all our lives hung.

We dropped our cookie, incendiaries and high explosives on the TIs then pulled up and away into the darkness once more, leaving the glowing mass of fire far behind us. The fighters, though, stayed with the bomber stream all the way back to the coast, and then, as we were crossing the North Sea, I received a message from Group telling us not to switch on our navigation lights as usual once over England; some of the fighters had stayed with the stream and were attacking returning aircraft as soon as their lights appeared.

At 00.35, exactly seven hours after take-off, we touched down again at Skellingthorpe and I felt that familiar rush of relief as the wheels raced along the concrete, the tension easing from me, the stress flowing out even as VN-B gently slowed and swung around the end of the runway and onto the perimeter track. Home again; nineteen to go.

In peacetime, lucky charms, mascots or traditional rituals are for most people no more than an innate, comforting connection with an earlier age, when deep superstition was central to a way of life. In wartime, when danger is a constant companion, it's very different. For us, having our lucky charms with us was as important as having ammunition for the guns or fuel for the engines. Whether these mascots really worked doesn't matter; what did matter is that we believed in them. They gave to each of us as individuals, something that we clung to, something that we believed would keep us safe, that would bring us back each time. Something that would help us survive the terror we faced every time we took off to battle with fighters, searchlights, flak, mechanical failure, collision, bombs from above, even the weather, and all in an aircraft packed full with high explosives, incendiaries, ammunition, petrol and electric sparks. In these circumstances, charms, mascots, rituals were all immensely important to each individual, often to the point of obsession, and to each crew as a whole; bad luck for one was likely to be bad luck for all.

On 50 Squadron we had a tradition, introduced before my time by W/C Macfarlane, of listening to the Andrews Sisters singing 'The Shrine of St Cecilia' before going on ops, but for each individual airman it was usually something more personal, a favourite cap, a wife's scarf, a girlfriend's suspender belt, garter or stocking, a rabbit's foot, a St. Christopher, anything at all that was important. Our bomb aimer Les Bartlett had a whole chain of lucky charms which he draped around his bomb-sight. For Fred Ball and me it was the Lincoln Imp we had each been given by Ena and Joan not long after we had started going out with them on a regular basis. We never flew without our little Imps pinned to our battledress jackets.

The Battle Order for January 21st had us down for ops again and at the briefing we found that, although the main force was going to attack Magdeburg, south-west of Berlin, we had the dubious honour of being part of a spoof raid by twenty-two Lancasters and twelve Mosquitoes upon the Reich's capital. Together with another Lancaster from the squadron, we were to link up with aircraft of 617 Squadron from Woodhall Spa and 57 Squadron from East Kirkby for the raid. At the same time that I was getting settled into VN-B, a few miles to the south-east at RAF Spilsby Ron Boydon, with his usual good humour and confidence, was climbing aboard his 207 Squadron Lancaster EM-B, preparing for the trip to Magdeburg. There was no good reason why I should have thought about Ron that night before we took off other than a moment's regret that we hadn't seen each other and been out for a couple of beers whilst the weather had stopped us flying, but I did.

In the darkness of that Friday evening just after 19.30, with a scattering of snow on the ground providing a little light and the four Merlin engines firing in sweet unison, testimony to the great care given to them by our ground crew, Michael eased the Lancaster out of the dispersal area and onto the perimeter track. We had barely gone fifty yards when Fred called out in desperation from the rear turret, "Reg, I've left my Imp in the billet. I'll have to get it, we can't go without it."

In the pilot's seat, Michael heard Fred's plea but was helpless to do anything about it. We were already moving down the peri-track in a growing line of Lancasters making their way to the head of the runway ready to take off, so simply stopping and letting Fred get out and go all the way back to the billet just wasn't an option. As if in answer to his prayer, at that moment I saw a corporal driving a Tilley, a small general utility pick-up vehicle, not far from the perimeter track and close by. I signalled to him with my torch and he drove across to us. Struggling against the backwash and the noise from the engines, he was given shouted instructions from Fred through the open front of the rear turret and sped off across the aerodrome to our site hut.

Meanwhile, the thirty or so aircraft from 50 and 61 Squadrons continued their slow convergence upon the head of the main runway, each one awaiting the signal to take off. Then the line of Lancasters began to shorten as one by one they started out, and as we moved further down the line there was no sign of the corporal or the pick-up. Then through my side window, I could see the Controller's black-and-white-chequered wagon and I knew we were very close to the head of the runway; there were only two Lancasters in front of us now and still no Tilley. Finally, we turned in on the main runway and stopped, waiting for the green Aldis light from the Controller clearing us for take-off. Michael ran up the engines and VN-B began to vibrate; we couldn't wait any longer, we were ready to go and would have to leave without Fred's Imp.

"He's here. Don't go yet, he's got it," came Fred's frantic voice.

Racing up behind us was the little Tilley with the corporal leaning out of the window, waving. He brought the pick-up to a skidding halt on the grass near the rear turret and, once more fighting to keep his balance against the powerful backwash of the Merlins, ran across to pass the little Imp to Fred through the open frame at the front of his turret.

"There's the green, Fred, we've got to go," came Michael's voice through the intercom, as the engines strained, the brakes came off and we started to roll; our seventh trip to the Big City.

"It's alright, skipper, I've got it. We're ok now," replied a very relieved Fred.

We all breathed a sigh of relief too. The last thing we wanted was a rear gunner who was convinced that we were going to get the chop. We flew with the main force for most of the way and then peeled off to Berlin, hoping to draw some of the fighters with us, but fortunately for us, the spoof didn't really work. Over the city there was very little flak and only a few fighters about. Just after we had dropped our bombs, I looked out through my side window in time to see the one Lancaster that we did lose from our little force attacked by what I think was an Me110. The aircraft was quickly engulfed by flames and spiralled down into the city beneath. I don't think that anyone managed to get out. Our flight back was uneventful and at 03.14 we dropped down onto Skellingthorpe's runway after nearly seven and a half hours in the air. The main force to Magdeburg lost thirty-five Halifaxes and twenty-two Lancasters. We had now been to Berlin more times than all our other ops put together. Eighteen to go.

There were no ops for us for the next few days and so I managed to get into Lincoln in the evening to see Ena. It was bitterly cold cycling along the roads, which were covered in ice and compacted snow, but it was always good to see her and spend some time together.

On 24th January we carried out a bombing and visual MONICA training exercise, which in itself was unremarkable, but after we had landed back at base and were in the crew locker room getting out of our flying kit, an RAF policeman came in to see us carrying a charred parachute harness which had been found in the nearby woods and handed in. He said that before he disposed of it, he thought we might be interested to see it, and he passed it to Michael. We couldn't really think why it would interest us, but Michael took it from the corporal anyway and turned it over. Although it was badly burned, we could clearly see the name and service number of the airman to whom it had been issued and who had last used it to bail out of a blazing aircraft; it was Arthur's, our first mid-upper gunner, who had come to Skellingthorpe ahead of us and been in that burning Wellington. It made me shudder, if that was what his parachute harness looked like, what on earth had Arthur's injuries been like? No wonder he didn't return to flying duties, he was lucky to be alive.

Thursday January 27th had us back on the Battle Order and at the briefing the target was of course Berlin. We took off at 17.17 and in the fading light managed a good solid place in the bomber stream. Being near the centre of the stream certainly did not guarantee survival, but those aircraft which flew at the edges of the stream were certainly more exposed and vulnerable to fighter attack. In an effort to disguise our intended target from the German controllers, the planned route was to take us out over the North Sea, crossing the coast at Cuxhaven and then on towards Hanover before turning east for Berlin. There were also diversionary mine-laying raids by other aircraft in an effort to draw the fighters away from the main force. This caused the night fighters to be committed early and some flew seventy-five miles out across the North Sea from the Dutch coast to meet us, and although they attacked some aircraft, we were left alone.

When we reached Berlin, the city was, as so often in the winter months, covered in cloud. Nevertheless, we bombed through it on the markers. The city defences were fairly active as the searchlights swept backwards and forwards through the sky in a criss-cross patchwork. Although the cloud was too dense for the beams to penetrate, seen from above they illuminated it like a vast silver cinema screen across which the darkened silhouettes of more than 500 Lancaster bombers slowly drifted. Instead of stooging around outside the target area waiting for the bombers to emerge from the flak, on this night the fighter pilots must have been ordered to get in there and mix it with us over the target. Just as likely to be hit by flak as we were, the fighters flew into the bomber stream, adding their own to the silhouettes passing across the silver screen that was becoming increasingly orange with each new explosion, each new fire far beneath it in the streets of the Reich.

The pilots were so committed to attacking the stream whilst over the target area that three times Les was forced to leave the bomb aimer's position and man the front turret before we eventually turned for home. We also had a relief mid-upper gunner with us for this trip as Jock had been hospitalised since our last mission on the 21st with a chest infection. On the return leg, whilst we were at about 25,000 feet, the gunner called me over the intercom to say that the Perspex of his turret was icing up and he was having difficulty seeing. This was very serious since it was essential that the gunners had as much visibility as possible to help them see an incoming fighter or even another friendly aircraft which might be drifting towards us on a collision course. I can't remember his name now, but he asked me to pass him an axe and reached down as I placed it in his gloved hand. The next moment, a shower of frozen Perspex came crashing down around me and over the bomb-bay floor, followed by the numbing -50°C icy air, which froze us all the way home giving us a taste of the freezing temperatures which the rear gunners endured night after night.

A little after two o'clock in the morning, after nearly nine hours in the air, we were in the circuit at Skellingthorpe and soon saw the red light on the towers of Lincoln cathedral, welcoming us home. Within a few minutes we were on 'funnels' and then coming in to land, racing along the runway, slowing all the time until finally we turned on to the peri-track and headed for the dispersal pan and our waiting ground crew. Seventeen to go.

50 Squadron were lucky that night; we didn't lose any aircraft, although P/O Toovey's VN-A lost an engine in a combat with a fighter. However, 61 Squadron on the other side of the aerodrome, who were shortly due to move to Coningsby whilst runway improvements were carried out at Skellingthorpe, were not so lucky; they lost two Lancasters and ten of the young men inside them.

We eventually got to bed at around 4.30am but after only a few hours' sleep were up again; operations were on that night and once more we were on the Battle Order. Jock was out of hospital now and was passed fit for flying duties. At the briefing we were told that it was to be a late take-off, and then the curtain was drawn back across the wall map. I couldn't believe it; Berlin yet again. This would be our ninth trip to the Big City and our third in a row. My heart sank. I felt certain that we couldn't keep going all that way to the enemy's capital and hope to survive; the law of averages was definitely against us. Still, there was nothing to do but grit my teeth and concentrate on the briefing.

Later, as we left the briefing room, I was walking along the pathway to the Mess with Jock and Les when it became obvious from their hushed tones that there was a problem with Jock's girlfriend, so much so that Jock ended by saying that he wouldn't mind being shot down then he wouldn't have to face the consequences of his amorous activities. Angry, I turned on them both, saying that I certainly didn't want to be shot down as Ena and I were very much in love. Even though I was twenty, I was still very naive about women and didn't realise the significance of their conversation, which became increasingly clear to my two friends as they continued. With no little astonishment at my ignorance, they gave me a quick lesson in the workings of the female anatomy. Well, how was I supposed to know! Nothing like that was taught at school and my parents certainly would never have spoken about such things. Happily, we weren't shot down and I think it turned out all right for Jock and his girlfriend.

We took off at 00.21 in the cold, crisp, clear air of that January night and joined the growing bomber stream gathering over Lincolnshire before heading out for the long journey to Berlin. The route this night took us far out into the North Sea before we turned in by Heligoland, where the heavy flak came close enough to buck our aircraft, rattle the sides with shrapnel and fill the inside with the smell of cordite. It continued until we passed near Flensburg on our way along the Baltic coast before finally turning in by Rostock and running down to Berlin.

By the time we reached the target in the fifth wave flying at 21,300 feet, Berlin was ablaze and through large gaps in the clouds we could see the ground markings which the Pathfinder Force had laid down. I was once more in the astrodome to ensure that there was no-one above us with their bomb doors open, and looking down, I could clearly see the seething mass of flames and explosions over four miles below. It was to be one of our most successful raids upon the city. The searchlights from the defences criss-crossed the sky, seeking to fall upon an unlucky aircraft whilst the deadly blue pencil beam of the radar-controlled light hunted with greater precision. Even at our height the scene was lit up with technicolour brilliance. Whichever way I looked, aircraft were flying through the canvas of the picture before me. Below, they were silhouetted black against the flaming cauldron that we had made of Berlin; around us, darkened undersides boasted a flickering orange glow beneath the camouflaged tops, which were betrayed only by knowing winks from Perspex turrets glinting in the fire light.

Les guided us in then called out, "Bombs gone." With relief, I felt the Lancaster lift, then the agonising wait while we flew straight and level across the target area to get the aiming-point photograph. At last, "Photograph taken, bomb doors closed," from Les. We started to pick up speed, anxious to leave behind the horror of the target area. I jumped back down to my wireless set, leaving that infernal devastation for Fred in the rear turret to contemplate. I had just finished receiving a message from Group when I heard our engines suddenly roar on full power and we began to climb steeply. At the same moment, Mike shouted over the intercom, "There's a fighter ahead attacking a Lanc. Les, get up into the turret and start firing at it."

Back in the astrodome, I was in time to see the underside of a Ju88 above and a little in front of us. Our bomb aimer, now in the front turret, was talking to the mid-upper, "Not yet Jock, wait till I say... now!"

Simultaneously, they fired their twin .303 guns. Four strings of tracer and bullets, shining in the dark like a Morse code message, whipped across the short distance of sky between us and struck the Junkers. Jock's line of fire was straight over my head and I instinctively ducked as I saw his tracer rake along the underside of its fuselage. Les in the front turret was scoring, too, and hit the wings as well as the body of the aircraft. Now we had to save ourselves from a counter-attack, but as Michael put us into a starboard corkscrew, the Ju88 continued steadily on its course still closing on the bomber ahead of it. Then I watched as very slowly it began to sink away to port and start to spiral into the cloud and haze. There was no flame or smoke from it, nor any parachutes. None of us saw it crash so we could only claim it as damaged, but I'm sure that the crew did not survive that amount of fire from such close range; it almost certainly killed the crew, leaving the aircraft to slowly lose control and spiral away as it did.

After nearly eight hours in the air, we landed back at Skellingthorpe at 08.16 and handed VN-B back to the ground crew. A rather excited debrief session with the Intelligence Officer followed, helped by a very welcome mug of hot sweet tea served by one of the many hard-working WAAFs. Then it was into the locker room to get out of our flying kit, breakfast and the sleep that we so desperately needed. God, I was tired. The adrenalin had stopped, the wakey-wakey pills had worn off. Fifty hours of night-time operational flying over Germany during January had taken its toll; we were all exhausted. Sixteen to go.

"The Beetham crew before Queenie: l-r Fred Ball, Les Bartlett, Mike Beetham, Frank Swinyard, Reg Payne, Don Moore, Jock Higgins"

Chapter Eleven

*"We were companions. We were young.
We were immortal – so we said...
For that which in the heart was sung
Could have no commerce with the Dead."*

- From '*The Fire*'; Hilaire Belloc

After this raid, we were given another seven days' leave, effective immediately. By the time I got up, it was too late in the day to go home to see mum and dad so I spent Saturday evening in Lincoln with Ena. It seemed ages since I had seen her and I was glad of the time to try to unwind a little as we sat in one of the many pubs having a quiet drink. Ena never asked me what it was like on operations, she was just glad that I was now nearly half-way through my tour. She asked me afterwards, when my tour was over, but during it she knew that I needed to think and talk about other things. Mostly we talked about our relationship, which was now growing very strong and, like most couples at that time, what we would do when the war was over, whenever that might be. I think that by early 1944, most people believed that we would eventually win the war; nevertheless, it had already been going on longer than the First World War and wasn't showing signs of finishing any time soon.

Early next morning, I collected my travel warrant and caught an almost empty local train into Lincoln, where I changed for the Kettering train, which was also quiet enough for me to have no trouble getting a seat. I got home just in time for Sunday dinner, much to mum's great pleasure, although she scolded me with tears of joy in her eyes for not letting her know that I was on my way.

I spent most of the first couple of days catching up on my sleep, relaxing and playing with my young brother Brian. Sitting at the table with mum and dad having my supper on the third evening, I told them that next day I thought I would go across to Ron Boydon's house to see his mother and find out if she knew when he would be home on leave, as I was sure that he would be due some by now. If he was already home, we could go out for a few beers and catch up. My mother dropped her knife and my father quickly took a large bite from his piece of bread. The silence around the table engulfed me, the room closed in, heavy with foreboding, the ticking of the clock like a blacksmith's hammer on my brain, the rain against the windows like a machine gun. My stomach tightened, my breathing stopped and in that moment, I knew.

"When?" I rasped. The word stuck to the back of my throat and was barely audible, although I already knew the answer; it was the Magdeburg raid.

"I'm really sorry, Reg," whispered my mother. "The telegram came at the beginning of the week. He's missing believed killed. He was such a nice young man." I could see the tears welling up in her eyes. She knew that she had been luckier because, even though Art was a prisoner, he was at least still alive. I think my father, who had been through the trenches on the Western Front in the Great War and had seen death on an unimaginable scale, had been told to say nothing; he didn't.

I had become used to losing familiar faces on the Squadron; it was just part of being on an operational station; crew who were at tea in the Mess before take-off were missing at breakfast. But Ron's death hit me hard; he was the first close friend that I had lost whilst on ops. We had been all through the hard days of our training together; two long years from that very first day outside Mrs Clegg's house in Blackpool, and now he was gone.

Sergeant Ronald Arthur Blake Boydon, 1435862, had been the wireless operator in Lancaster Mk1 R5895 EM-B flown by Pilot Officer JM Read. Stationed at RAF Spilsby with 207 Squadron, they had taken off at 20.11 on the night of 21st/22nd January 1944 to attack Magdeburg, part of a force of 648 aircraft. I had flown on the same operation but had gone to Berlin on the diversionary raid. They had fallen victim to a night fighter and had crashed at the village of Dannigkow about ten miles south-east of Magdeburg. The other five crew that night, were, Pilot Officer RW Sharp, Pilot Officer C Travers, RCAF, who was an American from Oakland in California, Flight Sergeant EC Clunas, RAAF, Sergeant LF Abel and Sergeant C Codling. None of them managed to escape from the burning Lancaster and all are buried in the Berlin 1939–45 War Cemetery.

I had never met Ron's father, Arthur, whose name he carried, and neither he nor his mother ever spoke of him. Ron was an only child and his mother Edith was devoted to looking after him, so when she was told that he had probably been killed she was totally devastated, unable to come to terms with the possibility of his death. After the war, by which time Ron's death had been confirmed, Edith Boydon had a complete mental breakdown and was admitted to the local psychiatric hospital for treatment. She never recovered and remained there for the rest of her life. Not long after her admission, she was joined by Kate Johnson, whose twenty-one-year-old son Arthur, another wireless operator from Kettering with 44 Squadron, had been killed on the ill-fated Nuremberg raid on the night of 30th/31st March 1944. Like Edith, Kate was destroyed by the death of her son although she did finally recover enough to return home to her family. I know that Art and I were both so lucky to have survived, even though Art had been seriously injured, something which would come back to haunt him in later life.

I stayed at home until the end of my leave for my mum's sake, really, and went out for a drink most evenings, but at the end I was glad to be back at Skellingthorpe so that I could see Ena. In a strange way, it was a relief to have the familiarity of the station and be with my crew again, and going out with Ena took my mind off things. We shared our billet with another crew who had joined the squadron at the same time as we had. They were a decent bunch, and we had got to know them well but when I returned from leave, there were new faces in the hut. The new crew didn't know what had happened, but we knew; one night they didn't come back. It was as simple and clinical as that, and this fresh-faced young sprog crew were their replacement, although there was no point in worrying them with that now, they would soon find out what it was really like over Germany.

We weren't on ops straight away so Fred and I could go into Lincoln to meet Joan and Ena in the evening after they had finished work. I didn't say anything to the girls about Ron, but Ena knew me well enough by now to know that something was troubling me, although she didn't ask. On Tuesday 8th February we were back in the air twice, with a daylight standard-beam approach bombing exercise and then a searchlight and night fighter interception exercise later in the evening when it was dark. On Thursday night there was a party in the Mess, but by Bomber Command operational crew standards it was a fairly mild affair with most people staying reasonably sober, although Les did tell me that the last thing he had seen was our rear gunner Fred Ball trying to play the bass drum. It seems, however, that later on he slipped on some spilt beer and put his foot through the drum, which did nothing for his popularity with the band.

Next day it was visual MONICA training, flying in formation. It was critical to the survival of all crews that they were kept as efficient as possible all the time. We had just returned from leave and the CO knew that we would have gone off the boil a bit and relaxed, so were detailed for a few days of air exercises to sharpen us up before the next mission. That evening I went into Lincoln on my own to see Ena. As I bicycled in from Skellingthorpe it started to drizzle, but by the time I left Ena and set off back to the aerodrome it was pouring down. When I got in to the billet my greatcoat was soaked through so I hung it up by the stove to dry. The room was bitterly cold as usual and now I was cold too from the rain when I got into bed. Every night I put my greatcoat on the bed to help keep me warm but not tonight, so I just shivered. I could hear my teeth chattering and then I heard Fred get up and felt him put his own coat over me to keep me warm.

After breakfast the next morning Fred and I rang Joan and Ena to say that we would see them that night following our scheduled routine fighter affiliation exercises in the afternoon. There was a 10/10 cloud layer over the east of England, but since the base was at 3,000 feet and the layer was only about 3,500 feet deep, the training was on and so, with full flying kit, we gathered around Lancaster W4119 VN-Q for Queenie that Saturday afternoon. We were to share the exercise with another crew; Pilot Officer Jennings and his two gunners had come to join us. Ten young men in the prime of life, cheerfully joking with each other huddled in a small group on the concrete of the dispersal pan in cold February air which blew straight off the North Sea.

Michael, who was the senior officer and would captain the aircraft, and P/O Jennings were talking to the ground crew before signing for VN-Q whilst the rest of us chatted at the foot of the ladder. As we did so, I noticed that our flight engineer was not holding his parachute.

"Don," I asked, "where's your parachute?"

"Oh, it's ok, Reg, it's only another training flight. I'm fed up with having to keep carrying it about. This is our fourth in as many days."

"You should always have your 'chute with you, Don," I replied with some dismay and alarm.

"You worry too much, Reg." He laughed and slapped me on the shoulder. "I'm not expecting trouble. I'll be ok."

We were to meet up with a Spitfire over south Yorkshire near the Humber estuary and practise evasion methods and corkscrewing in particular. By 15.10 we were airborne and heading north with Michael at the controls. We climbed up through the cloud layer into the bright winter sunshine above where we rendezvoused with the Spitfire. The two aircraft pilots were able to speak to each other over the radio link, and when everyone was ready, the exercise began. The Spitfire attacked us from different angles and directions. Michael dived, climbed and rolled Queenie through the corkscrew manoeuvres while our gunners tried to shoot the fighter down with blank ammunition, their efforts being recorded on the cine cameras fitted to their turrets; the rest of us simply hung on to our seats and tried not to be thrown about too much.

After about half an hour, Michael radioed the Spitfire pilot to tell him to hold off whilst he and P/O Jennings changed places, as did the gunners, and then the exercise continued. Our bomb aimer had nothing to do on this trip so had come up from the nose of the Lancaster and was standing close to my table in the astrodome taking photographs of the Spitfire. The fighter dived in to attack Queenie again and the rear gunner shouted, "Fighter, fighter, starboard quarter, up. Prepare to corkscrew starboard. Corkscrew starboard, go."

Jennings put the Lancaster into a very steep dive to starboard, and then as he pulled her back to climb to port, Don shouted, "The port outer's on fire!" I quickly looked out of my side window and saw a mass of orange flame engulfing the engine and the wing immediately around it. Jennings levelled the Lancaster, cut the engine and ordered the fire extinguishers to be activated. At the same time, Michael ordered us to prepare to abandon the aircraft. I reached into the bracket close to my table and retrieved my parachute, quickly clipping it on, and in that moment, I caught sight of Don Moore. He was passing Michael's parachute to him and as he did so, just for a second, he paused and looked at me, fear in his eyes, regretting his decision not to bring his own. Down in the tail of the aircraft, Fred Ball had his 'chute on and was helping Jennings' rear gunner out of the turret, passing the man's own life-saving bundle to him, whilst Les, Jock and the fourth gunner got the rear door open.

My heart was pumping fast as I turned my attention back to the fire in the engine, and it was with some relief that I watched the flames die down and then go out in a cloud of steam. But as soon as the extinguishers were empty, the fire blazed up again and once more quickly engulfed the engine and the wing around it. Suddenly, Les scrambled back over the main spar to the astrodome to retrieve his camera and was now busy stuffing it into his battledress. I looked out at the wing once more. It was starting to glow as the fire grew in intensity. The flames, fanned by the wind, had completely covered the engine and the outer wing. We had just a few precious seconds to get out before it dropped off and Queenie turned into her last dive.

Michael, too, had been watching the fire; he knew that the Lancaster was now doomed and that it would not be long before the heat burned through enough of the spar to cause the wing to break away and drop off. He gave the order to abandon the aircraft, not knowing that his flight engineer didn't have a parachute, although it wouldn't have made any difference if he had, it just saved him the agony of the inevitable decision.

By now, Les was at the rear door again and sitting on the step. As soon as Michael gave the order to abandon he rolled out and was gone. Then Jock stepped forward, still wearing his flying helmet with the intercom attached. Like me, he had seen the intensity of the fire from his turret and in the desperation, of the moment, he forgot his training and simply jumped into space. Luckily, as he went out, the lead pulled his helmet off but the slipstream caught him straightaway and whipped him onto the tailplane where the force of the wind held him tight. For precious wasted seconds we watched from the doorway, transfixed by his plight, but then his 'chute opened and in an instant he too was gone. The remaining three gunners stood around the open door, hesitating, the wind swirling in and buffeting their flying suits, their faces stark with fear. We hadn't trained for this; we had never jumped out of an aeroplane before, never stepped into that abyss praying to be caught by threads of silk.

"Go on, Fred, get out quick," I shouted over the thunderous noise of the straining engines and howling slipstream, but, too frightened to jump, they all stepped back and beckoned to me to go first. There was no time to waste; I knew the whole wing was on fire and that once it dropped off the chance to get out would be gone forever, trapped in the plummeting aircraft. Michael and Frank had already gone out through the forward escape hatch and I had seen Jennings put the aircraft on automatic and go down to the hatch too.

Don was there, too, standing beside me at the open door. Never before or since have I seen a man consumed by the absolute terror that gripped him as he faced certain death brought about by his own decision, but in the moments before I bailed out I looked into Don's eyes and saw it then. The blood had drained from his face, his hands were shaking and, although he was looking at me, it wasn't me he saw. His eyes were wide and had glazed over; he was staring through me at someone or something behind me, perhaps the image of death itself, but I hope that it was his wife and young daughter that he would never see again. There was nothing I could do for him. I put my hand out and touched his arm in farewell, sat on the step and rolled out. My last image of Don was of him scrabbling his way back along the fuselage desperately searching for a spare parachute.

A moment after I had rolled out, I was horrified to find myself back in the aircraft; the slipstream had thrown me up into the doorway. Thankfully, one of the gunners pushed me out again and this time I fell clear of Queenie and started to tumble through the cloud without any idea where I was going to come down. When the fire started, we had been over Spurn Head by the Humber estuary and my great fear was that we were still heading out to sea. Thanks to all those happy childhood hours I had spent in the Ise Brook, I could swim very well, but this was the middle of February not June and it was the North Sea waiting for me; nor was I wearing my Mae West. I would not last long in those bitter cold waters.

I quickly counted to three and then pulled on the ripcord of my parachute: nothing happened. I pulled it again. Still it wouldn't open. In desperation I pulled again and again as I plunged and somersaulted through the wet mist of the cloud layer, the cold wind ripping at my flying suit and tearing at my face. After falling for around 3,000 feet, I burst through the murk into clear air. It was with mixed feelings that I saw the solid earth beneath me. I wasn't going to drown but I was still going to die if I couldn't get my parachute to open. Finally, as one so often does in such circumstances, I prayed to God and as I did so, I realised that I was not pulling on the ripcord but on one of my harness handles. In an instant, I gave a grateful tug on the D-ring and, with an overpowering sense of relief, felt that life-saving jolt as my parachute ballooned above me, slowing down my headlong dash to the earth to a more sedate pace. My prayer had certainly been answered with not many seconds to spare, and bringing me down over land rather than the cold sea.

However, I was to be punished for my carelessness; when I had put my harness on I had not tightened it up properly. Probably a bit like Don, I had become a little blasé about short training flights and had been wearing it far too slack. As the parachute had opened and caught the air at the end of my helter-skelter descent, it had pulled my shoulders out of the harness, leaving only my legs in. In the nick of time, I realised what had happened and managed to duck under the straps and grab hold of the flapping canvas above my head, hanging on for dear life. Had I missed my hold, I would have tipped forward and slipped out of the harness altogether, parting company from my parachute and this world.

Content that I was now secure, I drifted down towards the Lincolnshire countryside. I could see for miles around me and my thoughts returned to Don Moore and how he should have been floating down as well instead of condemned to die in the Lancaster. Then, some distance ahead of me, I saw a great orange flash and a large pall of thick black smoke begin to rise, followed a few moments later by a muffled boom. I knew that I had just witnessed Queenie hitting the ground and the instant that Don had died. I felt sick at the realisation that I had lost another friend; first Ron Boydon and now Don. Thoughts raced through my mind. I hoped that Fred had managed to get out, too, but I knew that there was so little time for all three gunners to follow me out. God, I hoped Fred was out. Not him, too, surely not. I couldn't lose two friends this afternoon. What could I tell Joan? She would be devastated. He must have got out.

I couldn't look at the rising smoke any longer and turned my gaze upwards, just in time to see the outer port wing from Queenie following me down. The engine had stayed on the main spar but the outer wing had burned through and here it was, floating down with me, lurching backwards and forwards like an autumn leaf gently falling from a tree. In the quiet interlude of my descent, with only the sound of the wind rushing through my parachute lines, I watched it see-saw through the sky, mesmerised by the beauty of its motion, all that was now left of Lancaster W4119 VN-Q.

As I drifted away from the wing, a seagull silently glided past on a current, casually turning its head to watch me with a mixture of curiosity and disdain that I couldn't catch the wind and stay aloft. Little did it know that staying aloft was not what I had in mind. But I now realised that if I had birds for company, then it was time to start thinking about where I was going to land. Ahead of me and not far from where Queenie had come down, I could see an aerodrome whilst below me a reservoir was looming up and I wondered whether I should take off my flying boots in case I came down in the water, but even as I was thinking about this, I had easily floated on beyond its shores.

Just then, I saw another parachute coming down close to me and a little above. I shouted out, "Who are you?", but he couldn't hear me so I turned my attention back to where I was likely to land. The burning wreckage of the Lancaster was ahead of me now but slightly to one side and I knew that my drift would not take me that far; I was heading for the nearer large ploughed field. I must have been down to my last two hundred feet because I began to get an impression of speed and of how quickly I was travelling. In no time at all, I could make out the details of the hedge at the front of the field, and then the furrows beyond. Then I was over the hedge and the ploughed ground was rushing past. I was below the tree tops of the nearby wood and could see stones mixed amongst the soil. Any second now. I was braced, ready, then it came, the jolt, a flurry of soft earth under my boots, and I was rolling over on the ground. I was down. I was safe. I had survived.

I got to my feet and started to slip out of what little of my harness was around my legs. As I did so the other parachute that had come down behind me drifted on a little further beyond the field and into the woods on the far side, crashing in amongst the leafless branches of the trees. I wondered if it was Fred, if he had overcome his fear and had got out behind me after all. Gathering up my 'chute, I heard a vehicle engine and looked round to see an RAF truck coming along the farm track towards me. It stopped a short distance away and two airmen came racing across the field to me.
"Are you all right, mate?" one of them asked me.
"Yes, thanks," I replied a little shakily, "but one of the crew landed in the woods over there."

The other airman ran off to where the parachute shreds could be seen hanging amongst the trees and a few minutes later returned with a badly shaken and bruised but otherwise unhurt P/O Jennings, who kept repeating, "Where are we? What happened?" It would be some time before he was passed fit to fly again. We made our way to the truck, threw my parachute in the back and climbed up. We were driven back down the farm track and entered the airfield I had seen; we had come down at RAF East Kirby, which today is the Lincolnshire Aviation Museum, home to NX611 *Just Jane*, one of only three functional Lancaster bombers anywhere in the world. It is a wonderful museum, a great tribute to RAF Bomber Command and a must to visit for anyone interested in the RAF during the Second World War.

We were taken to see the Medical Officer straight away. After a fairly cursory examination, he seemed happy enough with me, but when the MO heard Jennings still rambling and obviously suffering from traumatic shock, he took the pilot into another room. I didn't see Jennings again until some weeks later when he returned to the squadron. Jock was the next one to arrive, nursing cracked and bruised ribs from his collision with the tailplane. The MO strapped Jock's ribs and then someone came in and told us that there were still four crew trapped in the aircraft when it hit the ground and would we go with them to help to identify the bodies. I knew that Michael and Frank had gone out through the forward hatch before P/O Jennings. Les, Jock and I had gone out through the rear door, which meant that the four in the wreckage were Fred Ball, Jennings' two gunners and, of course, Don Moore, whose fate had been sealed the moment he had decided not to take a parachute with him that day.

These were our friends, people we knew well, men we had entrusted our lives to. We had flown fourteen missions together, had been to Berlin nine times, faced the horrors of night fighters, flak, searchlights, bombs from above, fog and icing; and now they had been killed in a training exercise. It was so unfair. The Lancaster had driven into the ground at over two hundred miles an hour and neither Jock nor I could face the thought of looking at the mangled remains of our friends and trying to identify what was left of them; we said no.

We were taken to the Sergeants' Mess and given a mug of tea. Whilst there, we learned that Les had landed safely some miles away. Five of our crew had survived. Post-Traumatic Shock Syndrome was unheard of at this time and the serious effects of such shock were only just being recognised by doctors, and so, in the absence of any obvious physical injury, Jock and I were simply left to get on with it. The evening meal was being served whilst we were in the Mess and, although not feeling particularly hungry, we knew that our next meal might not be until tomorrow, so we joined the queue for fish and chips. As we waited our turn, one of the airmen from the station recognised Jock and called across to him,
"Hello, Jock, what the blazes are you doing here?"
"I came out of that Lancaster that crashed here earlier today," he quietly replied.

"Yeah, line shooter," came the response followed by much raucous laughter from those around us. But Jock and I weren't laughing; we had lost good friends that afternoon.

Back in Lincoln, Ena and Joan were beginning to wonder what had happened to Fred and me since we were now very late for the date we had arranged after breakfast that morning. Finally, when seven o'clock came and we had still not shown up, they rang through to our Mess. The news of the crash had been reported to the squadron but there was not much definite information about survivors. The unfortunate sergeant who answered Ena's call asked her to hold on, but after a minute or two of whispered consultation with the others there, told her that our aircraft had crashed and some of the crew had been killed but he didn't know who and could she ring back later. The girls were distraught, but there was nothing they could do but wait and hope.

It was fairly late when we were taken back to Skellingthorpe that night. Together with Jock and Les, I went to the Mess where we relived our escapes to the many eager listeners. Les, as usual, was shooting the best lines but we all needed to get it out of our systems; we were still in shock and the adrenalin had made us excited. Thoughts of having lost Fred, Don and the other two gunners were put out of our minds for a little while as we revelled in the attention of the moment. Then the MO arrived and put an end to it all, insisting that we turn in, and he gave us each a tablet that he said would help us to sleep during the night. He watched us take our tablets and then put the three of us in an ambulance with orders that we were to be taken back to our billet. Sitting in the ambulance, I suddenly felt desperately tired. The others must have been the same because we all fell very quiet and I was more grateful than ever to climb into my bed, close my eyes and quietly slip into a blissfully peaceful drug-induced sleep. The guilt of surviving would come later.

On the MO's instructions, we were to be left to wake naturally the next morning, and when I did, the pale winter sun, still low in the morning sky, was shining through the window behind me and striking the hut wall opposite my bed. I gradually came round and my head began to clear from the effects of the MO's tablet. The other crew we shared with had long since slipped out quietly for breakfast. Jock and Les were both sleeping, their steady measured breathing barely disturbing the stillness. From the trees outside, the soft coo-cooing of an optimistic wood pigeon filtered through the window. The distant spluttering sounds of a Merlin engine being worked upon by its ground crew drifted across the aerodrome while the muffled rhythm of the great hoofs of a passing Shire horse pulling its heavy load along the Skellingthorpe Road kept time with the pigeon and whispered around the room, as if fearful to intrude.

I sat up slowly and started to recall the events of the previous afternoon. Across the room lay the two neatly made beds where Fred and Don should have been sleeping and I felt the sadness that came from knowing I would never see them again. For a few moments I gazed over at Fred's tunic hanging where he had left it on the peg above his bed, wondering what on earth I would say to Joan. Lost in my thoughts, the minutes ticked by, the sunlight silently crept along the wall until it reached Fred's battledress and cast a vivid shaft across the lapels. From within that yellow strip of light, something caught my attention, something that seemed to be reaching out to me, to shine out from the pale blue tunic, sparkling in the brightness. I looked hard to see what was glinting, almost moving across the material, and then I realised; it was Fred's little golden Lincoln Imp. Piqued at having been left behind, he seemed to be laughing at me, mocking me with the consequences of being forgotten.

I flopped back onto my pillow, a lump in my throat. I glanced up at my own Imp, sitting contentedly on the breast pocket of the jacket I had taken off the night before. Do lucky charms really work? I wondered. Who knows? But I do know that I had worn my Imp and survived; Fred had left his behind and he hadn't.

Presently, the other two awoke so I roused myself and shook off the melancholic start to the day. I washed, shaved, dressed and then wandered over to the Mess to see if there was any breakfast left. Surprisingly, there was; the MO had ordered that we were to be fed whatever time we turned up. Breakfast made me feel better. I telephoned Ena to let her know what had happened, but she already knew. The two of them had rung the Mess again later and been told who the survivors were. Joan was devastated at Fred's death. I arranged to meet Ena that evening in Lincoln.

When I returned from the telephone, there was a message to say that all surviving crew from Queenie were to report to the CO, Wing Commander Anthony Heward, after lunch. P/O Jennings was in sick quarters somewhere. Whilst the rest of us were waiting outside the W/C's door, Les and I started to poke each other and I began to laugh; I suppose we were still suffering from a degree of shock. As soon as I laughed, Michael turned on me very smartly and told me to cut it out. He said that he had been speaking to the CO in the Mess the night before and told him that the incident and the loss of two of our crew had taken it out of us all a bit and that he thought we could do with a 48-hour leave pass, so stop fooling around and look miserable.

We were granted our leave but it was delayed for a few days whilst the Court of Inquiry sat to determine the cause of the accident. Michael gave evidence and it was found that when P/O Jennings had put Queenie into the steep corkscrew dive, a glycol pipe in the port outer engine had fractured and spewed the inflammable liquid out over the red-hot exhausts of the engine, starting the fire which the extinguishers would never have been able to douse. The pilots were completely cleared of any responsibility for the loss of the aircraft and the four crew members. After the Inquiry, we started our leave, but it came with strings attached. The CO, whose sobriquet was 'Smiler', was older and wiser, he knew all the tricks and how to come out ahead; we could have our leave but on the second day we were to attend Fred's and Don's funerals. Michael, Les, Jock, and I were to be bearers for Fred in

Birmingham, whilst Frank travelled to London to be with Don's family.

Michael made his own arrangements whilst Les and Jock came home with me to Kettering, the plan being that we would all meet early on the second morning on Leicester station in time to catch the train to Birmingham. We arrived home quite late in the evening, not having left Skellingthorpe until well into the afternoon, and I hadn't had chance to let mum know that we were coming. However, she was quite used to me just turning up with my RAF pals in the same way that Art had done before he was shot down.

After the evening meal which mum put on for us, we stayed in and chatted to my parents, who gave me some news from Art in the prison camp. It was all a bit of a squeeze for the three of us in the one bedroom since, as well as my brother Brian, my sister Doris was also still at home. We managed, though, and the next morning following breakfast, washed and shaved we went into Kettering, had a few drinks and a lunchtime snack at the NAAFI before going back home for tea and a brush-up ready to return to the pubs. That evening, we really let ourselves go, mixing with the Americans in the town, who, when they heard of our close shave were quick to buy us a beer, and enjoying the attention of the girls who hung onto our every word as well as our arms. We were RAF boys who really had jumped out of a burning Lancaster bomber and floated down to earth on the end of a parachute, and now we floated from pub to pub borne on the breath of night life that blew through the town, drinking in the joy of being alive.

There is no doubt that we drank far too much that night, but who could really blame us? Mum and dad certainly didn't when we eventually returned home. I think my dad knew just how close it had been for us and understood. Mum was, as always, simply pleased to have me safely at home for a few hours and, despite the continued rationing, she still managed to have some supper on the table for us. Happy, fed and content, we went to bed and made ourselves as comfortable as three grown men sharing a double bed could do. However, it wasn't long before the beer worked its way through to three bladders and relief was needed. It was cold, it was winter and the lavatory was downstairs in the porch outside the kitchen door. In what seemed like a relay, we used the pot under the bed and when it was full, tipped it out of the window into mum's garden. I'm not sure how many times we emptied it, but it was at least twice.

It was an early start that morning to catch the train for Leicester, where we met Michael, and then on to Birmingham, a subdued journey from the sadness of our duty and sore heads from the night before. Michael had been ordered to ensure that under no circumstances were Fred's family to be allowed to open the coffin. When he told us what his orders were, I remembered that day in 1940 when I was in the Home Guard and had been out to the crash site of the Blenheim bomber, and I knew exactly why the Wing Commander had given him these orders. Fred's parents were better to remember their son as he was when alive, not the wreckage of him that I knew was in the coffin.

We arrived at the family home and were shown into the front parlour, where to my horror, I saw one of Fred's brothers with a screwdriver undoing the last remaining fixings of the coffin lid. Another five minutes and we would have been too late. Michael was brilliant. He used his authority as an RAF officer and Fred's aircraft commander to stop what was about to happen and got the screws replaced, but he did it in such a kind way that the family didn't object or feel deprived of a last look at Fred, which was just as well because it would have finished his mother, who was barely able to control her grief as it was.

It wasn't long before the undertakers arrived and we became the official bearers. Fred's family were strong Catholics and I didn't follow the long service very well, much of it being in Latin. Finally it was time to lay Fred to rest. We carried the coffin to the grave and I was upset to see it being lowered into the three or four inches of water which had gathered in the bottom. Almost unable to stand, Fred's mother leaned over and looked down at where her son was resting, and had someone not been holding on to her tightly, she would have fallen in. I thought about Don Moore's funeral taking place at the same time in London and that this was how his wife must be feeling, and of how Ron Boydon's mother must be. It had been a terrible few weeks.

Back at the house, the family had obviously pooled their ration coupons and had put on quite a spread, which filled the large dining table. I don't know what Michael had had for breakfast, but for the rest of us it had been a boiled egg and a piece of toast, and we were ravenous. None of the other mourners seemed to be hungry and it appeared that the only ones who were steadily working their way through the food like four locusts were these RAF chaps. Fred enjoyed his food and wouldn't have wanted us to have wasted it. Understandably, the family wanted to know all about the crash and how Fred had died. There was no place for line shooting now, just the bare facts. It was very hard but eventually we had to leave them to get our train back to Lincoln.

Fred was a good friend and I missed his company. On Sunday morning, the day after the accident, the ground staff had come into the billet and removed all of Fred's and Don's belongings; however they didn't take Fred's greatcoat, which was still on my bed where he had put it over me on the Friday night to keep me warm. It had been his last night alive and this Christian act of caring concern for me was so typical of him. I kept it for a short while and then gave it to a very grateful ground crew airman, whose own coat was covered in oil and grease and in a terrible state from working on our aircraft out in the biting cold of the open windswept aerodrome.

Now when I went into Lincoln to meet Ena, I went alone, and this seemed to bring us closer together, made us focus on our own future more. I suppose because of Fred's death, Ena became more conscious of what the other ATS girls were finding; increasingly they wouldn't date RAF aircrew more than two or three times. Too many of them had fallen in love with an airman only to find that they were left waiting one night in the cold and the rain for a man who was never going to show up.

The morning after the funerals I cycled across to the parachute room to find the WAAF who had packed my 'chute to thank her. It was customary for an airman who had bailed out of a doomed aircraft and had felt that life-saving tug as his parachute blossomed in the sky above his head, gently carrying him to the earth, or sometimes the sea, to find the WAAF who had packed his 'chute and reward her not only with thanks but also with a pound note. As I gladly handed my money to the young WAAF, she told me, with a little flush in her cheeks, that she had packed five of the six survivors' parachutes: it had been a good day's work for her and an even better one for us.

Fred and Don were replaced on the crew by two of the most experienced officers on the squadron, who we were very lucky to have. Flight Lieutenant Ted Adamson, the squadron engineer leader, took over as flight engineer and Pilot Officer Johnny Blott, the squadron gunnery leader, became our tail-end Charlie. Although they were both tour expired, they volunteered to fly with us until we finished our own tour which, since we were barely halfway through, was a huge compliment to us as a crew and to our skipper in particular.

Exactly a week after Queenie had crashed, we were once more on the Battle Order, but the CO wanted to make sure that we were psychologically as well as physically fit and so, later that morning we took our own trusted VN-B up on a thirty-minute night flying test and to do a few corkscrews. We drew our parachutes that day with renewed respect and enthusiasm for them.

On that flight, we carried an extra crewman who had been receiving special treatment for chronic airsickness. I suggested that he sat close to me on the rest bed where I could look after him, remembering how terrible Frank had been when we were training on Wellingtons, and I took the precaution of giving the man a bucket just in case his treatment hadn't been very successful. The general flying test went well and then Michael said that we would try a few corkscrews. I clung tightly to my seat waiting for Johnny Blott to give the word to the skipper and then for the Lancaster to suddenly drop and turn. I looked at the airman sitting on the edge of the bed, he was as white as a sheet and the aircraft had hardly started to fall when he was violently sick into the bucket; so much for his special treatment. I think that the poor man left the squadron soon afterwards. No matter how keen he was, he would be a liability to the rest of his crew like that. In some ways I felt very sorry for him but he was at least out of what we were once again going into.

That night the target was Leipzig, south of Berlin and deep into Germany. It's a good job that I didn't know then what I know now. This was the first of three disastrous raids for Bomber Command which would take place over the next five weeks. Leipzig would be followed by Berlin again and then finally by the catastrophe of Nuremberg. These three raids would cost the Command 263 aircraft, the lives of nearly 1,500 young men and bring the Battle of Berlin, which had been fought since 18th November 1943, to an end. We were destined to go on them all.

It had been three weeks since our last operation and all the familiar fears and anxieties returned as we waited through that long evening for the late take-off time. Then, just after ten o'clock, at last it was time to start getting ready. It seemed strange not having Fred and Don with us in the kit room as we dressed, but we all knew how experienced Ted and Johnny were. Then it was outside into the bus that would take us to our Lancaster waiting patiently with our trusted ground crew on the dispersal pan.

I climbed up the short ladder into the back of the aircraft and felt the comforting familiarity of VN-B surround me, settling me into my routine. After checking all my radio equipment and the extra items I was responsible for, I slipped back down the ladder and joined the others sheltering from the cold night air under the wing. As the time approached, nerves started to gnaw away at my insides, a fear that always accompanied the waiting of each operation, the doubts of a safe return, heightened this time after Queenie's crash. I knew the others felt the same, as, one by one, they too drifted off into the dark at the side of the concrete pan. Through the trees I could hear the unmistakable sound of someone from another crew vomiting violently. This wasn't a game we played but a deadly job; each time we left, our lives hung by a thread, and everyone knew it.

Around the aerodrome aircraft engines began starting up. Michael signed for our aircraft, was asked by the corporal in charge of the ground crew to bring her back in one piece, and then it was time to go. I felt better; we had a job to do now. Engines throbbing, the Lancaster eased out of her bay and onto the peri-track close to the head of the growing line of bombers making for the main runway. Even though it was nearly midnight, there was still a small crowd of girlfriends and hardy well-wishers gathered around the Controller's black-and-white-chequered wagon parked close by to wave to each aircraft, and at five minutes before midnight he flashed the green Aldis light and we were cleared to go. The steady throbbing of the idling engines changed as the power came on, building up the revs ready for that frenetic dash down the runway to reach more than 100mph if we were to get off the ground at all. Still Michael held her on the brakes, the airframe vibrating, the noise deafening. I felt the tail come up and she started to roll, slowly at first, gathering pace. Out of the window beside me I could see the flames leaping from the exhausts on the port engines, each second stretching them farther back across the wing as the air pressure built up and the sparks began to bounce off the upper turret.

Then the noise of the tyres on the runway faded and we slipped over the hedge on the Doddington Road, starting our steady climb. Before long, we were into cloud and starting to ice up but soon broke through, up into a clear bright starlit night.   Glancing through my window, I could see other aircraft joining us as the bomber stream began to form and head out across the North Sea for the Dutch coast.

The raid went badly from the moment we crossed the enemy coast. The flak was very moderate and it soon became clear why; the German controllers were not fooled by the diversionary raid to Kiel and their fighters picked us up very quickly.   To make matters worse, the Met reports were inaccurate, with much stronger tail winds than had been forecast, which had the effect of pushing us along to the target ahead of schedule. The first wave, which included us, arrived ahead of the PFF and we had to orbit Leipzig waiting for the Pathfinders to mark the target. The German ack-ack batteries took their toll. I jumped up in to the astrodome and in the first few minutes saw four aircraft go down, leaving a trail of fire in their wake. Then a massive explosion over to starboard caught all our attention. In the general mêlée of circling bombers, two had collided. Moments later, that appalling spectacle was repeated as the paths of two more converged.

It had been a long time since a target area had frightened me so much and we hadn't started to bomb yet. The city was covered with cloud, so the Pathfinders used sky markers. With so many aircraft on hand desperate to unload high explosives and incendiaries, this meant that the bombing was very concentrated, but then creep-back and scattering started as the markers became obscured by the cloud and the fires on the ground. I wasn't sorry to leave that carnage as we turned for home. After exactly seven hours' flying we touched down at Skellingthorpe once more, physically exhausted from the long flight and concentration, emotionally drawn from the losses we had seen. 50 Squadron had been incredibly lucky and lost no crews, but it was far from a jubilant report which we gave to the Intelligence Officer that morning; and there was much worse to come. Fifteen to go; half-way.

Like every base, Skellingthorpe had its fair share of 'chop girls'. These were the handful of WAAFs who, like Rita at RAF Cottesmore, were by any measure exceptionally attractive and consequently very popular with aircrew and ground crew alike, at least to start with. It did seem, however, that as soon as an airman became seriously involved with one of these girls, his crew was shot down, got the chop, hence the name chop girls, and so such relationships were vigorously discouraged by the other members of affected crews.

In April 1944, Skellingthorpe's runway improvements were completed and 61 Squadron returned to the base from their temporary home at Coningsby. It wasn't long before Bill Rudd, the flight engineer in Flt Lt Bob Acott's crew, whose aircraft was QR-T, became involved with one of these girls. One of the main tasks of the flight engineer on take-off was to help the pilot with the engine controls, in particular to push the throttle levers forward and 'through the gate' to get the extra power needed to lift the heavy, fully laden aircraft into the air whilst the pilot kept both his hands on the steering column to hold the aircraft straight and steady as it gathered speed to well over 100mph. Arthur Atkinson, the wireless operator in that crew, told me what happened to them one night.

The crew's Lancaster slowly moved around the peri-track, making its way to the head of the runway and the start of another mission. As usual, it was carrying a 2,000lb overload and so would need all of the runway to gain enough speed to lift the huge weight off the ground and up into the air. It wasn't long before they were at the front of the remaining aircraft and waiting by the Controller's chequered wagon for the green on the Aldis. Standing in the fading light of that late spring evening was the CO, accompanied by other officers, a few aircrew not on ops, some ground crew, and a group of WAAF girlfriends, amongst them Bill Rudd's girl enthusiastically returning his eager waves.

Then the Aldis flashed, Bob Acott opened up the Merlins and QR-T began to edge forward, leaving the group of well-wishers behind. Wanting another look at his pretty WAAF as she blew him a kiss, Bill leaned forward to give her a last wave from the starboard side of the cockpit canopy, unaware that as he did so he had stretched too far and his intercom lead had popped out of its socket. Gathering speed, the Lancaster thundered down the runway towards the halfway mark, the point of no return, as Acott concentrated intensely to prevent any swing that could spell disaster. They reached halfway, now it was lift off or crash. The pilot called for Bill to push the levers through the gate; Bill didn't move, he just stared ahead at the passing runway rushing underneath them. Over the deafening roar of the engines Acott shouted at him, but still there was no response as the hedge at the end of the runway came into view.

Almost out of concrete and in final desperation, the pilot risked a swerve, took his right hand off the column and punched Bill's arm indicating to him to push the levers through the gate. Finally, Bill got the message, the engines got their boost and QR-T got off the ground; but only just. They shot over the hedge with only inches to spare and it took all of Acott's skill to wrestle the cumbersome weight of the bomber over the fields south of Lincoln and up into the darkening sky. It had been a close shave for the crew, caused by a girl who had only become available to Bill because all her previous boyfriends had got the chop. The choice words of the crew and their skipper are not recorded but the following day Bill terminated his relationship with the WAAF. The crew survived and went on to complete their tour.

For me, the next operation was on 25th February, when the target was Augsburg in Bavaria. A lazy, icy breeze cut across the flat land of Lincolnshire that day. The air was bitter around the aerodrome, a dense cold that clutches at the throat and hurts the lungs to breathe. The ground was frozen, the water pipes were frozen and I was frozen. After breakfast we were detailed to fly another crew to Barford St. John, a satellite of Upper Heyford, to recover an aircraft that had been forced to land there returning from the raid on Schweinfurt the night before. This was quite a good way to spend the morning for me because the wireless operator's position was so warm and certainly a lot warmer than our freezing cold billet.

When it came time for the operation, we took off for Augsburg at 18.35, quickly ran into cloud but then broke through into the bright, clear evening light and the setting sun. It was another long eight-hour trip during which it wasn't so much the enemy who troubled us as the gremlins. By 20,000 feet it was -50°C in Johnny Blott's rear turret. His intercom froze up and I took a spare helmet down to him. When I opened the doors to the turret, the searing cold in the blast of air that came through the open front of the turret nearly tore my face off. I don't know how those tail-end Charlies survived. The new helmet didn't make any difference, it was just so cold.

Next, Jock complained of severe stomach pain. These were serious problems for the pilot to consider, because a rear gunner with intermittent communication and a possibly sick mid-upper could spell disaster for us all, but no-one liked turning back, not least because it meant landing with a full bomb and fuel load. In the end, we decided to press on.

The route down to Augsburg took us close to the Swiss border and, reminiscent of Sweden on our trip to Stettin, it was lovely to see all the lights of the little snow-covered towns and villages twinkling in the darkness like a scene from a fairy tale. It seemed such a long time ago that Britain's streets had been lit. We reached the target amid a mass of searchlights and heavy flak, but the city hadn't been attacked since a daylight raid on 17th April 1942, when Squadron Leader John Nettleton had been awarded the Victoria Cross, and they weren't prepared for us. Very quickly the defence co-ordination broke down and we were able to get in and out again without too much trouble and were soon on our way home.

Then the gremlins were back. Our bomb aimer passed out; his oxygen lead had pulled out. It was half an hour after Ted Adamson reconnected him before he felt better. It was then only a short time before the pilot and flight engineer became concerned about the oil temperature in the starboard outer engine. The gauge was showing the engine running hot but the revs were fine and it certainly sounded all right to me. Rather than risk a fire from an overheated engine, which would spell the end of us, they decided to shut it down and try to fly the rest of the way on three whilst our navigator kept us well away from heavily defended areas. The worry was not the aircraft; the Lancaster was a fantastic machine and could actually fly on just one engine if not bombed up, but we would be slower now, take longer to get home, be at greater risk of fighter attack and be unable to corkscrew effectively.

Despite all the minor problems, at just after half past two in the morning we slipped smoothly onto the runway at Skellingthorpe, relieved to be home again. In the morning the ground crew told Mike that the engine was fine, it was the gauge that was faulty. I don't know whether that made me feel better or not. Fourteen to go.

Augsburg brought our flying for February to an end and although we had only done two operations, it had been a month that I would never forget. The first day of March was our next operation, this time to Stuttgart. The days were beginning to lengthen now, which meant that take-off times would become steadily later. On that Wednesday evening our heavily laden bomber lifted off the runway at 11.20pm and at 7.30am gracefully landed again. We had quickly climbed up into 10/10 cloud which lasted all the way to Stuttgart. The risk of collision was always greater in cloud, but it also prevented the night fighters getting to us.

We didn't see any combats at all that night and, although the sky markers over the city soon disappeared into the cloud, its thickness prevented the searchlights getting through to us, so the flak was fairly ineffectual. The raid was successful and Bomber Command lost only four aircraft, although we could easily have been a fifth. Every half hour, I received a broadcast from England which I had to take down in code. These messages gave us information such as wind speeds, weather conditions at our home bases and if German intruders were amongst the returning bomber stream. Not far from the target, as I was busy writing down the message coming through, I saw smoke starting to pour out of the back of my wireless receiver. When the message finished, I switched off the set and the smoke died away but when I turned it on again for the next message the smoke started once more, although by now I had a fire extinguisher handy. This went on for the whole trip with the smoke getting worse each time I tuned in, and I fully expected the set to burst into flames at any moment. The next day the wireless mechanic told me that it was a faulty transformer in the receiver which was overheating and dripping pitch onto the hot valves causing the smoke. Thirteen to go.

There were no operations for us during the next two days but on the 4th our names were on the Battle Order again, Munich the target. Then, just as we were jumping down from the back of the truck in front of our aircraft, the message came through that the mission had been scrubbed. It was early enough in the evening to get changed and go to the pub, so off to Skellingthorpe village we went and got drunk. The following day was Sunday and Munich was the target again, but once more the operation was scrubbed at the last minute so we spent the night drinking in the Mess. On Monday the target was Kiel and yet again it was called off, but we couldn't afford to get drunk for a third night in succession, so it was a much quieter night in.

"The Beetham crew after Queenie: l-r standing Jock Higgins, Ted Adamson, Mike Beetham, Frank Swinyard, Les Bartlett, sitting: Johnny Blott
[left] Reg Payne"

Chapter Twelve

"The invasion so long dreaded and expected came suddenly. For Earth had made the Giants and hidden them away in great caves far to the north of Greece until the moment came when they were strong and fierce enough to assail heaven."

- From '*Tales of the Greek Heroes; The Battle of the Giants*'.

In the spring of 1944, there was a general feeling that the Allies were going to be launching an invasion of Europe sometime soon. The country was not just full of Americans but was full of equipment as well. From our vantage point in the skies whilst flying on daytime tests and exercises, we could see all sorts of activity below us on the land and around the coast, even though we had no idea what was happening. In the run-up to the invasion, Bomber Command would be required to attack small special targets in France, bombing from around 10,000 feet instead of our usual 20,000 feet in order to minimise French casualties around the target. The plan was for a small number of aircraft to be detailed to attack a specific target. Having arrived over the target they were to orbit it until the Master Bomber was satisfied with his marking. When he was ready, he would use the radio to call in half the force to bomb the target, then he would review the success and if necessary call in the other half; if not, it was home for everyone. Radio messages were to be repeated in Morse code to minimise errors.

The first inkling that we got that the invasion was not too far away came on 7th March when we were detailed to carry out a fairly low-level night practice on a selected target. We had with us as an observer, Air Commodore Arthur Hesketh, CO of RAF Waddington and Deputy C-in-C No.5 Group. He wanted to see for himself how the communications between the Master Bomber and the attacking aircraft would work in practice and chose to come along with us; he sat next to me for the whole exercise. It was very unnerving to have such a senior officer watching my every move but he was very pleasant and didn't interfere at all during the two hours we were airborne.

"I must say, Beetham, your crew are very well disciplined and behaved," the Air Commodore said to Michael after we had landed back at Skellingthorpe and were waiting to be collected by a WAAF driver.

"They are, sir, but I rather think that your presence on board might have had a lot to do with it too," offered Michael.

"Oh, do you think so," replied Hesketh, laughing heartily as the WAAF arrived. "Good show, anyway." And we climbed into the waiting bus.

Two nights later we put that practice into operation. At the briefing, the red tape on the map stretched out into the Atlantic and then turned into the Bay of Biscay, then south-east across France and over to Marignane, just north of Marseille. The target for tonight was a particularly satisfying one for bomber crews; it was our nemesis, the Junkers Ju88 night fighter assembly plant.

By the time we went out to our aircraft, the fog was already settling across the Lincolnshire countryside and gathering around the aerodrome, silent fingers of mist feeling their way from the fields on the breathless air, enveloping the waiting bombers and the men of the ground crews as they fussed over their precious charges. It was touch and go whether the operation would be aborted, but just before 8.45pm, with propellers churning through the grey mist, we hurtled down the runway and climbed above the murk into a clear bright moonlit sky. Since the first part of our route took us over England, I tuned into the BBC Light Programme and picked up a broadcast of dance-band music which may have been from the Queensberry All-Services Club, Rainbow Corner or Crystal Palace. Like many wireless operators, I did this whenever I could at the start of a mission and put it through the intercom for everyone to listen to. It wasn't always possible, but when it was the music got us off to a good start.

The forty-four Lancasters of No.5 Group, their Rolls Royce engines throbbing in steady unison, thundered above the foggy streets of the darkened towns beneath, then on across the sleeping fields of the English countryside, slipping out unseen over the Devon coast. The mist stayed behind with the land and far below the midnight blue sea was speckled with dancing flashes of fire as the radiant moonlight played upon its surface, hiding in the shadows of the waves before ambushing their crests with scimitar thrusts of silver light.

Leaving Brest to the east, on we struck, full of purpose, that little band of finely tuned men and machines racing down Biscay towards our goal, the flames from engine exhausts licking back across the wings like the salient messengers of Prometheus. Presently a change of course, banking to port and then ahead of us the unmistakable string of pearls that were the Atlantic rollers crashing upon the French coast throwing up glittering phosphorus stars like sparklers in the hand of a child. On we flew unmolested; the rising land of the Central Massif coming up rapidly to meet us, only to flash by a few hundred feet beneath, left behind in the urgency of our mission, the thunder of our engines rumbling through its valleys.

Then, there in front of us like sentinels of a celestial kingdom stood the snow-covered French Alps shining in the brilliant moonlight. The great bulk of their bright cream-coated shoulders thrusting up battalions of towering peaks from the darkened plains beneath, rising to challenge us and stretching towards the heavens, defying us to cross their path. Wallowing in the clear platinum light of a full moon, jagged peaks and cavernous valleys created a treacherous monochrome kaleidoscope of ice and snow and shadow; a gigantic glistening, sparkling, shimmering icing-sugar cake that had been vandalised into the magnificence of the landscape that lay before me.

The elements had been kind and on this one night had allowed me to see this wonder of the natural world, though I struggled to reconcile the purpose of our mission with the immense beauty and frightening power of those mountains. But we were not to tangle with these geological goliaths this time; they could rest easy, our fight lay on this side of the Alps and we were nearing our target; there was work to be done and the spell was broken.

It was the most peaceful operation I had ever been on. We were untroubled by fighters and only light flak greeted us at the aircraft factory. We bombed very accurately from 10,000 feet. The high explosive and incendiaries slipped out of the bomb bay, the photo flash going with them, and in the clear conditions that night the camera took a good picture of our efforts. We climbed to 12,000 feet, circled until we received the order to leave, and then gladly turned for home. Just before six o'clock in the morning, with the first pale palette of the dawn reaching out from the east to greet us, we arrived over a fog-bound Lincolnshire. Beneath us, a dense impenetrable grey cloak stretched for miles in every direction with no clue as to what lay shrouded within. Only the great square triple towers of Lincoln cathedral stood out high on the hill above the rolling sea of undulating mist like an immense three-headed primordial creature rising from the swamp to greet the day.

Tired and hungry after the long journey, it was not what we had wanted but, having taken off in fog, it was what we expected. We were diverted to nearby RAF Fiskerton where they had FIDO, 'Fog, Intensive, Dispersal, Of' or sometimes 'Fog Investigation and Dispersal Operation'. It was an ingenious if somewhat risky means of moving the fog from the runway and consisted of a long iron trough placed down each side of the landing strip filled with flaming petrol which burned so fiercely that it evaporated the condensation hanging over the runway. When in full operation it was very petrol intensive, using around 500,000 gallons to clear the air up to about 300 feet above the runway. It was also sometimes used to melt falling snow to keep the runway open for returning aircraft. Quite honestly, we didn't care how much petrol it took, getting down safely was what mattered to us and FIDO was the salvation of many crews, and that included us.

The use of FIDO for our return in the early hours of this particular night, 9th/10th March 1944, was the first time that it had been used by Bomber Command, and Fiskerton together with RAF Ludford Magna were the first bases to try it out under true operational conditions. Its success undoubtedly greatly contributed to the safe return of all the forty-four aircraft that had been on the raid and been diverted to the two stations. We had to circle above the fog for some time before it was our turn to land but eventually we were called in. Landing a heavy four-engine bomber between two walls of blazing petrol is not for the faint-hearted, especially after having been in the air for nine hours. Like all the other pilots that night, it was Michael's first FIDO landing; he brought VN-B down dead centre and we whizzed along the concrete strip, fanning the flames with our backwash as we went, gradually slowing until we turned onto the perimeter track and joined the nose-to-tail line of Lancasters parked there to await collection when the weather cleared. It had been the longest trip of our tour to date and would in fact remain so. Twelve to go.

The 9th March had been a particularly good day for Les. Just before the briefing he had been told that his commission had come through and with it his immediate promotion to Pilot Officer, leaving Jock and me as the only NCOs in the crew. Also, later the next day when the bombing photographs were developed, we had an aiming-point picture, which meant that our bombs had landed right on target in the middle of the Ju88 factory, something which gave us particular pleasure as this was where they built some of the fighters which stalked us night after night.

After this raid we were given nine days' leave and as usual I went home to my family. I travelled home on Friday afternoon but stayed in that evening; I was tired and was happy to sit and talk to mum and dad. It was strange the way things worked out that I was at home this weekend. It was well into Saturday morning when I woke up; the blackout curtains were still drawn and the room was dark but I could hear Brian playing outside and mum busying around downstairs. I lay there a little longer before I got up. Today was my twenty-first birthday. Was it really three years since I had lain here on that bright spring morning, excited at being eighteen and old enough to join the RAF like Art? And now, here I was, feeling much older than my twenty-one years, Art a prisoner of war somewhere in Germany and me almost two-thirds through my tour. It had been nothing like I had imagined it but I didn't want to dwell too much, it was my birthday and time to get up; I was hungry.

I did not expect any celebrations for my birthday but after my late breakfast I went into Kettering. I had a beer in one of the pubs, couldn't see anyone I knew so decided to go to the cinema, after which I wandered home again.

My mother met me at the door saying, "Where have you been, Reg? Quick, get down to the railway station to meet Ena, she's coming to stay with us for the weekend."

I didn't stop to ask any questions, I was just so pleased and almost ran to the station. I walked to the end of the platform and it wasn't long before the engine was clattering past me surrounded by swirls of smoke from the funnel and gushing hissing steam from the pistons, whilst the brakes on the carriages squealed like a herd of frightened pigs. Uniforms of every colour adorned the people who leaned out of the windows of compartments and doors, waving to loved ones waiting for them on the platform. As the train slowed, the doors began to open and the young men, some carrying kitbags, jumped from the still-moving train and ran to the arms of sweethearts and wives.

Finally, the train jerked to a stop amid escaping steam and noisy complaints from the couplings. As the first rush of passengers eased, I eagerly looked along the line of carriage doors at the women who were more carefully stepping out onto the platform, a Wren, two WAAFs and a housewife; disappointment began to creep upon me. Then, through the swirling white mist of steam, I saw Ena in her ATS uniform walking towards me. I ran to meet her, put my arms around her and kissed her. I was so pleased to see her; what a wonderful twenty-first present.

A few weeks earlier, whilst the weather had brought a halt to ops, Ena and I had been to some sort of fairground and had won a stuffed rabbit which she thought would make a lovely present for my little brother Brian. At the ATS offices, Ena had access to brown paper and string so she had wrapped up the rabbit and sent it to my mother. It seems that she had enclosed a note with it, including her address. Of course, my parents already knew all about Ena because I always went back to Lincoln early at the end of my leave to try to have some time with her before returning to Skellingthorpe. It seems that my mother had written to Ena thanking her for the rabbit and inviting her to spend the weekend with us next time I had some leave. That evening we went out and I introduced Ena to friends and family. I suppose it was then that it really struck me that Ena and I had become very serious about each other and that if I survived the war it was likely that our future lay together.

When I returned from leave there was great excitement amongst the crew; Mike and Frank had each been awarded the Distinguished Flying Cross and Les the Distinguished Flying Medal. We celebrated in customary style. Whilst on leave, Les had been to London to be measured for his officer's uniform and when he returned to Skellingthorpe he moved out of the billet and into the Officers' Mess, so Jock and I also moved out, having found a smaller room in one of the other huts.

Ops tonight, but surely not Berlin again? The groans went around the briefing room. After our last trip to Marignane I had hoped we would have finished with Berlin; and just to make matters worse, the Meteorological Officer told us that Skellingthorpe would be fog-bound again by 02.00. This would be our tenth mission to Berlin and once more I wondered how many times we could expect to visit the city and hope to survive.

We took off just before 7pm and headed out over the North Sea. The route would take us across to Denmark then along the Baltic coast, making land around Rostock and then down to Berlin, returning by a more southerly route avoiding the defences around Hanover, Osnabrück and the Ruhr, making the Dutch coast to return home. With several diversionary raids going on as well, it all sounded so simple, but then it always did. There were varying amounts of cloud but as we got nearer to the continent, the wind became stronger. Frank was a wind-finder, that is, he was one of several nominated navigators who would calculate wind speeds every half hour throughout the mission and pass the information back to Bomber Command through their wireless operators. Each time Frank passed the information to me for transmission, he grew increasingly concerned about its strength coming in from the north. It was already clear that the bomber stream was becoming scattered by the wind.

At Rostock we turned south for Berlin and at 21,000 feet, chased by a strengthening 80 knots wind, we were soon over the target. The wind was even stronger here, blowing at around 100 knots; the sky markers drifted off to the south-west and it was that part of the city and the outlying towns and villages that took the full force of the raid, which lasted for about twenty minutes as some 800 heavy bombers passed through. Looking out of the astrodome and my side window, I saw three aircraft going down near the target, victims to fighters, no doubt, but it was on the return leg that we took such a terrible battering. The wind continued to gain strength and scattered the fleeing bombers like autumn leaves, with many aircraft being blown into the path of the Ruhr defences. Far away to port, I could see the explosions and blazing trails of those lost bombers.

Crossing the North Sea, I received a signal telling us to divert to RAF Foulsham in Norfolk since Lincoln was, as expected, once more covered with dense fog. As we approached the aerodrome, a large single searchlight shone up into the sky, helping us in, and at 02.20 we touched down at Foulsham. Having parked VN-B, we were transported to the debriefing where I was given a large mug of steaming hot tea heavily laced with rum, which was just what I needed. Eleven to go.

This raid, which became known as the night of the strong winds, was to be the last major raid on Berlin, but it cost Bomber Command dearly again; we had lost seventy-two crews, fifty of which were shot down by flak on the return journey. First Leipzig, where we lost seventy-eight aircraft, and now Berlin. But there was worse to come yet, much worse.

Two nights later, the red tape on the wall map stretched to Essen in the heart of the Ruhr. This was the German powerhouse, the centre of its industrial output. The daring raid by 617 Squadron on the Ruhr dams in May 1943 had been intended to cripple the factories and mines here by cutting off their water supply. This was the most heavily defended area of Germany, and whilst we knew it as Happy Valley, it could equally have been called the Valley of Death. Had he lived a hundred years later, Alfred Lord Tennyson, that son of Lincolnshire who had been born at Somersby near Spilsby, could have called his epic poem, 'The Charge of the Heavy Bombers'. Flying into the teeth of the German guns defending the Ruhr at this stage of the war had many similarities with that suicidal cavalry charge into the mouth of the Russian guns at Balaclava on 25th October 1854; 'into the Valley of Death flew the six hundred'.

As the hours of darkness began to shorten, so the targets drew closer to home and Essen could be reached quite easily under the cover of night. Take-off was 19.50 and we had an uneventful trip across the Wash then over to the Dutch coast, where some dangerous light flak came up at us; but Essen so nearly got us. Flying above the layers of shifting cloud, we came over a great gaping hole and were instantly caught by the thin blue pencil beam of a radar-controlled searchlight. The battery of lights quickly locked on to us and filled the fuselage with a dazzling white glare. Michael swung the aircraft from side to side but still we were held in the deadly glare. The flak became more intense and nearer as the radar-controlled guns began to get our range. Then we were falling through the air in a series of tight dives and corkscrews, twisting and turning in a desperate attempt to lose our tormentors.

Holding on tightly to my seat, I watched helplessly as first my flask, then my logbook and then my parachute went hurtling past me and over the main spar on their way to the rear of the aircraft. If we were hit now, I was in trouble. Using all his strength and experience, Michael continued to coax our fully laden aircraft through the immense stresses he was putting it under to escape from the searchlights. Everything that wasn't bolted down was now flying around inside the fuselage, crashing into everything else. Another diving turn and Frank's chart and navigational instruments went clattering down the fuselage after my parachute, followed by the packs of 'window' which had been on the floor.

Up we came again, twisted over, then as we dived once more, I was horrified to see the 120 volt HT battery rip loose from its housing underneath the navigator's table and head straight for me. I ducked just in time as the heavy battery plunged over my shoulder, bounced on the main spar and careered on down the aircraft until it lodged at the tail. With the loss of the battery, we had lost the intercom and it was a few seconds, struggling against the pitching of the aircraft, before I could get enough purchase to flick over the switches on my main set to the emergency circuit. All this time the flak had been getting so close that shrapnel had been rattling against the fuselage and the inside had filled with the smell of cordite. Then suddenly, we had lost the searchlights, the overspill faded, and blessed darkness closed around us once more. We levelled off and the engines picked up their steady rhythm; they had so nearly got us. We had used up another life.

Now that we were flying straight and level again, I connected myself to a portable oxygen canister and set about clearing up the mess. I recovered the battery, which fortunately wasn't damaged, plugged it back in and restored main communications. Then I retrieved my parachute and the bundles of 'window', and helped Frank find his charts and instruments. By comparison, the rest of the trip was quiet and just before one o'clock in the morning we landed back at Skellingthorpe. Ten to go.

There were no major ops for Bomber Command on the next three nights, which gave me time with Ena. It was the end of March and spring was here. The sun had gained warmth again; the cheerful colours of the early flowers brightened the hedgerows after the long winter and the smell of spring hung in the air. Cycling through the lanes to meet Ena, I felt good to be alive. In the afternoon of days when we weren't on ops, I would cycle to Mrs Fatchett's house in Lincoln where Ena's mother was staying. Mrs Fatchett always made me very welcome and during the cold winter days would make me a cup of tea and tell me to sit by the fire whilst I waited for Ena to come off duty at around 5pm. If I had been flying the night before she would let me lie down to catch up on some sleep. After Ena finished work, we would go for tea in Lincoln, sometimes to the NAAFI or to the Boots restaurant, and then often it was on to the Unity pub where we had first met to enjoy a quiet drink before I walked her back to her billet for the ten o'clock curfew.

30th March 1944. Nuremberg. With Bomber Command's heaviest losses of the war, the raid would even overshadow the recent disasters of Leipzig and Berlin and bring to an end the Battle of Berlin. It was arguably Air Chief Marshal Harris's worst decision, not only of target but also of timing, to send his crews so far into Germany on a clear bright full-moon-lit night. Ironically, it would be this last raid which would produce the only Victoria Cross of the battle.

The city of Nuremberg was in many ways the spiritual home of the Nazis, having hosted a rally there each year from 1933 to 1938. These were immense displays of growing military power, and by 1936 Hitler had more or less completed the transformation of Germany from a democratic civilian society to a military dictatorship. The city was a legitimate target, and even though there was no particularly vital industry, it was an important link in the rail and waterway connections in the area. Although the name was familiar, it meant nothing to us at the briefing that night other than being just one more German city, but that would all change long before we got back and the name would become anathema to Bomber Command.

Notwithstanding the full moon, when traditionally crews were stood down and rested, the raid had been planned on the basis of a Meteorological report that there would be cloud cover for most of the way there, with a clear target on arrival. However, a Meteorological Squadron Mosquito made a reconnaissance flight late in the day and reported just the opposite: clear all the way to Nuremberg with a two-mile thick cloud bank over the city! The operation planners ignored the report.

The morning had dawned bright and warm. After breakfast, together with Jock, I looked at the Battle Order on the noticeboard; we were down for ops again. At the briefing in the late afternoon, the route was shown as out over the North Sea once more, crossing the Belgian coast then heading in a long straight 200 mile leg to a point sixty miles north of Nuremberg before turning and flying for eighteen minutes to the city.

"Good luck, sir. Bring her back safely, won't you," the corporal in charge of the ground crew had said to Michael as we mounted the ladder, each of us uneasy in the light of the full moon. Then, a little before 22.00, our trusted Lancaster taxied out of the dispersal pan onto the perimeter track at the head of the procession; we were to be first into the air. Leaving the runway lights behind, we climbed up into the clear bright moon-lit sky, circling into the bomber stream. We crossed the Belgian coast at 20,000 feet and very soon ran into trouble. The German Controller ignored the diversionary mine-laying raids and grouped his fighters around two radio beacons which just happened to straddle our course to Nuremberg and readily picked up the signals as each wave of bombers switched on their H2S radar sets. They had correctly guessed our route and the fighter pilots, some in their enthusiasm with their navigation lights still switched on, quickly encircled and preyed upon the bombers like sharks around survivors of a sinking ship.

The moon was so bright it was like flying in daylight. A silver glow hung over everything, lighting up the bomber stream. I could easily see dozens of other Lancasters across the sky, the fuselages of those nearest so clear that I could read their squadron codes. Moonlight conditions like this were lethal to bomber crews because, when looking up from below as the fighter pilots were doing, the brightness opened up the sky like an illuminated canvas upon which each aircraft in the stream was portrayed in great detail. Looking down to the darkened earth beneath, as our gunners were with the moon above, there was only an inky blackness in which it was almost impossible to see anything. We were totally exposed to the enemy whilst we could see nothing of what was coming up at us from the dark; it was an airman's worst nightmare which became reality for so many crews.

The Luftwaffe's familiar red fighter Very flares littered the skies and then the battles started, not just with an odd aircraft going down but in twos and threes. It very quickly got so bad that Frank, who normally charted the position of downed aircraft on his maps, told Jock and Johnny Blott in the rear turret to stop telling him because he couldn't keep up with their reports. The fully laden bombers were easy targets, and once struck, quickly turned to flaming infernos as, almost in slow motion at first, they peeled away, before with gathering speed, twisting and tumbling to the earth, there to erupt in a mass of blazing high explosive and incendiary.

I had never seen anything like it and soon believed that we would all meet the same fate; I couldn't see how the fighters could miss any of us. I had been nervous on previous missions, even frightened, but this night I knew the meaning of real terror. My stomach was so tight I wanted to vomit. Cold sweat trickled down my face and back, my breathing came fast and shallow and I had my parachute on the seat beside me. But with great fear came a heightened awareness and I sat at my table straining my eyes into the MONICA screen for any sign of a fighter trying to creep up on us. I thought of Ena and whether I would live to have the life that we had started to plan after the war. I remembered my brother Art and what he must have felt in the moments before his aircraft exploded, blasting him out through the roof into the night sky at 20,000 feet. We were one of the most experienced crews on the squadron, but tonight that would only count for very little; if we were to survive at all it would be by the Grace of God and a great deal of good luck.

I couldn't stand the suspense any more and climbed into the astrodome to watch what was happening. Stretching out behind us as far as I could see, the burning wrecks of dozens of bombers littered the ground of Belgian and German soil. Even at 20,000 feet, the combined effect of all these fires was to further light up the sky, adding to our woes. Suddenly, over to starboard, a massive explosion of greens and oranges and reds and yellows as one of our aircraft simply blew up in mid-air, the coloured images hanging in the sky slowly drifting away. I would witness another three like that before we got to Nuremberg.

Then, to make matters worse, I noticed that, like everyone else, we were leaving four great condensation trails behind us as we sped across the sky on that deadly 200-mile leg. Michael eased us up a thousand feet or so but to no effect, then he tried dropping us down two thousand feet, but it made no difference at all, we were still streaming that perfidious banner of invitation to the prowling enemy. On our port side, I watched another Lancaster that was flying close by and level with us. There was no immediate danger of a collision but our courses were converging so the skipper slowly eased back a little on the throttle and let us drop a hundred feet to allow the other aircraft to cross safely.

"Look out!" My shout was as useless as it was instinctive and a stream of 20mm cannon fire and tracer zipped past my head and plunged into the body of that Lancaster now just 200 yards away to starboard. The stricken bomber seemed to stumble in the air and then dipped away with flames gushing out of its wings and fuselage as it started its final spiralling descent to earth. I remembered Queenie and knew the terrible fear which would be gripping those poor young men inside for their last few moments of life. I ducked down and looked hard at the MONICA screen; there was nothing there to show a fighter in range. The German pilot had crept up unseen and had chosen the upper aircraft as his target. Had we not throttled back and dropped down we would almost certainly have been his target; such was the gossamer thread upon which life and death hung.

The wind over Germany was much stronger than predicted and started to scatter the bomber stream, which now made us even easier targets. However, we had been to Berlin so many times that we knew where the Ruhr defences were and, although the wind tried to blow us towards them, Michael was able to keep us to the south. But there were plenty of aircraft which drifted into the range of the flak batteries and paid the price. The wind was largely behind us and this did at least help to push us all along that corridor of hell. Even so, it took an hour to fly those 200 miles and we lost sixty aircraft, one every minute, one every three miles, and their burning remains were stretched out along the line of the route, grievous and woeful beacons of our plight.

By the time we turned for the run down to Nuremberg, Bomber Command HQ knew that we were in trouble. The radio station at Kingsdown, which was listening to and monitoring the German wireless traffic, had picked up all the claims of victories from the fighter pilots and the excited chatter amongst the controllers. Even allowing for an element of over-exuberance, experience told our operators that the raid was becoming a debacle and we were being put to the sword.

Over Nuremberg, most of the sky markers just disappeared into the thick bank of cloud which, as predicted, cloaked the city. Others were dropped in the wrong place, but some were accurately placed, and as soon as Frank was sure we were over the target, the bomb doors opened and Les bombed Nuremberg. There was no point in waiting for an aiming-point photograph, so with the doors closed again, we sped away from the city. A few minutes later, we reached the first turning point of the homeward leg and Michael's voice came over the intercom, "Frank, there is still plenty of fighter activity going on ahead of us. I'm going to turn ten degrees to the south to try to avoid it. Keep your eyes open everybody." "Okay skipper, got that," replied Frank in a monotone voice which he afterwards confided to me belied the physical sickness and deep psychological fear he felt at the thought of having to run the gauntlet of annihilation all over again. He was not alone. I think every airman who made it through to Nuremberg that night, must have experienced the same terror. I know I did.

Many crews strayed too far north, missed the turning point altogether and bombed Schweinfurt, whilst others bombed Lauf to the east. There was no Master Bomber to guide the main force in and too many PFF aircraft had been shot down on the way. The bombing was scattered across the city and the creep-back extended for ten miles as crews were just glad to get somewhere near the target area, unload their bombs and get away. Within seven minutes of the main force turning south to return home, the Luftwaffe pilots had been given the new course and more crews became their victims on the homeward leg. Even higher losses were only prevented because the German pilots were forced to return to base before running out of fuel. Eventually, the moon dipped below the horizon and blessed darkness began to close around us as the last of the bomber stream left Nuremberg behind.

Another hour passed by whilst each of us, intent upon our tasks, counted off the minutes and the miles towards home and safety. My eyes hurt from the glare of the MONICA screen, searching it for the irregularity that would betray an enemy, but nothing came. I could identify the bombers that were returning with us by their steady pattern and consistent course, it was the out-of-place blip that I was looking for. In the two turrets, the gunners, their night vision restored with the return of darkness, searched equally intently for the dark shape coming from behind and below, the flash of an exhaust flame where there shouldn't be one, but still nothing. On we flew, the engines throbbing, seeking their home as we did ours. Far in the distance, the poignant dots of light that were the still-burning remains of lost bombers from the outward journey led all the way back to Nuremberg.

"Coast ahead, skipper," came the welcome message from the bomb aimer and we passed over the French coast at Calais, eighty miles north of the planned route, but opening up the shortest stretch of Channel, and then we would be over England.

At a quarter to five in the morning, with a relief which is impossible to re-live, I felt the wheels of VN-B touch down at RAF Skellingthorpe. She raced along the concrete, the brakes slowed her, the rear wheel dropped down, and we taxied round to the dispersal pan, where the sudden silence when the engines stopped enveloped me. For a few moments in that silence, I closed my eyes and thanked God for our salvation: and I meant every word of that prayer. We were amongst the first crews back and our ground staff met us without celebration but with unconcealed relief.

The transport to the debriefing was waiting. The WAAF driver had kept the engine running but the grim expression on her face told its own story; news of the mission had already filtered down. I gathered up all my bits of kit and joined the others in the truck. I felt numb from the relief, the horror, the strain, the weariness, of what I had witnessed and experienced. It was a sombre gathering of surviving aircrew that crowded into the debriefing room that early morning.

The general hubbub in the room was the usual mix of chatter amongst crews awaiting a seat at a table to answer the questions from one of the Intelligence Officers, but tonight there was no laughter; disbelief and shock at what we had been through permeated the atmosphere. I felt someone touch my arm and turned to see one of the volunteer WAAFs offering me a mug of steaming hot tea. I thanked her and sipped it gratefully as she did her best to manage a thin smile. I vaguely recognised her as the girlfriend of a sergeant in one of the other crews. I can only imagine what she must have been feeling that night, what emotions were churning through her as she waited silently, patiently, agonising for the return of his aircraft whilst handing out mugs of tea to the lucky ones who were back.

The Flight Officer called us across to her table and we gratefully flopped onto the chairs just vacated by the previous crew. She went through all the usual questions about the raid, the route, the Met forecast, the winds, the target, the flak, the marking, and then she asked how many of our own aircraft we thought had been shot down. We all looked at Jock, knowing that he had seen more than any of us.

He paused for a few moments and then, almost in a whisper offered, "Aboot a hundred I should think."

"Oh, come off it, sergeant, it wasn't that bad," the WAAF officer scoffed.

His piecing bloodshot eyes looked straight at her, his face set hard. The strong Glasgow accent rasped his reply, leaving her in no doubt. "You've nae idea what it was like, ma'am. I know what I saw. We've lost a hundred crews the night."

And he was right; ninety-five aircraft failed to return from Nuremberg and a further fourteen crashed whilst trying to land back in England. Exhausted though I was, it was a long time before I fell into a short and troubled sleep. 50 Squadron lost three aircraft at Nuremberg, and on the other side of the aerodrome, 61 Squadron lost another two; it was a bad night for RAF Skellingthorpe but many other squadrons had fared much worse. Whoever planned that operation should have been there to see it. The raid was a complete disaster. It had achieved nothing and cost the lives of 535 airmen, with another 180 captured as prisoners of war or lying injured in hospitals across England. On that one night, Bomber Command lost more men than did Fighter Command throughout the entire Battle of Britain. It was our worst night of the war and brought the Battle of Berlin to an end. Nine to go.

Whilst the raid was a catastrophe of the highest order, the courage of twenty-two-year-old Pilot Officer Cyril Barton, the captain of Halifax LK 797 with 578 Squadron, was also of the highest order but of a different kind. Still some seventy miles from Nuremberg, his aircraft, carrying a full load of incendiaries was attacked by a Ju88 fighter which destroyed the intercom system. A few minutes later, an Me216 joined in, rendering the Halifax's machine guns useless and damaging one of the four engines. The now defenceless aircraft was attacked several more times by the fighters but incredibly without further major damage, so Barton elected to press on to the target. However, in a communication mix-up, his navigator, wireless operator and bomb aimer bailed out, leaving the four remaining crew without their navigation team. At last, against all the odds, they arrived over Nuremberg, where P/O Barton released the incendiaries himself. But just as he turned his heavily damaged Halifax for home, the propeller blades of the stricken engine broke up and flew off.

Flying on three, he began the long struggle to bring his battered aircraft and remaining crew back to England through those lethal skies that night. With only three engines running he should have had plenty of fuel, but his FE soon realised that, even allowing for the strengthening head wind, his petrol was going down too fast; the fighter attacks had punctured two of his tanks and precious fuel was seeping away. Using the experience of eighteen previous ops, he managed to avoid the heavily defended areas and, despite the desperate condition of his aircraft, he brought it over the enemy coast and headed towards Yorkshire. Without his navigator, though, he didn't realise the wind had pushed him out over the North Sea and by the time that he sighted the coast near Sunderland he was ninety miles north of his base at RAF Burn and almost out of fuel.

By now the starboard outer engine had given up and the Halifax was rapidly losing height. Knowing that he was too low for his crew to bail out, he ordered them to take up their crash positions as he desperately searched the built-up area below him for somewhere to land. Then, when flying over some houses, the second port engine spluttered and stopped, all its fuel spent. The aircraft was shaking violently as it approached stalling speed and, with only seconds left in the air on the one remaining starboard engine, Cyril Barton fought with immense courage and skill to save his crew, finally crashing in the railway cutting at Ryhope Colliery. In those last moments, the pilot saw some miners' cottages but there was little he could do to avoid them as his aircraft was now without power. It hit the end cottage then ploughed along the back gardens, demolishing the footbridge over the railway, killing coal miner Mr Head, who was crossing the bridge. The Halifax careered on with a deafening rending of tearing propellers, wings, fuselage and railway track, skidding and slewing along the ground until eventually coming to a shuddering stop in a cloud of debris.

In the quiet that followed the chaos of the landing, with the dust and soil settling upon what was left of their Halifax bomber, the two gunners and the flight engineer scrambled from the twisted wreckage with only minor injuries; but their captain lay dead at the controls. It was a cruel stroke of fate which had robbed the brave young pilot of his life in the last moments after he had endured so much during the previous eight hours and brought his remaining crew home.

The Victoria Cross, which was awarded posthumously to Pilot Officer Cyril Joseph Barton on this very last mission of the Battle of Berlin, which had raged since the night of 18th/19th November 1943, was both the sole VC of the battle and also the only one during the war to a Halifax airman.

The morning after the raid, I managed to telephone Ena to let her know that I was safe. I thought that she was going cry. There was a long silence at the other end of the telephone, then finally she said, "Oh Reg, I was so sure that you had been killed. They said on the news that over a hundred of our aircraft hadn't come back last night. Thank God you're safe." Well, I am until the next one anyway, I thought, but I didn't say that to Ena.

There were no major raids for the next few nights as Bomber Command reflected upon Nuremberg and the cost in lives and machines. The break from ops gave Ena and me time together, time in which we could also reflect upon our good fortune to still be able to have that time. Although many crews socialised together where one or perhaps two were officers, it was more difficult for Jock and me because the other five were all officers. There were occasions when we went out as a whole crew but not often, and since I was walking out with Ena, and Jock with Joyce, the blonde WAAF corporal from our Mess, it rather suited us.

Our next operation came on 5th April when we attacked the aircraft factory at Toulouse. Just as the briefing ended, Les Bartlett heard that his wife had given birth to their daughter Diane, but with the briefing over, Les had to go on the trip before getting any leave to go and see Margaret and their new baby. This was the mission on which Wing Commander Leonard Cheshire, who when made Group Captain at twenty-five was the RAF's youngest Group Captain and who would end the war as its most highly decorated officer, first used the fast twin-engine de Havilland Mosquito for target marking. The tactic worked so well that Harris allowed 5 Group to mark its own targets rather than rely on the Pathfinders of 8 Group and he ordered 83 and 97 Squadrons of the PFF to return to 5 Group.

It was also the mission when flak took out all our engines over the target. We had just released our bombs and I was receiving a radio message intended for the following waves not to bomb below four thousand feet, when there was an almighty bang as a flak shell exploded just below our central fuselage. The aircraft shuddered, stuttered and one after the other, the engines died in turn. I was sure that this time we had bought it. My stomach turned over and I reached for my parachute. The Lancaster quickly lost speed, dipped and started to head nose down towards the earth. Pilot and flight engineer frantically flicked switches and then, one by one, each engine fired up and roared into life again. Normal service had been resumed and we were on our way.

"Ok everyone, we're back in business. Is everybody all right?" Michael calmly asked over the intercom and with much relief each one of us replied that we were. Eight to go.

Six days later it was another new target when the ribbon on the map stretched to Aachen, which gave us some satisfaction, since the city had been a thorn in our side for a long time, with its heavy defences and as a night fighter gathering point. We were allocated Lancaster LM435 VN-E for a change as our trusted LL744 was still having the engines checked. It was only a short trip of four hours and passed without incident, except that on the way back, even though I had let out the trailing aerial and switched on the IFF, we were fired at by some of our own coastal defences. Over-enthusiastic ack-ack batteries always posed a danger for returning aircraft, especially those off-course or damaged looking for an early landing ground, and too many crews needlessly met their end that way. I fired off a couple of Very cartridges with the colours of the day and we were left alone. Seven to go.

The April days were growing longer as the spring turned towards early summer, and with the ending of the Battle of Berlin and the shorter nights, the large massed raids over Germany were becoming fewer. The Allies were also preparing for the invasion of Fortress Europe, and Bomber Command had an important role to play in that preparation. Many of our targets were now in France and this required a different approach. The targets were usually very specific and relatively small, such as a factory complex or railway marshalling yards. Avoiding civilian casualties was essential and at briefings we were instructed that if we could not clearly see the target then we were not to release our bombs but to return with them.

The rail network was very important for the Nazis to move their troops and heavy armour quickly over long distances and so was a prime target for us at this time. The Reich knew that the invasion was coming and expected it to be in the Pas de Calais area. However, the 'Desert Fox', Field Marshal Erwin Rommel calculated, correctly as it transpired, that the invasion would come in Normandy and Hitler appointed him to oversee the defences all along the Channel coast just in case. Fortunately, he didn't have the resources to strengthen them as he would have wished. He did, though, want the railways clear so that he could move tanks, men and armour quickly, and part of our job was to destroy the major marshalling yards to prevent such movements.

In between other ops we had been training for this and just before 21.00 on 18th April, back in LL744, we took off for the railway yards outside Paris at Juvisy. We circled very low, about thirty miles from the target and then, when it was clearly marked, we came in and bombed it very accurately, almost completely destroying the yards. Two days later, we repeated the mission by going with 617 Squadron to the railway yards at La Chapelle to the north of Paris and destroying them with more very accurate bombing. Five to go.

One morning the whole crew were told to report to Wing Commander Heward's office. We were nearing the end of our tour now and all getting a little nervy about reaching the thirty ops mark safely. However, the CO wanted to know if we would be prepared to carry on and go straight into a second tour. Michael was one of his flight commanders and we were one of his most experienced crews. He knew that he would be losing us all soon if he couldn't persuade us to carry on, but we needed a rest. We were tired and we had definitely ridden our luck. I was also thinking about my parents, who knew that they would not see Art again until the end of the war and probably only then if we won. I declined the CO's kind offer.

Saturday 22nd April dawned bright and sunny. We were down on the Battle Order for ops that night. At around 11.40am we took off in LL744 for a night flying test, with instructions from the CO to head out over the Wash and empty the machine guns into the sea as they had not been used for some time; he didn't want them jamming when needed in combat. The idea was to drop a smoke float to fire at but when we got there I could see a complete Halifax sitting on a sandbank, clear of the water. We circled the stranded Halifax a few times whilst the two gunners, Les and I all took turns letting off some three thousand rounds of .303s at it. Satisfied with the results, and by now well out to sea, it was time to return home. It was such a lovely day so I went and stood in the astrodome to enjoy the view. We were seven young men living very dangerous lives which could end at any moment. We had the most powerful, reliable and exquisite flying machine in the world at our disposal and after all we had been through recently it was time to have some fun with it.

Les suggested that we should do some wave hopping, so, somewhat uncharacteristically, Michael took us joyriding. He dropped the Lancaster right down to the sea and opened the throttles. The mighty engines roared as we thundered straight and level barely ten feet above the surface, carving a wake through the gentle swell which would have been the envy of any MTB skipper. The sun glinted on the water as it flashed beneath us at over 200mph whilst the spray flew up behind in a cascading curtain of white foam.

Crossing the coast, we barely rose thirty feet as VN-B continued its headlong charge over the fields, farms and homes of the Lincolnshire countryside. Directly ahead, I could see the neat farmstead with the sturdy round haystack in the yard, carefully built to withstand the winter gales that blow in from the North Sea looming up. Nearer it came, as we rushed towards it, so close now that I could see the chickens pecking around on the top. With a volcanic roar, the aircraft skimmed over the stack and in an instant was past, cavorting on far down the lane leaving behind a comedy of startled chickens catapulted into the air and swirled round by our backwash only to flutter safely down to the earth amid an explosion of hay and dust. Fields, hedges, trees, houses, all passed beneath us in a blur of exhilaration as our joyride swallowed up the miles back towards Skellingthorpe. But then it was over before anyone got our number. I heard the change of note in the engines and felt the Lancaster gaining height. It was time to return to reality and focus on tonight's operation, wherever it might be.

When I see boy-racers today trying to get a thrill out of driving their mother's car too fast, and badly at that, I do have to smile; they really have no idea about thrills and adrenalin rushes. Flying in a Lancaster bomber ten feet above the sea at 200mph, that's a thrill; flying in one at 20,000 feet through a flak barrage, that's an adrenalin rush.

The operation that night was to Brunswick in northern Germany, not far from Hanover. For 50 Squadron, it was the minor target of the night, the main force having gone to Düsseldorf. However, the raid is important in the history of Bomber Command because it was the first time that 5 Group carried out low-level marking on a major German city. As we neared the target, I slipped up into the astrodome to keep watch for other aircraft. I hadn't been there many minutes when, well into our bombing run, I looked up to see another Lancaster just above and slightly behind us with its great thirty-three-foot long bomb-bay doors gaping wide open.

I alerted the crew to the danger. The pilot said 'OK', the bomb aimer swore and the rear gunner said it was closing the gap. The skipper gave permission for a warning burst to be fired across the Lancaster's front if he got any closer and I don't think that any of us ever watched another aircraft with such intensity before or since. We were stuck on our run-in so if his bombs didn't get us, we would lift up into him when the weight came off as our own slipped out of the bay. Eventually I think the other bomb aimer must have seen us because the aircraft held back. We unloaded our cookie and incendiaries and got clear pretty sharpish, landing back at

Skellingthorpe at 05.20, six hours after we had taken off. It had been a good raid for the squadron as all the aircraft returned safely. There was still a long way to go in the war, with many crews yet to be lost, but history would show that the tide had turned; the Luftwaffe night fighter squadrons had passed the zenith of their success. And we still had four more ops to go.

The first of them came on 26th April when the target was Schweinfurt, far away near the Czech border. Although we were airborne for nearly nine hours, it was a fairly uneventful trip. However, the same could not be said for Sgt Norman Jackson, the flight engineer of a 106 Squadron Lancaster from RAF Metheringham.

An engineer by trade, when the war came, despite being in a reserved occupation, Norman Jackson volunteered for RAF aircrew and trained as a flight engineer. In July 1943 he and his crew, led by Flying Officer 'Miff' Miffin, were posted to 106 Squadron, then stationed at RAF Syerston. They were a successful crew and in October moved with the squadron to the new station at Metheringham to the south of Lincoln.

By 24th April 1944, they had completed twenty-nine operations and were almost at the end of their tour. The squadron was on ops that night, the target Munich, although the Miffin crew were not on the Battle Order. However, the flight engineer of another crew was not available so Norman Jackson filled in. The aircraft returned safely in the early hours and with it Jackson had done his thirty ops, his tour complete. The next day, 26th April, he was overjoyed to receive a telegram from his wife Alma to say that she had given birth that morning to their first son, Ian.

That night, the squadron were called upon to attack the ball-bearing factory at Schweinfurt and the Miffin crew were on the operation. This was to be the last op in the tour for the rest of the crew and so Norman Jackson volunteered to do an extra trip to stay with his crew to the end of their tour.

They reached Schweinfurt safely and bombed the target, after which F/O Miffin climbed to 22,000 feet and sped away from the area. However, within a few minutes they were attacked by a Focke-Wulf 190 fighter, which raked the Lancaster, wounding Jackson in the leg and shoulder with white-hot shell splinters as he was thrown to the floor, and starting a fire in the fuel line between the starboard inner and the fuselage. Jackson activated the wing fire extinguisher, but as soon as it was empty, the flames flared up again, fanned by the force of the wind, licking back over the wing. He immediately realised the great danger to the aircraft and crew if the fire reached the fuel tanks in the wing and asked Miff for permission to climb out with a fire extinguisher to douse the flames.

I can only wonder at the incredible courage of a man who, already wounded, would volunteer to climb out onto the burning wing of a Lancaster bomber flying at 200mph at 22,000 feet over Germany with a fire extinguisher in his hand, knowing too that an enemy fighter was still out there somewhere, but that is exactly what he did.

The pilot, struggling to control the damaged aircraft had little time to consider Jackson's idea and gave permission. The flight engineer stuffed the extinguisher into his Mae West, put on his parachute and then pulled the 'D' ring. As his 'chute opened, he handed the canopy and rigging lines to the navigator and bomb aimer to act as a safety rope. He opened the cockpit escape hatch and climbed out into that 200mph hurricane. By now the fire had spread to the starboard inner engine, but as he almost reached the wing, he slipped, managing, though, to catch hold of the air intake on the burning engine. Fighting against the immense strength of the slipstream, he pulled the extinguisher from his Mae West and turned it into the blazing engine. Just as the flames began to die down he felt a searing pain in his legs; the Focke-Wulf had returned, the burst of cannon fire hitting his legs. Then the Merlin engine exploded, burning Jackson's hands and face, setting fire to his parachute and the rigging lines and blowing him off the wing.

He was caught in the slipstream, held by his burning parachute lines, twisting and turning in the air like a leaf in a storm flicking around on its stalk trying to break away from the tree that holds it. There was no chance that he could be saved and the two airmen inside had to let the parachute go before it and their friend burned where he was. They released the cords and watched helplessly as he was snatched away by the night, disappearing into the darkness, only the glow of his burning parachute marking his descent to earth.

Norman Jackson tumbled away towards German soil four miles below. His parachute, however, although ripped and continuing to burn, did fill enough to give him some support whilst he tried desperately to put out the flames in the burning cords with his bare hands. He hit the ground hard and felt the unmistakable stab of intense pain as his ankle broke on impact. He lay still for a few moments as his smouldering parachute fluttered to the earth behind him. He was badly burned, his hands were useless, he was wounded in the legs and shoulder, he was alone and disorientated, but from the intense pain he felt, he knew that he was at least alive.

High above him, the intensity of the fire on the Lancaster's wing grew by the second and the crew knew that despite their flight engineer's great courage, the aircraft was doomed. Inside, as he began to lose control, Flying Officer Miffin, DFC, gave his last order telling the crew to bail out; neither he nor the rear gunner F/Sgt Johnson would survive.

As daybreak dawned, Jackson realised that escape was impossible; what he needed was help, but there was no sign of anyone. Desperate and in great pain, he began the agonising crawl to a nearby village, dragging his broken ankle over the rough terrain, the mud and the soaking wet undergrowth. At the first house and almost at the end of his endurance, he summoned the strength to knock upon the door. An old man answered, but he couldn't see anyone there. As he turned to go, he heard a gasp and looking down saw the dishevelled heap of Jackson lying at his feet. He quickly realised that he was looking at an RAF airman and, despite Jackson's appalling injuries, set about cursing him as a 'Terror Flieger'. Fortunately for the sergeant, the man was pushed aside by two young women from the house who were nurses at the local hospital. They took him inside and bathed his wounds, but even as they were helping him, the old man had alerted the Gestapo, who arrived soon afterwards and arrested the Englishman. Sgt Jackson's injuries were so great that he spent the next ten months in hospital before being transferred to a prison camp.

The remaining survivors of the Lancaster's crew were one by one picked up and taken prisoner, too, but after the war when they came home from the Stalag Luft they told the full story of Norman Jackson's actions that night. On 13th November 1945, Warrant Officer Norman Cyril Jackson, accompanied by his wife, Alma, and eighteen-month-old son, Ian, received the Victoria Cross from King George VI at Buckingham Palace for one of the most remarkable feats of courage by any airman during the war; the only flight engineer to be awarded the VC.

"5th October 1945. Reg and Ena on their wedding day"

Chapter Thirteen

"There's a one-eyed yellow idol to the north of Kathmandu,
There's a little marble cross below the town;
There's a broken-hearted woman tends the grave of Mad Carew,
And the Yellow God forever gazes down."
- From '*The Green Eye of the Yellow God*';
J. Milton Hayes

We were very nearly at the end of our tour and two days after the Schweinfurt raid were listed on the Battle Order again. It was with a mixture of nerves and excitement that I sat in the briefing room waiting for the CO to unveil the target, to see what fate awaited us; it was the explosives factory at St. Medard-en-Jalles, near Bordeaux. It was a long but uneventful trip of eight hours but, just as we were about to start our bombing run after having circled the target for quite a while, I received a radio message not to bomb but to return to base. Smoke covered the target making visibility too poor to ensure a pinpoint attack so we turned around and flew back to Skellingthorpe.

The prospect of landing a Lancaster bomber with ten tons of high explosives and incendiaries underneath us in the bomb bay occupied all our thoughts on the way home. The total weight was about forty tons and would put a colossal strain upon the aircraft. Any weakness in the undercarriage or the tyres would mean disaster for us.

In the early light of that misty Saturday morning, the skipper brought the Lancaster past the great towers of Lincoln cathedral and gently eased her down over the fields to approach the runway. I heard the familiar clunk as the wheels locked down and we were ready to land, but she seemed to hang in the air a little longer than normal, hesitating, unwilling to take the risk of returning to the earth, as if aware that these might be her last moments. She wasn't alone; we were all thinking that this might end in a blinding flash, and so close to the end of our tour, too. Lower we sank, the aircraft still hesitant, almost resisting, then we were over the runway, the wheels touched with the faintest of bumps and we were down, racing along the concrete strip. Two to go.

The next night we did it all over again on the same target, only this time we bombed in clear visibility and seven and a half hours later I climbed down the rear ladder onto the dispersal pan, once again safely back at Skellingthorpe. Only one more.

Inexperience made crews vulnerable during their first five missions, then again at the midpoint of their tour as complacency crept in, and finally during their last five trips as nerves began to bite and the allure of the finishing line distracted them. Too many crews like Norman Jackson's had come to grief on their last trip and I didn't want to join that unenviable list.

Waiting for that last operation could be a very nervy time for crews, and a long wait because of bad weather was not good. But we were lucky again, and on 1st of May we were called for the very last time. The target was the aircraft assembly factory at Toulouse, which, unmolested by fighters or flak, we attacked in ideal conditions, giving Les a clear aiming-point photograph which he still has today. We had taken off at 21.35 and, nearly six hours later, the skipper switched off the engines of our trusted, lucky bomber as she settled at the dispersal pan, much to the relief and delight of our ground crew. I gathered up all my kit and walked away from Avro Lancaster LL744 VN-B; I would never fly in her again.

We had beaten the overwhelming odds that had been stacked against us and completed our tour. When we started, our chances of survival had been less than one in four, but we had survived collisions, bombs from above, fighter attacks, searchlights, flak, engine failure, fuel shortages, fog and a bailing-out. We had been to Berlin ten times and made it through the terror of Nuremberg, but that night as I drifted into the most relieved sleep I had had for a long time, I thought of Fred Ball and Don Moore and how sad it was that they were not here to share the moment.

Perhaps we only just finished our tour in time; that very first mission looking for the ditched crew close to the enemy coast probably saved our lives. The next operation for the Squadron after we had finished was the raid on Mailly-le-Camp on the night of the 3rd/4th May. Led by Wing Commander Leonard Cheshire, the target was the German military barracks just outside the village of Mailly. Cheshire marked the target and called in the main force, but the Controller, Wing Commander LC Deane, could not transmit the order to the waiting Lancasters; his VHF radio set was being drowned out by an American Forces' programme of dance-band music. Before Deane's deputy, Squadron Leader Sparks, was able to take over and order the bombers in, the Luftwaffe arrived, with devastating consequences. Forty-two Lancasters were shot down, including Sparks, who nevertheless managed to bail out and then evade capture, returning to England soon afterwards. More to the point, 50 Squadron lost five aircraft, its worst night of the war and even worse than Nuremberg. It could so easily have been us.

After a lie-in, I got up to go for breakfast and telephone Ena. It felt wonderful to have finished my tour, the relief was immense. Cycling across the camp in the warm sunshine to the Mess for breakfast, I started to whistle, I was so happy because now there really was a chance that we could have a future together. Ena had been desperate for me to finish my tour and I knew she would be thrilled to know that it was finally over. We had planned to go out and celebrate; however, I had to tell her that it would not to be tonight.

One of the traditions was that on completing a tour, the crew would take their ground staff out for the night to thank them for looking after the aircraft that had brought them safely home so many times. When I broke this news to Ena she was very far from happy, a situation not helped by me telling her that I thought she was being selfish; taking the ground crew out was very important to us all. Mac, Alan, Jock and Fred had spent endless hours working on our Lancaster out in the open of the windswept dispersal pan all through the bitterly cold weather of the winter. They had worked in freezing temperatures, their fingers numb and raw from touching the iced metal, to keep us safe by ensuring that VN-B and the other aircraft we flew did not let us down through mechanical failure, as well as patching up the damage we had taken from flak and fighters. It is not an over-statement to say that our lives depended upon the dedication of the ground crew, the men who are all too often over-looked in the Bomber Command story but without whom we could never have done what we did. In the end, Les and I went to see Ena and talked her down a bit but it left an unpleasant taste. Well, it did until I had had a few beers that evening.

Everyone chipped in and we went to one of the pubs in Lincoln, which put on a buffet spread for us. Not surprisingly, we drank far too much as the relief of finishing the tour sank in, but we had a great deal to celebrate: being alive, to start with. We were all destined to survive the war but, sadly, our Lancaster was not. She was lost three weeks later attacking Brunswick on 22nd/23rd May along with all but one of her new crew.

I met Ena in Lincoln the next night and we enjoyed a much quieter celebration, but it did bring home to me how deep her feelings were, which was just as well, because I then had to tell her that I was going home on leave the next morning for a few days. I did promise to return early so that we could have some time together before my next posting. We were both very conscious that once I left Skellingthorpe, I could go anywhere and that we would probably see a lot less of each other than we had done so far.

At lunchtime next day, I arrived home and, as always, mum was over-joyed to see me. But when I told her that I had finished my tour she didn't know whether to laugh or cry, she was so relieved. That evening, she and dad took me out for a small celebration to one of the local pubs in Kettering. It's the only time that I can ever remember doing anything like that with my parents as a young man and is a measure of just how much they loved me and were excited by the news, news which seventy-six per cent of aircrew parents never heard.

The following day I called to see Edith Boydon and ask whether there was any news about Ron; there wasn't and she seemed even more desolate than the last time I had seen her. She was pleased to see me, though, and thanked me for calling, but I knew that it was so hard for her. She was still clinging on to the slenderest hope that Ron would be alive in a prison camp somewhere. I didn't tell that I had finished my tour; that would have been too much for her.

When I returned to Skellingthorpe, I had my next posting; it was to No.17 OTU RAF Silverstone. It could have been worse, but I had hoped for a station nearer to Lincoln. I delayed leaving as long as possible by slipping off into Lincoln, but after a few days the Orderly sergeant saw me at breakfast one morning. "Good God Reg, haven't you gone yet? You were supposed to have left two days ago. Get over to the Orderly Room and collect your travel warrants and instructions."

The game was up and I was on my way. I just had time to telephone Ena from the Mess before the transport left to take me, my two kitbags, suitcase and bicycle to St Mark's LMS railway station, one of two in Lincoln close to the River Witham. I had to change stations in Birmingham from New Street to Snow Hill but when I found a taxi the driver refused to take my bicycle as well, so whilst he drove off with everything else, I cycled behind keeping up in case he disappeared with all my kit, although I had taken the precaution of noting his number first. Pedalling along through the streets of Birmingham chasing after the taxi, I remembered the words of the old music hall song and started to laugh:

"My old man said foller the van
And don't dilly dally on the way;
Off went the van wiv me 'ome packed in it,
I follered on wiv me old cock linnet,
But I dillied and dallied, dallied and dillied

Lost my way and don't know where to roam,
You can't trust a Special like the old time coppers
When you can't find your way 'ome. "

I caught my connection to Banbury where the RTO, the Railway Transport Officer, arranged for someone from Silverstone to come and pick me up. I arrived at the base around 4pm and was shown to the billet used by the sergeants and flight sergeants in charge of various sections, such as the Sergeants' Mess, clothing store and so on. Consequently, there was always a ready supply of whatever you wanted, particularly bread and cheese. I was the only aircrew sergeant there and, although they accepted me, they were not over-friendly.

My job at Silverstone was to act as wireless operator on the training flights, where pilots who had finished their tour on heavy bombers were starting to learn to be instructors. The first step was to re-familiarise themselves with the twin-engine Wellington and, although they could fly without a navigator, they always had to take a wireless op with them: me. The flying that I was doing was not at all enjoyable as the pilots were undergoing emergency action training, such as single-engine landings and stall correction, often at night. However, I was only there for a few days before being posted to the satellite station at RAF Turweston, near to Brackley.

I reported to 'B' Flight Signals where I found Flying Officer Clarke in charge. He was a decent sort of chap to work for and it was nice to be back amongst aircrew again, most of whom, like me, had completed a tour of ops. I had arrived just in time for D-Day, 6th June 1944, the long-awaited invasion of mainland Europe. Our Wellington engines were upgraded to 100 octane fuel and we were divided up into crews ready to fly over the Normandy beaches should it be necessary. My pilot was WO Lovell, DFM, but in the event, the landings went well enough not to require my further attendance in the skies over Europe and we were stood down. Not long afterwards, my Crown came through and I was promoted to Flight Sergeant.

The accommodation arrangements at Turweston were fairly basic and we only did about twenty-four hours flying in a month, which gave me a fair amount of free time. Getting home to Kettering was easy enough but to see Ena in Lincoln was more difficult. However, by organising my days off each week I could usually manage a two-day break, which would give me time to hitch-hike to Northampton and from there up the Great North Road to Newark and on to Lincoln.

As soon as I arrived, I would go to the Salvation Army hostel by the River Witham and book a bed and breakfast; clean sheets to sleep between and a lovely fried breakfast next morning for just a shilling. I was eternally grateful to the 'Sally Ann', because without them I would hardly have seen Ena during this time, and even today I always put something in their collection boxes.

Life was very different as an instructor than it had been on an operational station. I missed the excitement, the tight bond of friendship, the tension of ops and the squadron pride. However, I also missed the deep fear, sometimes terror, that an operation brought, the draining weariness and the sadness at the loss of friends. Even so, we did have a lot of fun at Turweston and I made some good friends.

When the pilots were doing air tests, they would often come into the Signals office to see if any of us wanted to go along for the ride and I was always glad of the chance. Monday morning 11th September brought one such chance when WO Lovell offered to fly over my house after the air test was finished. Arriving at Kettering, we flew really low over the Co-op clothing factory, the roar of the engines bringing people out to see what was happening. Then we did a tight turn and I pointed out our house as we flew along the Stamford Road. Another tight turn and a very low pass over the Henry Gotch School brought the children and staff running out to see this Wellington bomber thunder by a hundred feet or so above their heads. Turning again over Warkton Lane, we swooped right down to roof-top level and flashed past the houses in Washington Square, the lines of clean white laundry gently blowing in the breeze until each in turn was whisked up by the backwash from our aircraft.

By now, the deafening roar of our engines barely fifty feet up had everyone in the area rushing out to see us and, sure enough, when I looked down there was my mum and her neighbours standing on the top of their Anderson shelters enthusiastically waving at us. On down the road we raced until, just in time, Lovell pulled up to avoid the block of flats at the end of the street.

"That's enough, Reg, let's get out of here before someone takes our number and we end up on the carpet," he laughed as he opened the throttles and we quickly disappeared into the distance. By 12.30 Wellington 3550 'O' for Oscar was back at Turweston, ready to deny all knowledge of the incident.

The social life at the base was very good, too, with dances in the Sergeants' Mess always riotous affairs. Everyone drank too much; beer and broken glass littered the lino floor along with drunken airmen and not a few WAAFs. These dances were very popular with us all, especially the less good-looking WAAFs, who could always expect to be well kissed if nothing else in the darkness of the Mess balcony.

That autumn gave way to a hard winter and just before Christmas we had a heavy snow fall which stopped the flying for a few days until it had cleared enough for training to resume. Late one afternoon I watched as a Wellington took off, climbing steadily into the crystal light of the winter sky. Just as I was about to turn and walk away, I heard the engine note change, then stall and the aircraft dived into the ground. From the muffled boom and tell-tale plume of smoke, I knew their fate. The crew had been through an entire tour of duty against the Luftwaffe and the flak over Germany only to be killed on a training flight. It was true when they said that your time as an instructor was often more dangerous than on ops.

Ena and I each managed to have a week's leave over Christmas, which we spent at my home. It was a lovely few days with family and friends, in stark contrast to the Christmas it might have been had I been the wireless operator in that doomed Wellington. The cold weather pushed well into January and so too did our troops in France, so much so that some of Ena's unit were being posted over there to continue their work nearer to the front line, although married and engaged girls were excluded from the posting. Ena didn't want to leave Britain and, since her CO, Captain Lewis, had already asked me when I was going to make an honest woman of her, we decided to take the plunge and get engaged.

Whenever I visited Ena in Lincoln, I would catch the late train back to Brackley to make sure I was at the base on time. One dark autumn evening, just as the train was pulling out of Nottingham station, a rather pretty WAAF came into my compartment and sat opposite me. The train rattled along through the countryside and in the dim light of the carriage, with my greatcoat pulled around me against the cold, I dozed off. I was awoken by the jolt of the train making one of its stops along the way and I began chatting to the WAAF. It transpired that not only was she stationed at Turweston but she worked in the cookhouse at the Sergeants' Mess, although I didn't recognise her.

Presently, the train slowed and came to a stuttering halt at Brackley. We left the compartment and walked along the darkened platform to where the ticket collector stood at the gate, vaguely silhouetted by the quietly hissing shielded gas light behind him. A carriage door slammed shut on the train, a whistle blew, along the platform a green lantern waved in the night and, with a whoosh of steam, the little train eased out of the station and on its way.
"How are you getting back to the camp?" I asked the WAAF.
"I'll walk, I suppose," she answered.
"Well, I've got my bike here and you are welcome to a lift if you want one."

She gladly accepted and clambered up onto the crossbar, though I could hardly see where I was going with her greatcoat collar directly in front of me. We managed quite well along the dark lanes, navigating by starlight, until almost at the base we ran into a section of road that was as black as pitch. I couldn't see a thing; I hit the verge, wobbled, lost control and toppled into the ditch followed by the WAAF and then the bicycle.

I lay there in a daze for a few moments, then asked her, "Are you all right?"

"Yes, I think so," she answered a little shakily.

"I'm sorry," I offered, "I couldn't see the road."

"It's all right, it's not your fault and we're nearly there now."

Fortunately, we had landed amongst the soft grass and earth in the ditch and were none the worse for wear, but we walked the last few hundred yards to the base and I said goodnight to her as she disappeared off towards the Waafery.

I didn't see her around the Mess as I had expected to, and a few days later asked one of the other WAAFs where she was.

"Oh, I didn't know that you knew her, Flight," she told me. "She was having a crossbar lift on someone's bike the other night and fell off. She had a miscarriage next day and has had to leave the Service."

In the spring of 1945, Ena and I managed to have a week's leave together which we spent in Kettering. A neighbour of my mother's was a seamstress and made a dress for Ena; it was the first time I had seen her out of uniform. I put on the one remaining civilian suit that I had and we went out, feeling two different people. However, when I got back to Turweston after my leave, I found that my bed was missing from the hut. It seemed that no-one had expected me back that day and someone from another hut was doing very well with a WAAF in the boiler house down in the woods and they had commandeered my bed to aide their comfort. My friend Bernard Dye helped me carry it back, but I made sure that I changed the sheets.

There was an electric buzz of excitement around the station one Monday morning early in May; rumours of an end to the war were rife. Finally, Winston Churchill came on the wireless and announced that the Germans had surrendered and that the war in Europe would officially end the following day, 8th May 1945. We were told to take the next day off as leave. I didn't wait. As soon as possible I collected my bicycle and set off for the two-hour ride to Kettering, arriving home at about 7pm. I knew that I couldn't get to Lincoln but I could at least get home. Dad was in town on his St. John Ambulance duties but mum was in the kitchen. I kissed and hugged her. At last, after nearly six long years the war in Europe was over. After a bite to eat and a quick tidy up, we walked into town to meet dad and join the celebrations which had already begun. Mum talked a lot about Art that night and I knew that she would not relax until he was home.

ATS Staff Sgt Susan Heald was a secretary at SHAEF [Supreme Headquarters Allied Expeditionary Force] and had typed the English version of the Act of Military Surrender that brought an end to the European war and it was she who, the day before, had sent the historic signal to London, *"The mission of this Allied Force was fulfilled at 02.41 local time, May 7th 1945."* At the time of her death in February 2009, Susan Hibbert, as she was by then, was the last British witness to the signing of the German surrender and was survived only by Eisenhower's staff photographer, Albert Meserlin, who died about six weeks after Susan.

It was around this time that I had news from my mother that Art had returned from the PoW camp. He was desperately thin and bore the scars from where he had been blown through the roof of his aircraft the night they had been hit. Art's Lancaster ED438 was one of two which 49 Squadron lost on 3rd November 1943. They were on their twentieth operation when caught by a night fighter near Cologne on the way to Düsseldorf. The Lancaster quickly became a mass of flames as his pilot, Flt/Lt CG Thomas, fought to hold the burning aircraft steady. Art, together with P/O JE Teager, who was on his second-dickie trip that night, and Sgt ND

Panter, the flight engineer, waited in the cabin area while the navigator and bomb aimer struggled to release the forward escape hatch. In the few seconds that passed before they could get it open, the intense heat of the fire reached the bomb bay and detonated the 4,000lb cookie. The Lancaster simply blew up in mid-air, hanging in the sky in the shape of the mythical scarecrow so much feared by aircrew.

Art, Teager and Panter were blown through the Perspex roof and were the only survivors, becoming PoWs. As he was hurled through the air, my brother was just conscious enough to pull the D-ring of his parachute before he passed out. When he came round again, his parachute had opened and he was floating down towards an unknown fate. Barely able to see through the blood pouring down his face, Art had no idea who or what lay beneath him, but luckily he landed on open ground. He couldn't move though and was quickly captured, but the seriousness of the injuries to his head and face was so obvious to all that he was taken straight to a German hospital where a Luftwaffe officer photographed him, unable to believe that Art was actually alive. Thoughtfully, he gave a copy of the picture to Art as a keepsake when it became clear that he would survive.

After hospital discharge, Art, whose PoW number was 261470, was sent to Stalag Luft 6, close to the Baltic in East Prussia, near Hydekrug, now in Lithuania. By July 1944, the Russian Red Army was advancing and had got close enough to the camp for Art to see the artillery flashes in the night sky, all of which made the guards nervous and trigger happy. On the 14th, ahead of this advance, the Germans began to evacuate the camp, a particularly harsh decision for those men already in desperate need of medical attention. Crammed into cattle trucks without food, water or sanitation, the PoWs were transported to various other camps; for Art it was Stalag IVB. On the River Elbe some sixty miles north-west of Dresden, it was one of the largest camps, through which some 300,000 prisoners from forty nations passed during the war.

By now I had been promoted to Warrant Officer and soon after VE-Day, aircrew who had completed a tour of ops and a tour as instructors could apply to retrain for ground duties without losing their rank. The alternative was to join the Tiger Force being prepared to go to the Far East to finish the war against the Japanese. My 50 Squadron pilot, Michael Beetham, had already contacted me and asked if I wanted to rejoin his crew, but Ena and I wanted to get married though had agreed not to do so whilst I was still flying, so I applied for ground duties on the promise of a home posting close by.

I handed in my flying kit and set off for Blackpool PDC. Standing there on the railway station in the sunshine, filling my lungs with the sea air, I remembered that October day four years earlier when I had arrived at the same station to start my RAF service with no idea of what lay ahead; now, back again, I'd come full circle. The eight-week course had barely begun when the atomic bombs were dropped on Hiroshima and Nagasaki, bringing the Second World War to an end and sparking more celebrations around the country.

On 5th October at London Congregational Church in Kettering, Ena and I were married. Her mother came down from Lincoln, her father returned from serving in the Royal Navy and Art was there to be my best man. He was staying at a rehabilitation centre on the east coast awaiting his demob from the RAF but had come home for the wedding. The night before, my grandmother came to see me and said that she had managed to get me a small bottle of whisky, which was in very short supply during the war.
"Thank you, Gran, that's very thoughtful of you. How much?"
"Seven and sixpence, Reg," she said without a blush as I counted out the money. She never gave us presents and she wasn't going to start now!

We were married by Rev. Wide, who had been an RAF padre, and after the ceremony we went back to mum and dad's house in Washington Square, where the neighbours had laid out a wonderful spread. They had been saving up their food coupons for weeks to make sure that we would have a good party. Art had a barrel of beer from the off-licence and people just called in all through the afternoon and evening, including a couple of local lads I had been to school with and who were on leave at the time.

My grandmother was sitting with some of the other older women and I went over to her. "Hello, Gran, what would you like to drink?"

"Oh, thank you, Reg, I'll have a little drop of your whisky, please." Well, fancy that, what a surprise.

We left the party around 8pm and spent that night at a hotel in Leicester and then went on to Blackpool for the rest of the week. Ena had never been to Blackpool before, although I had seen quite enough of it. One day, whilst walking through the town, we bumped into Mrs Clegg, my landlady when I had started training in 1941.

"Aren't you one of my boys?" she asked looking at me hard.

"I am, Mrs Clegg. It's Reg Payne. How are you?"

"Very well, thank you. What happened to the other two boys you shared with?" she asked.

"Ron and Arthur were both killed over Germany," I answered with sadness.

"Oh dear. I'm so sorry, but I'm glad you made it."

She saw Ena's wedding ring and I introduced them. She wished us luck and I realised how much I had grown up in the years since I had stayed with her. The week slipped by so quickly and all too soon it was time for Ena to return to Lincoln. I went home for a few days and then it was back to PDC Blackpool yet again to await my next posting.

Ena in Lincoln and me in Blackpool may not have been an ideal start to our married life but that was nothing to what awaited me at the North Pier Pavilion when we were given our postings. I had been promised a station near Kettering or Lincoln, but in true military fashion, the opposite was applied and I was sent to 56 FRU [Forward Repair Unit]. I had no idea where that was, but worse still, the RAF in Blackpool didn't know either. Was it somewhere in Britain? If not, maybe France or Germany? Eventually, I found out; it was South East Asia Command. I couldn't believe it. Moreover, not until I reached Karachi would I be told just whereabouts in SEAC I was destined.

After spending a few weeks at various transit camps, the cold, snowy day that was the 11th December finally brought the orders to pack our kit and board one of the waiting Liberator bombers for the first leg of the trip to the Far East. The aircraft took twenty-five men at a time; no seats, nothing to drink, just emergency rations and an uncomfortable floor to sit on. After seven hours' flying over France, Italy and Sicily, we landed in the warm sunshine at Castel Benito airfield near Tripoli, where we were given a mug of tea, a meal and, best of all, some oranges; I hadn't had an orange in years.

We were billeted for two nights in tents pitched in the desert sand amongst the remnants of war. Italian and German aircraft littered the airfield, and Tripoli harbour was full of sunken ships, with just their funnels and superstructure above the water. Then it was on to Cairo, where my accommodation couldn't have been more different. We landed around midnight and were taken to the Heliopolis Palace Hotel, where a good meal and a real bedroom with its own bathroom and balcony awaited me. That night I slept like never before and awoke to the warmth of the sunshine as it streamed through the slats of the window shutters, whilst the gentle hum of the early-morning activity in the street below washed into my room. I got up and stepped out onto the balcony and was greeted by a sight to behold; there in the distance stood the pyramids, one of the Seven Wonders the World, symbol of the majesty and power of ancient Egypt. We had learned about the pyramids at school but never in my wildest dreams had I thought that I would actually see them.

After two days of comfortable rest at the Heliopolis it was back to the floor of the Liberator and on to Shaibah in Iraq, then Mauripur near Karachi, at that time in India. It was here, having been told I was going on to Rangoon, that I spent Christmas 1945, lying in the sunshine drinking Canada

Dry, eating fresh fruit and wishing that I was at home with Ena. Yet what a difference two years made; the challenging, dark, fearful, exhausting days of the Battle of Berlin seemed a lifetime away, and in many ways, they already were.

The 28th brought the next leg to Chakulia some distance from Calcutta. On the way, the pilot did a circuit of Delhi so that we could look down upon the Taj Mahal and later he gave us a wonderful view of the Himalayas. There was nothing at Chakulia except the hawks, which would swoop down and snatch the food off the plate of any unwary airman. The journey to the base at Calcutta was by train, and whilst there, we were confined to barracks because of the unrest amongst the local Indian population, who were seeking independence from Britain and resented our presence. From there I made the final leg of my long journey to 56 FRU by Dakota to Mingladon airfield just north of Rangoon. The whole place was literally a bomb site and we even had to build our timber beds with hammer and nails before going to sleep that night. The base had been bombed by the Japanese on their march through Burma and then again by the RAF to recapture it. So much for the promise of a posting near home; I couldn't have been much further away and could happily have strangled the posting clerk who no doubt thought it a great joke.

My job here was to supervise the recovery of all the equipment that was left behind by the RAF squadrons which had been disbanded. The war was over and the new government was in a rush to dismantle the structure and demob the troops to save money. Any equipment which was in working order or needed only slight repairs was put on charge, that is listed as available stock; anything else was destroyed as scrap. As a Warrant Officer, I also had other responsibilities: Duty Officer, Fire Prevention Officer, Anti-Malaria Officer and Officer-in-Charge of petrol issues and receipts for vehicles on the base.

The air in Rangoon was always hot and sticky and we sweated profusely. However, a tea wagon came around several times a day to help to keep us hydrated. I know that during the battle for the Arnhem Bridge in September 1944, a German general is quoted as saying of XXX Corps that the trouble with the British was that they drank too much tea. Well, out in Rangoon, that was certainly true and a necessity, because, apart from a little bottled beer, there was nothing else to drink since the water infrastructure had been destroyed by bombing and every drop had to be boiled, and tea kept us hydrated.

I had managed to write to Ena on the journey out and now that I was settled, her letters started to come through. They took about a week to arrive from England and one of her first letters brought good news; she was to be demobbed from the ATS in about March, Art was soon to be released from the RAF and our sister Doris had married Bob. With Doris going to live with Bob's parents, there was room for Ena to live with my parents until I returned home.

Life was different again here from an operational squadron or a training station and it took me a little while to settle to the routine of not flying any more. Our weekends were free from midday on Saturday so we often went to the Victoria Lakes to canoe in our self-built craft or swim in the cool refreshing water.

Rangoon lies about 17° north of the equator, deep in the tropics and the passage from day to night is very swift. There is no lingering blazoned dusk, no Turner grandeur as the earth rolls on to wake our brethren beneath the western sky. In just a few minutes, the vermillion disc that was the sun that had baked us all day long slipped below the horizon, darkness settled over the land and the creatures of the night emerged. Cries and calls, shrieks and wails gave witness to a world beyond my view. Bats, much larger than anything I had ever seen, swirled through the air, whilst fireflies danced and courted in a frenzied swarm of fairy lights around their chosen tree.

Life in the city could be brutal and its end swift. Rabies was rampant and any dog found on the camp with the disease was immediately dispatched with the aid of a Sten gun. It was violent but it was quick, saved the dog immense suffering and helped to protect our troops from a disease for which there was no cure. For the same reason, organised dog shoots were conducted on a regular basis. Advance notice was given of the date and times so that owners could keep their pets at home, then military marksmen would patrol the city and shoot any dog seen roaming the streets.

But it wasn't only rabid dogs. Rangoon Jail hosted many Japanese officers accused of war crimes. Each Thursday morning at 11 o'clock, the next group of convicted prisoners sentenced to death faced the firing squad. As the hour approached, the area around the jail would fill with local Burmese, who, although unable to see anything, would wait to hear the rifle shots then quietly move on with a sense of satisfaction, and for some, perhaps, the beginning of closure.

Before the war, a woman on my main office staff, together with her husband, had owned the Rangoon race track. They lived with their young son, and one day in 1943, Japanese soldiers arrived at her home whilst the family were eating. They rampaged through the house, knocked her to the floor and then dragged the three of them outside to the dusty courtyard. The soldiers were commanded by an officer of the Imperial Japanese Army and, upon his orders, her husband and son were forced to kneel in front of him. She was held tightly by two soldiers, one pulling her hair back to force her head up whilst the officer poured scorn and abuse upon them all. Finally, his tirade came to an end and, as the dust from the commotion settled gently over her kneeling family, she realised the appalling horror that was to follow. The officer slowly drew his sword and brutally beheaded the two people she most loved and cared for in this world. Their crime was that they were of mixed Anglo-Burmese race. She was spared for the entertainment of his men.

In the closing days of the war, this officer was captured and imprisoned in Rangoon Jail, where he was subsequently tried and convicted. When I arrived at my office on the Thursday set for his execution, there was a palpable air of anticipation. By 10.45, the usual bustle of activity in the busy room had died away until the only sound to be heard was the steady metronome ticking of the clock on the wall. Work was put aside for the moment, and the windows were pushed wide open. The woman, together with the other female staff, sat perfectly still at their desks, listening intently, each absorbed in their own thoughts, reflecting upon what had been and what was about to be. As the hands of the clock moved inexorably towards 11am, the world outside seemed to have stopped. In the silence of the room, the tension and sense of expectation was overpowering. There was no sound of breathing, there was no birdsong from the trees outside, no sound came in from the streets; it was if the whole city was holding its breath, waiting for the moment of ultimate justice.

11 o'clock. The tense, still, stifling air was split by the sharp crackle of rifle fire. It was done. A moment later, the women stood up, beaming smiles lighting up their faces, shook hands and hugged one another. The birds began to sing again, the tension in the room poured out of the windows and the noise of the city streets flooded in. I was greatly moved by the dignity of these women who had suffered unimaginable brutality at the hands of their captors, and for the next few minutes I knew that this office was not the place for me; I quietly slipped out and left them to the sanctity of their own emotions. I cannot even begin to conceive what these women had endured, but I do know that for them, and that one woman in particular, true justice offered no other option but the firing squad.

June 1946 brought me the news I had been waiting for. Forty-six was my demob number and at long last it had come to the top of the list; I was on my way home in the troopship SS *Orduna*, which would ply the Far East route for another three and a half years before leaving Gibraltar for Great Britain on her final voyage in December 1949. When I boarded her in Rangoon, I was told that the voyage was to take thirty days, that there was no library on board, no form of organised entertainment and no bar, not even for fruit juice, there was only tea. Whatever might be said about the Americans at war, they certainly looked after their troops a great deal better than our people looked after us. The prevailing philosophy for the British was always 'make it as hard and uncomfortable as possible for our troops'.

We started out across the Bay of Bengal in monsoon rain and heavy seas. As each hour passed, the *Orduna* found it increasingly hard to climb each giant wave only to crash down into the trough on the other side. I was lucky because the Warrant Officers' Mess was in the middle of the ship where the motion of the sea was at its least, but even here I could feel the old ship strain at the effort and shudder with every impact. After several days we found relief in Colombo harbour where we took on fresh water and more troops.

Here, I moved my hammock out of the Mess and up onto the deck where the air felt a little less stifling and smelled a lot less putrid. The *Orduna* slipped Colombo harbour late in the afternoon and set out across the Indian Ocean and up the Red Sea to Suez for another stop. By now it was July, the calm of the Mediterranean very different from the storms of the Indian Ocean, so we were able to make good progress. The quick call at Gibraltar for more home-bound troops broke the monotony for a few hours, and then it was off again, through the Bay of Biscay on the last leg of our voyage to Liverpool.

Happily, Biscay was benign but the Western Approaches were chilly and so I moved my hammock into the shelter of the Mess deck stairwell for the last two nights of the trip. Finally, after thirty days at sea, through the grey light on that last early morning, I saw the cloud of murk that hung over the Mersey and knew that we were home at last. By mid morning the ship was tied up, disembarkation had begun and I was on my way once more to RAF Kirkham, near Preston, where I had done my stores equipment course a year earlier. That night, most of us went into Preston to celebrate being back in Britain, almost at the end of our service. There had been little or no beer available in Rangoon so we certainly made up for lost time and I know that I drank far too much.

Over the next two days, I received my grey chalk-stripe demob suit, shirt, shoes, a hat I didn't want but knew my dad would like, over sixty pounds in back pay, my travel warrant home and, best of all, my release papers. The Royal Air Force, which five years earlier as a teenager I had been so desperate to join, had finished with me and I with it. Now it was time to build a fresh life with my new bride in the country that we had fought so long and hard to keep free and for which so many had died.

"Christmas Day 1945 en route to Rangoon. Reg is front right"

"1946. Relaxing at Victoria Lakes, Rangoon"

"Sgt WA Payne, Wireless Operator, 49 Squadron"

"1943. Art in his flying kit, taken a few days before he was shot down"

"No25 Thomas Road being built, 1947"

Chapter Fourteen

"Life is mostly froth and bubble,
Two things stands like stone,
Kindness in another's trouble,
Courage in your own"

- 'Life is mostly froth and bubble';
Adam Lindsay Gordon

Ena and I were living at my parents' house. This was a normal arrangement at the time as very few people could afford to buy their own homes and the local authorities were not yet able to build in the numbers they were to do so in the 1950s to replace all the war-damaged houses and slum clearances. Mum and dad had given over one of their downstairs rooms for us to have as a bedsit, otherwise we fitted in with the family. My little brother Brian was nearly seven now and growing up fast. It was nice for me to have time with my family again and get to know Brian better, but more than anything, I needed a job. For the last five years, the Royal Air Force had paid me wherever I went and whatever I did, but now that had stopped and I had a wife to support and a home to find. With thousands of men leaving the Services every month, finding a job quickly was my priority. The British Legion which I had worked for when I left school had moved to Nottingham, so that was out of the question; I would have to look elsewhere. The trouble was, there was not a lot of call for wireless operator/air gunners in Civvy Street.

Art had been taken on as a trainee lathe operator at Timpson's in Bath Road, one of the local engineering firms, and was enjoying the work, so I decided to see if they would have me too. On seeing details of my service in the RAF, they employed me on a six-month trial for £4-10s-0d a week. If at the end of that period I was suitable, I could stay with five shillings a week rise and a further five shillings in another six months; if I was not suitable I would be sacked. Although this was a big drop in income from my Warrant Officer's pay, it was a start.

Ena also found a job in the offices of another engineering firm. She started straight away and was shown to her desk, which she began to organise. After a few minutes, a rather perplexed-looking manager came hurrying over to her. "Excuse me, Ena, but you are a single lady, aren't you?" he enquired.

"No, I'm married," she answered smiling.

"Oh, we couldn't possibly employ you if you're married."

"Why not?" protested Ena.

"Well, I mean, what guarantee would we have that you will still be here in twelve months' time. I'm sorry, we thought you were single. You'll have to leave, I'm afraid."

With that, Ena left the building having been employed for about five minutes.

I wasn't due to start work until the following Monday, so Ena and I used the time to walk into Kettering and meet up with some of my old friends who had survived the war. Some, like me, were now married and just starting out in Civvy Street, others had been all over the world during the war, so one way or another, we had plenty to catch up on. One person I did take Ena to see was Edith Boydon. Now that the war was over, she still clung to the desperate hope that Ron would yet turn up. She was so pleased to see us, made us very welcome and wished us luck. It was a few weeks later that she received the official letter she had dreaded for so long; Ron wasn't coming home. Edith completely went to pieces after that and I didn't see her again; no-one outside the psychiatric hospital did. Who was there? Her son was all she had.

Ena soon found a job with the Board of Trade, which had a much more enlightened attitude to employing married women. As it worked out, the previous firm helped us because the BoT job was much better paid with more sociable hours. With two incomes, we could start to save towards our own home. Art, who was now courting a lovely and very pretty girl called Christine, and I both gave mum part of our wages towards our keep. I know that this was a big help to our parents, not just for food, much of which was still rationed, but also with the rent and the bills, and enabled them to have some spare money to enjoy after so many years struggling to bring us up and then getting through the war.

1947 had not dawned long when it began to snow, and it just kept on coming, day after day, week after week. Even though we were used to hard winters with plenty of snow in those days, this was too much and gradually Britain ground to a halt under the great white blanket that covered the land. The rural roads were the first to be blocked, then the larger roads away from the towns became impassable, and finally the town roads filled with the incessant white flakes. Short spells of daytime thaw turned to a smooth sheet of ice at night upon which more snow settled, layer upon layer. Road transport was all but impossible, the trains couldn't run a regular service, and in the end, the RAF was called in to drop food supplies to isolated villages, farms and livestock in the fields. Even large stretches of the Thames through London froze over, affording public skating on a scale not seen since Charles Dickens was writing *A Christmas Carol*.

Like most buildings constructed before the war, there was no roofing felt beneath the tiles on our home, allowing the fierce east winds to blow the snow under the eaves and into the attic, so Art and I had the regular task of getting up there with a dust pan, brush and bucket to sweep up the snow before it melted and brought the ceiling down.

Almost all of the factories in Kettering closed down, and the workforce signed on at the Labour Exchange for unemployment benefit. The power stations were running short of coal and only generating a limited supply and, anyway, miles of electricity cables across the country hung limp and useless, snapped by the weight of snow and ice that had built up on them. Timpson's remained partially open and I went in to do work in the pattern shop that did not require electricity. Ena's office was open too and I would meet her afterwards. The two of us would then slip and slide through the dark treacherous streets, groping our way home; it was worse than the blackout of the war years.

In the middle of all this metrological chaos, an item appeared in the *Evening Telegraph* advertising plots of land for sale on the West View Estate, where new homes would be built once the weather broke. On that Sunday, Ena and I went to see the show house in Bryant Road. It was wonderful, of course, with an upstairs lavatory and bathroom with its own water heater, another water heater in the kitchen, three bedrooms, and all for £1,140. The next day, I secured plot number 21 for £140 deposit. I managed to get a mortgage for the balance from the Co-op, but it was based solely upon my basic wages; bonuses, overtime and Ena's wages were not taken into account.

April at last brought an end to the great freeze with the great thaw and the great flood, but the summer that followed was beautiful. Timpson's failed to honour their commitment to both Art and me to increase our wages after six and twelve months' service, and so when the opportunity came along, we left and went to work at Whitfield's, a rival engineering firm which paid better money and included a bonus scheme.

It was around this time that Ena found out that she was expecting our son David, who was born on 30th September 1947. After that, I discovered that the reality of married life was going to work, looking after David and having no money or time for stepping out. I spent Christmas Eve 1947 sitting on the floor of our room with a glass of brown ale, rocking David's cot trying to coax him to sleep. It was all very different from our time in Lincoln when we were single.

Twelve months after I had paid the deposit on our new house, the builders started work and each Sunday I would push David in his pram out to what was to become No.25 Thomas Road to watch the progress. There were, though, little added extras to be paid for in the build which today, when houses come with fully fitted kitchens, carpets throughout and legal fees waived, seem incredible. Every 15amp socket fitted cost me an extra £1-10s-0d, consequently, we could only afford one 15amp and one 5amp in each room.

Inevitably, living with my parents especially now that we had David, created tensions in the house, particularly between mum and Ena in the age-old battle surrounding motherhood of experience versus modernity. I am eternally grateful to my parents for taking us in when we needed somewhere to live after the war, but our own home beckoned and the building progress seemed painfully slow. Finally, in the autumn of 1948 we moved out of 19 Washington Square into our own house. I think that there must have been a sigh of relief all round, because Art and Christine had got married a few weeks earlier and were trying to manage in Art's small room at home, so at least they could now move into the larger rooms we were leaving.

My priority was to my family, and there was a lot to do. There was no money left at the end of each week from my wages after I had paid the mortgage and all the outgoings, so I took over an allotment on which I grew all our vegetables to help ease the cost of food and supplement the rations. I also carried out various alterations to the house, including building a porch at the front door, and knocking down the pantry to increase the size of the kitchen.

The pace of change during the twentieth century has been staggering, especially after 1945, but in the immediate post-war years Britain seemed to hold its breath. The war had virtually bankrupted the country and our debt to the Americans was so great that we received aid under the Marshall Plan. There were relatively few car owners and commuting to work was not a phrase anyone outside the South East would recognise. People went to work on foot, bicycle, bus, tram or train.

These were years of great austerity where wartime rationing and coupons were still in general use. The television-driven consumer economy had not yet arrived from America and much of David's early childhood reflected my own. I made him a canoe as I had for myself twenty years earlier, he would play out in the street with the other children or along the brook by the allotments as I had done at his age in the Ise

259

Brook, and we would go swimming at the Baths. However, by the mid 1950s the austerity began to ease, things became more comfortable, and we were able to have an annual holiday. And when, in 1957, Prime Minister Harold MacMillan told the country in a speech about the state of the British economy: *"Indeed let us be frank about it… most of our people have never had it so good,"* usually paraphrased to "you've never had it so good," he was so right, both then and now. Although people have more material possessions now, they are definitely less content than we were. Life today it seems is driven by acquisition rather than fulfilment and can therefore never be satisfied. Contentment becomes an illusion rather than an achievement, which is why MacMillan was right.

My experiences and memories of the most violent and devastating war to have raged across our planet had to be buried deep in my subconscious in the years immediately afterwards if I was to survive the transition to peace and make a future. It was this focus on the necessity of the moment which helped me to keep the dark memories of the Battle of Berlin locked away, but I couldn't escape the nightmares which relived the horrors of those missions. I would wake up, soaked in sweat, convinced that our aircraft was on fire and I was trapped at my wireless operator's table. At other times it would be Don Moore's face that I would see, his haunted stare as he looked at death then turned away to search for a parachute; but I never told Ena about these dreams as she lay sleeping quietly beside me. The armchair moralists who blame the young men of Bomber Command for carrying out the decisions of our political masters have no idea of the burden which we have carried down the years to give them the freedom to blame us. Only those who have faced violent death can understand.

Over the years, there have been precious few occasions when any British government has truly acted in the best interest of its people, despite what the politicians would have us believe. The creation of the National Health Service in 1948, still the envy of the world, is a rare shining example. Conceived by Sir William Beveridge in his 1942 report, the idea of a 'cradle to grave' welfare state was opposed by Winston Churchill, a stance which cost him dear in the 1945 General Election. But if 1940 was the British people's finest hour, then the treatment of injured Service personnel by post-war bureaucrats was certainly not the government's.

When Art cheated death in his exploding Lancaster, unbeknown to him as he went through its roof, the gods arranged a cruel retribution, and by 1949 he was in trouble. About a year after he and Christine were married, when their first daughter was just a few weeks old, he started to have dizzy spells when getting up in the morning. These quickly became worse and affected him at work during the day as well. Art went to see Doctor Ogle, who suspected a brain tumour and sent him to Oxford for further tests which confirmed the doctor's diagnosis. Major surgery quickly followed, but the tumour could not be removed, only drained. Art was given radiotherapy and three months to live.

The treatment was much more successful than expected and Art lived for another thirty years. The tumour's growth had been slowed, but during those years my brother had to regularly return to the Oxford hospital for further draining operations and radiotherapy. He could no longer work and support his family, so RAFA, the Royal Air Force Association, took up his case and tried to obtain a war pension for him from the government through the local tribunal, but without success. Undeterred, RAFA instructed a solicitor to present Art's case to the War Pensions Appeals Tribunal in London. In its findings, the Tribunal said that although it was most likely that the tumour was caused by the injuries to Art's head when he was blown through the roof of his Lancaster, the evidence was not conclusive and consequently no pension could be awarded. Hardly their finest hour; at best, a callous decision particularly in view of the prognosis for Art, and at worst, deliberately punitive.

As a family, we could never have afforded the surgery and radiotherapy treatment but, thanks to Sir William Beveridge and the Atlee government, the NHS, created on 5th July 1948, was there just in time to treat Art and Christine when they needed it. During the 1950s, Christine was diagnosed with leukaemia and regularly had to visit the same Oxford hospital as her husband to have a complete blood transfusion. For a while afterwards she would pick up, but the visits gradually became more frequent until the day came when the treatment no longer worked. For all we expected to lose Christine, when it came in 1960, she died very suddenly. Art was devastated, as were their three girls who were still quite young. It was soon clear that my brother couldn't manage the girls on his own, so Christine's sister Beryl and their mother more or less brought them up.

Over the years Art's own condition continued to worsen and the tumour could no longer be drained. In time he lost much of his mobility and spent long periods in hospital. The local authority managed to find him a bungalow along the Stamford Road, but in his later years he could do so little for himself. Mum would go and look after him most of the time, until he moved back home to Washington Square where our parents could take greater care of him. After a long hard struggle, he finally died on 27th March 1982, just two months after dad. Poor Art and Christine, life had dealt them both such a cruel hand.

As the 1950s progressed, I took on another allotment and was able to sell or barter the excess produce, which made us more or less self-sufficient. Not long after moving into our new home, I had framed a couple of pictures to hang on the walls. My framing skills were soon noticed by friends, neighbours and visitors alike and I was asked to frame pictures for other people. Then a couple of local photographers heard about me and suddenly I was getting work framing wedding photographs. Of course, they always wanted the finished pictures yesterday, which meant working late into the evening on many occasions, but Ena would help me and we were glad of the income. These were hard but very happy years in many ways for us and with the little extra cash from the picture framing, I was able to buy a small second-hand Italian Berrini moped. Instead of cycling to work each day, usually against a head wind, I could now ride with ease simply by twisting the grip a little and turning up the power; what pleasure!

By now I was a foreman at Whitfield's, but the hours were long, too long with the overtime, and after seventeen years there, I needed a change which would allow me to spend more time with Ena and David. I saw an advertisement for a vacancy in the engineering department at Kettering Technical College, I applied and was appointed to the post. I knew quite a lot about the college as all the young apprentices at Whitfield's attended day-release courses there. Although Whitfield's offered me the same wages that I would be getting, which was only one pound a week more, it was a staff appointment, the conditions were better, the holidays were longer and the hours were shorter; it was exactly what I wanted.

Whilst I worked my week's notice, several of the charge hands came to persuade me to change my mind and stay. I knew the management had sent them, but wouldn't come to talk to me themselves. On that final Friday afternoon, I packed my tools away and walked to the door for the last time. At the far end of the workshop stood a group of managers, deep in conversation and looking over to me as I left. After seventeen years of service, never having lost a day's work, not one of them came to say goodbye, let alone wish me luck; I knew I had made the right decision.

John McKinlay, the principal of the college, was a formidable army officer during the war, and I think that sometimes he thought that he was still in the Forces. He was the man who directed my work and to whom I was responsible, which suited me very nicely, since whenever I found myself pulled in too many different directions, I just referred the matter up to McKinlay; no-one ever argued with him and it made for a quiet life for me. He was very direct, called a spade a spade and expected a lot but we got on well together and I know that he greatly respected my Bomber Command record. My years at the college were very happy and I never regretted joining the staff.

Throughout these years, I kept in touch with the other four members of our original crew. Our navigator, Frank Swinyard, the oldest member of the crew, was a chartered accountant. He took on the role of company secretary and accountant of the Merchant Seamen's War Memorial Society, to which he devoted so much time and effort to ensure its success before his death in 1991.

Mid-upper gunner Jock Higgins joined the Palestine Police Force in the days leading up to the creation of the State of Israel, after which he returned to Glasgow where he married Fay before moving to Canada in the 1950s. He did, though, manage to return to Skellingthorpe in 1989 for the unveiling of the 50/61 Squadron Memorial. Perhaps because he had a keen eye for the target, Jock dearly loved playing golf and always said that when his time came he hoped that he would be on a golf course. In 1993 the Almighty granted him his wish.

Before the war bomb aimer Les Bartlett had been a pharmacist, the profession to which he returned and followed until his retirement.

Flight Lieutenant Michael Beetham, DFC, our young pilot and the youngest member of the crew by a few weeks from me, remained in the RAF and made it his career. During 1946, there were a number of events commemorating the end of the war, including the Victory Day parade on 8th June, during which Michael piloted Lancaster TL-A in the flypast over London. Later, he was posted to Africa where he did much important aerial survey work. Record-breaking flights, ADC on a staff tour of the USA and Canada, the V bomber force, pioneering work with air-to-air refuelling techniques and much more vital work accompanied ground tours, overseas postings and staff college appointments.

As the post-war years unfolded, Michael's career continued to gather momentum and promotions followed, as did recognition of his many contributions to the RAF. In 1977 he became Chief of the Air Staff, a post in which he remained for five years, longer than anyone had done so since Lord Trenchard. He was appointed Companion of the Order of the British Empire in 1967, Knight Commander of the Order of the Bath in 1976 and Grand Cross of the Order of the Bath two years later. Finally, on 14th October 1982, Sir Michael was appointed Marshal of the Royal Air Force, the very highest rank of the RAF.

He had come a very long way from the young pilot who flew our Lancaster bomber through the Battle of Berlin and yet, even as his outstanding career was unfolding with postings as far afield as Aden during the terrorist campaign of the 1960s, he never forgot the friendship which had been forged in the skies over Germany. From time to time over those years, we would meet up or talk on the telephone, opportunities which greatly increased in retirement. Today we are no longer the carefree young men of a closely knit bomber crew who would wrestle on the grass under the wings of our aircraft on a sunny afternoon, just two elderly gentlemen who remember and value a friendship which has spanned seventy years.

By now I had been appointed Chief Technician at the college, but there is nothing quite like family life for stealing time. It didn't seem so long ago that Brian was born, and yet on 3rd December 1966, he married Janet in Worcester; no longer my baby brother but a qualified draughtsman in an engineering firm and a married man. David, too, had grown up, left school, passed his driving test and was earning a living as a journalist on the *Evening Telegraph*. As soon as he was old enough, David had passed his motor cycle test and used my old scooter to get around on, later exchanging it for a more modern one. After a series of accidents, some quite serious, Ena and I were pleased to see him pass his driving test and have four wheels under him.

Like so many youngsters did in those days, he had an old car to start with, graduating to a better and more reliable one, something which coincided with his greater interest in girls, and it wasn't long before we met a rather special one. Annette lived in Rushden and had been the Carnival Queen the year before, and I could see why. She was every bit the 1960s' girl, very pretty with long blonde hair, like the singers Marianne Faithful, Twinkle, Mary Travers of Peter Paul and Mary and the actress Judy Geeson. Marriage followed in 1968 and they lived with us for the next two years until their own home was built, just as Ena and I had done with my parents some twenty years earlier. I have three lovely grandchildren, Joanne, Kerry and David.

One Saturday morning in 1974, a rather official-looking envelope dropped through our letter box. Always wary of such things, I made a cup of tea and opened it with some diffidence. Unbeknown to me, my brother Art was doing exactly the same that morning with a similar official-looking envelope that had dropped through his letter box, too. We had both been invited to travel to the RAF Museum at Hendon as guests of the Irvin Parachute Company to receive our golden caterpillars. Mine was as a result of bailing out of VN-Q before she crashed at East Kirby and Art's was for having his life saved by his parachute after his Lancaster blew up on the way to Düsseldorf.

Membership of the elite Caterpillar Club is reserved for that fortunate group of people whose lives have been saved by their parachutes in an enforced bail-out. The free parachute, that is one where the ripcord is pulled by the airman during descent rather than being attached to the aircraft as it is for paratroopers, was invented in 1919 by the American-born Leslie Irvin, who at only nineteen years of age, tested his own invention in front of the US military. Within two years, Lieutenant Harold R Harris became the first person to have his life saved by an Irvin parachute after being forced to abandon an aircraft which was about to crash. Happily, I am one of over 45,000 men who have come to owe their lives to Leslie Irvin's invention. The emblem given by the Irvin

Parachute Company to its members is a little solid gold silk worm with real ruby eyes, a reminder that until just after the war, all parachutes were made from pure silk.

At Hendon, Art and I were warmly met and directed to the hospitality bar, where the refreshment soon eased the shyness and inhibitions of the assembled company. Les Bartlett was also there that day and I was able to introduce him to Art. An enjoyable evening meal followed together with some very interesting speeches, after which it was back to the two bars. By now the party was in full swing; it was like old times, with off-duty RAF lads doing what they do best, having a good time. It was a very mixed crowd of people, mostly former wartime personnel, although there were a couple of serving officers who had recently bailed out of a jet fighter off the Norfolk coast.

Former rank meant nothing that night as we all had the one thing in common, but for all that there were a couple of notable chaps there, one of whom was the night fighter ace Group Captain John 'Cat's Eyes' Cunningham, CBE, DSO**, DFC*, AE, who famously downed an enemy bomber one night without firing a single shot by diving upon it though cloud and forcing it to the ground.

If the Luftwaffe Nachtjaeger force was the nemesis of Bomber Command, then John Cunningham was theirs, with twenty aircraft to his credit. His first victory came on 19th November 1940, but after he swapped his Blenheim for the 'Whispering Death' Bristol Beaufighter, his tally rapidly mounted. There is no doubt that Cunningham had exceptional night vision so the government used his success in a propaganda campaign urging us all to eat plenty of carrots to help us see in the blackout, and thereafter he became known as 'Cat's Eyes' Cunningham, a name which stuck with him for the rest of his life. Carotene is certainly good for the eyes, but the truth behind his remarkable success was airborne radar together with the considerable skill of his radar operator, Jimmy Rawnsley, which in 1940/41 was a closely guarded secret. This was a double campaign for the government in that it gave us all practical encouragement to eat home-grown vegetables as part of the Dig for Victory campaign but also provided a veil for the radar secret.

Cunningham was awarded his first DSO, a DFC and a bar to his DFC in 1941, followed by bars to his DSO in 1942 and 1944. He had made Group Captain in 1943 at only 26, but after the war he walked away from a career in the RAF which would almost certainly have seen him become an Air Chief Marshal to return to de Havilland. Within a year he became its chief test pilot, most notably flying Comet, the world's first jet passenger aircraft. He was appointed OBE in 1951 and CBE in 1963. I was rather surprised to see him at the dinner since I had not heard that he had ever been shot down, but it seems that in 1939 he had to bail out of a doomed Moth Minor, and nearly thirty-five years after the event, he was there to receive his membership of the Caterpillar Club and his golden silk worm; well, it does take a long time for a worm to make a whole parachute. I wear mine with pride and enduring thanks to Leslie Irvin, a brilliant and courageous young man and, of course, to the hard work of those industrious little silk worms.

In 1978, Ena and I drove down to Surrey to visit Frank and Pam Swinyard. I hadn't see Frank since the end of our tour although we had kept in regular contact. Whilst we were there, Frank showed us around the 400 acre Springbok Farm that was part of the Merchant Seamen's rehabilitation training centre and an important part of Frank's work for the Society.

The following year, I returned to East Kirby for the first time since that fateful day when I landed there after jumping out of Queenie. There I met a local man who lived on the site and, when he found out that I was a survivor of the crash, he took me to the field where she had come down. Telling me to wait by the hedge, he picked up a bucket and walked along the rows of potatoes, stopping every now and then to pick something up and put it in the bucket. After ten minutes he returned and showed me several pieces of Perspex and metal. Then he handed me a large circular piece of bone, which I took from him without thinking too much about it. As I turned it over in my hands and looked at it, the realisation came to me that this was part of Fred, Don or one of Jennings' gunners. It had lain in that field for thirty-five years. I felt the lump in my throat as their faces looked back at me.

I took the various pieces of Queenie away with me, including the piece of bone. I showed the bone to the biology lecturer at the college, who was very interested. Then I gave it to a pal who worked at Kettering General Hospital for analysis. It turned out to be part of a pelvis from someone with blood group B, which is an unusual blood group, so identifying whose pelvis it was would have been fairly easy, but I let it rest; there was nothing to be gained from pursuing it. Another friend melted down the metal and made some lovely castings of a Lancaster, one of which I still have today.

It was not long after this that I started to paint. At first I used watercolours and was quite pleased with the results. After I had finished a few, I took them in to the art lecturer at the college who told me that they were indeed quite good but that I was painting in the style of oils rather than water colours and suggested that I tried oils. This led me on from copying landscapes on calendars to my love of World War Two aviation and the Lancaster in particular.

Friday, 2nd December 1977, saw the start of a weekend re-union for Frank, Les and me with Sir Michael, by then Air Chief Marshal and Chief of the Air Staff, which he had arranged at RAF Waddington, just outside Lincoln. Jock was in Canada and couldn't get over. We had a wonderful time and were definitely spoiled by the station airmen; well, after all, we were the wartime crew of the Chief of the Air Staff and in RAF circles that is a lot of street cred. The highlight of the weekend was a flight over Lincoln. It had been thirty-three years since I had seen Lincoln from the air and it brought back so many happy memories. It was good to be together again in an aircraft.

My long-standing friend Roy Christie owned an apartment in Majorca and during the summer of 1981 he invited Ena and me to use it to take our two granddaughters, Joanne and Kerry, for a holiday. The girls were teenagers by now and they had their mother's good looks, so although we had a lovely time, I couldn't really relax until they were safely in bed at night and away from all the young lads who were holidaying in the resort. When we came to fly back home, I mentioned to the stewardess that I had been a wireless operator on Bomber Command during the war and that I would love to see the flight deck if possible; sadly something which would be out of the question today. She said she would ask the pilot and I thought no more about it.

It was a night flight and quite late, but just as everyone had settled down, the stewardess came along the aisle and whispered in my ear, "Would you care to come with me, please, Mr Payne, the Captain would like to see you." And with a warm smile, she led me through to the cockpit.

I was surprised how little room there was for the two pilots and how many dials and switches there were. It turned out that both pilots were ex-RAF and that they knew Mike Beetham. We chatted for a little while about what it was like on operations during the war and just before I left, the Captain said, "Well, we're flying over France at 40,000 feet now but don't worry, Reg, the German night fighters can't get you at this height."

I went back to my seat reflecting upon the fact we were flying at twice the height and twice the speed that we had cruised at in VN-B. I closed my eyes and remembered those days; days of close friendships, excitement, fear, danger and being instrumental in the achievement of ultimate victory and peace. It was a job to be done and we had done it well.

Our crew met up again shortly after this holiday when Sir Michael once more arranged for Frank, Les and me, together with our wives, to join him for lunch one Sunday at his official flat in Knightsbridge. Although it was a very private affair, the staff were there to wait upon us and see to our every need. We had a lovely time talking about our years together in Bomber Command and also finding out a little more about the life of a Chief of the Air Staff, but no official secrets, of course!

By contrast, these were also the last months of my brother's life. He was now a permanent in-patient at St Mary's Hospital, but it was, at least, next door to the college and so I could see him during the week as well as my weekend visit to him with Brian each Sunday. Art was able to go home for a few hours on Christmas Day 1981, looked after by his daughters, but that night back at the hospital he fell out of bed and hit his head on the hard tiled floor, an accident which virtually paralysed him. After all he had already been through, the gods were still taking their retribution for his survival.

The year turned and brought sadness with it. Dad had by now completely lost his sight and during January became very ill. He stayed at home but could no longer get out of bed so it was brought downstairs to help mum, who was also in her eighties by now, with looking after him. However, after a week or so, dad slipped into a coma and died on the 19th January. On the other side of town in St. Mary's Hospital, Art deteriorated quickly and, on 27th March, he followed dad. It was not a good start to the year.

"Civvy Street. Reg the family man in their new home"

"Reg's brother Brian with David"

"Reg's father and son David"

"Ena's mother Mildred, Reg and David"

"David on Reg's scooter around 1963"

"Reg's parents around 1965"

"Reg [2nd left] and colleagues at Kettering Technical College, around 1971"

"RAF Waddington, 2nd December 1977
L-R, Reg Payne, Les Bartlett, Frank Swinyard,
Sqn Ldr Morrison, Sqn Ldr Richard Head"

Chapter Fifteen

"Higher still and higher
From the earth thou springest
Like a cloud of fire;
The blue deep thou wingest,
And singing still dost soar, and soaring ever singest."
- From '*To a Skylark*';
Percy Bysshe Shelley

After VE-Day, Skellingthorpe aerodrome continued in RAF use for a short time. In June 1945, our two wartime squadrons moved out to RAF Sturgate and 619 Squadron moved in, only to be disbanded the following month. It was replaced by 463 Squadron, but that too went the same way in September as the government drastically reduced all the Services with unceremonious haste, a policy which led to so few aircraft being preserved for posterity, preference being given to scrap metal dealers or simple disposal in the ground. There was a proposal in 1948 to use the site as a civil aerodrome but nothing came of it and, after a period of use by No.58 Maintenance Unit, RAF Skellingthorpe was finally closed in 1952. During the following years, the concrete runways that had seen all those crews take off on operations, some for their last time, were broken up, the buildings gradually fell into ruin and the land became the Black Moor pasture once more.

Located on the outskirts of Lincoln, it could not escape the housing pressures of the 1970s and 1980s and low-grade pasture land quickly acquired premium residential development value. The builders moved in and Birchwood provided homes for the city where once our own wartime home had been. However, for a short time, RAF Skellingthorpe had also been home to Flying Officer Leslie Manser of 50 Squadron, who on the night of 29th/30th May 1942, was the captain of an Avro Manchester taking part in Operation Millennium, the first 1,000-bomber raid.

Shortly after take-off, F/O Manser discovered that his aircraft did not have the power to climb above seven thousand feet, well below the bomber stream. Nevertheless, he continued across the North Sea and, an hour and a half later, approached Cologne, already a mass of raging fires which seemed to consume the whole city. Flying so low, he was quickly picked out and coned by some ten searchlights and targeted by very heavy flak, but Manser remained totally focused and, despite his aircraft's inadequacies, did not take evasive action but held her steady for the bomb aimer, Flying Officer 'Bang On' Barnes, who delivered a direct hit on the target.

Manser turned his aircraft away and almost at once the bomb-bay doors were hit by flak. He dived down to eight hundred feet through a curtain of 20mm cannon fire to gain the relative safety of darkness. Hit several times, the Manchester was now full of fire and smoke, and the rear gunner, Sgt Naylor, had been wounded by shrapnel.

Despite the damage to his aircraft, Manser, determined to get it and his crew back to England, nursed the ailing Manchester up to two thousand feet where soon afterwards the port engine burst into flames, threatening the fuel tanks. At this point, he greatly inspired his crew by calmly continuing to fly homeward until the flames slowly died away. However, the Manchester became increasingly difficult to control on the remaining engine and there was nothing the pilot could do to prevent their gradual descent as the engine overheated. By now over Belgium with the aircraft at stalling speed, he ordered the crew to bail out, while he remained at the controls, knowing that if he tried to save himself the Manchester would immediately stall and dive into the ground, now only a few hundred feet below, killing them all. Co-pilot Sgt Baveystock was the last to leave, and a few seconds later the bomber ploughed into nearby woods and burst into flames. Flying Officer Manser had given his life for his crew; they could have asked nothing more of any captain.

Manser's crew survived, and all but the navigator evaded capture and made it back to England as he had hoped. From the information which they gave at their debriefing and the details of their captain's courage, F/O Leslie Thomas Manser was awarded a posthumous Victoria Cross, the only Manchester crewman to receive one. Unusually, though, the rest of the crew were also decorated for their courage that night and, whilst there may be other examples of an entire seven-man bomber crew being decorated in the same action, I don't know of them. Today, he is still remembered: in amongst the houses of the Birchwood estate stands the Leslie Manser Primary School and every pupil who passes through its doors is taught about the outstanding courage of this extraordinarily brave young man.

In the early summer of 1986 I received an unexpected telephone call from Keith Coldron, a friend who lived in Lincoln, suggesting that a permanent memorial to all the men and women who served at RAF Skellingthorpe with 50 and 61 Squadrons should be erected at Birchwood, the site of the old aerodrome. Together with Les Bartlett and four others, I served on the fund-raising committee and started giving talks about my RAF days to raise money. Then, just before Christmas, I had a telephone call at work; my mother had died. Gone was the final link with my childhood, with that world I had known before the war and the RAF. For me, it really was the end of an era.

After more than twenty years at the college, my work there had become very demanding, and as I approached sixty-four I began to long for the retirement I would have the opportunity to take then. In addition to my memorial fund-raising efforts, I had been a member of RAFA since 1953 and every year put a lot of effort into the window display at our local Anglia Building Society offices, together with collecting at Sainsbury's during Battle of Britain week. I was also the Welfare Officer for the Northamptonshire Air Gunners Association and would visit sick members or their widows and take them presents at Christmas. Retirement would give me more time for such things and I longed for the warm sunny days when I could sit with Ena in the stone alcove I had built in our garden at Thomas Road, enjoy a cup of tea and not have to think about going to work.

Finally, on 11ᵗʰ March 1987, my sixty-fourth birthday arrived. The Principal, Mr Hammond, treated me to lunch and then afterwards I was presented with a book in which everyone I had worked with over the years had written something. I enjoyed my time at the college and have many fond memories of those years.

Destiny is a strange and unpredictable companion. Ena had worked in the college general office since 1980 and decided to retire at the same time. Sarah, a very pleasant young woman who was always willing to help Ena, shared the office and they had become very friendly. It wasn't long after we had retired that Sarah invited us to her wedding to David Skelham at Kettering Roman Catholic Church. After the service, as Ena and I stood in the warm sunshine watching the family photographs being taken, I couldn't help but notice David's widowed mother, Freda, radiant in a large-brimmed pink hat which saved her from squinting in the sunlight on all the pictures.

I continued raising money for the memorial fund and during that summer Lincoln City Council became involved, presenting us with the site at Birchwood Leisure Centre where the memorial was ultimately erected. Just a few yards away, at the edge of the playing fields, there remains a short stretch of the original peri-track which has been preserved. Each time I walk along it I remember that dark winter of 1943/44 and how lucky I was to survive.

For the next twelve months, Ena and I enjoyed a relaxing retirement now that the pressure of work was lifted and I had time for my allotment, to paint and to sit quietly in the alcove with Ena, just the two of us in the sunshine. Then one day, Ena was gone. Late at night on 15ᵗʰ August she suddenly became ill and was rushed to intensive care. Three days later, she died, her death caused by a blood clot. My world collapsed. I couldn't believe that Ena would no longer be at my side. The pretty young ATS girl that I had met and learned to care for and love, the girl I had married and made my life with, was gone. I was devastated.

In my sadness, I was very lucky because I had some wonderful friends and family to help me through the hardest times; Gerry Shutes and his wife, Terri, Fred and Margaret Allen, my brother Brian, and Janet, and Bernard Chapman, with whom I had worked at Whitfield's and then at the college for most of the years since I left Timpson's. Margaret and Cecil Beard, too, who lived on the other side of Thomas Road and with whom we had been great friends for many years. When we retired, Ena had been able to spend more time with Margaret and I would often hear them laughing together. After Ena's death these two lovely people were a lasting support to me. I know that Margaret missed Ena as much as I did in her own way and there were many times that we unashamedly cried together in our grief.

I spent Christmas Day 1988 at my son David's house but was on my own again on Boxing Day, so I walked over to Roy and Mavis Christy's in Northampton Road. As always, they made me very welcome with a couple of glasses of sherry and a meal, after which I returned home around one o'clock, just in time to see Margaret and Cecil getting ready to go out for a ramble. I asked if I could join them on the walk and, although I didn't know it at the time, the page had turned, a new chapter in my life had begun and destiny was about to give me a nudge.

It was Easter 1989 before I joined the Kettering Ramblers again and I could hardly have chosen a worse day; the weather was dreadful. It was cold with a biting wind that seemed to blow the rain into our faces no matter which way we turned. Walking with Margaret as we neared the old Desborough aerodrome, I noticed the lone figure of a woman ahead of us plodding through the rain, head down and well muffled up. Barely lifting her head to the driving rain, Margaret nodded towards the retreating figure. "That's Freda Skelham up there, Reg. You know, Sarah's mother-in-law. Why don't you catch her up and say hello," she suggested.

I quickened my pace and caught up with Freda. She had her collar turned up and her hat pulled right down so that I could barely see anything of her face. It was difficult to visualise her as the same woman I had last seen nearly a year ago at Sarah's wedding wearing a pretty dress and that broad-brimmed pink hat. Through tight lips, heads down and barely a glance at each other as the rain cascaded off our clothes, we chatted easily about the wedding and the link with Sarah through the college which had led to our invitation. I didn't have to tell her about losing Ena as by now most people knew anyway. When we reached Pipewell, the small Rothwell contingent which included Freda said goodbye and turned down a different path to the rest of us. It would be some months before I saw her again.

More than ever, I took refuge in my painting, sometimes in the early hours when sleep deserted me. I decided to use one Lancaster picture that I was particularly pleased with to raise money for the memorial fund. It was taken to Lincoln and hung in the RAF Recruiting Office window, where raffle tickets for it were sold at one pound each; to my great satisfaction it raised over £1,000. By that summer, our work on the memorial committee was completed. We had raised the £26,000 needed, Lincoln City Council had generously donated the land and we had settled the design for the fine Norwegian granite memorial. The committee asked me to design the detail of the aircraft to be engraved onto it, which I happily did – twice, as the first set of drawings went AWOL in the post.

Then, on 3rd June 1989, Marshal of the Royal Air Force, Sir Michael Beetham, GCB, CBE, DFC, AFC, FRAeS unveiled the memorial. It was an immensely proud moment for everyone there but particularly for those of us who had been in the crew of the young Flight Lieutenant Beetham, who had then gone on to reach the highest rank in the RAF and was here now to unveil the memorial to all those from both 50 and 61 Squadrons who had made that ultimate sacrifice from this very place.

The unveiling was attended by about a thousand veterans from the two squadrons, including our mid-upper Jock

Higgins, who had come back from Canada for the occasion. He had put on a couple of stone and exchanged his strong Glaswegian accent for a Canadian drawl, but it was wonderful to see Jock again; I was just so sorry that Ena wasn't there to see him. She liked Jock, but then all the girls liked him. He was a good-looking lad who had the personality to go with it.

During the early summer, at one of the college retirement lunches, I met a woman I had worked with for many years. Now widowed, she asked me to call round for a coffee one morning. She knew that I was very handy at all sorts of jobs around the house and she certainly had plenty for me to do, but always prepared a lovely lunch for me each day as I worked through her list of jobs. After some months when all the jobs were done, she found as many excuses not to invite me again; I was clearly of no further use to her. Too late, I remembered the warning Mary Donald, one of the college lecturers, had given me just after Ena died: "Beware of widows, Reg. They are ruthless." How right she was, but I had learned the hard way.

My next trip with the Kettering Ramblers was very different from the previous one; it was a blazing hot day along the Norfolk coast. It was the first time that I had seen Freda since that bitterly cold wet day at Easter and during the walk we once more chatted easily to one another, discovering a common interest in painting. I promised to frame one of her own paintings and a few days later collected it from her office at Loake Brothers, the shoe makers. I think nearly everyone of my generation in Kettering has at one time or another worked in some part of the boot and shoe industry. A week later, I arranged to return it to her but she invited me to her home for an evening meal as a thank you. After my previous experience with widows, had it been anyone but Freda, I would have declined, but we had already got on so well and seemed to have so much in common, I accepted. I am so glad that I did, because Freda had such a warm genuine personality that we had a lovely evening.

At the next ramble, Freda invited me for Sunday lunch the following weekend when David and Sarah would also be there. Later on that same ramble, another widow approached me and invited me for coffee. She was someone I had known since my teens and it was clear from the conversation that what she really wanted was a painter and decorator. Not for the first or the last time, Mary Donald's warning rang in my ears; I made my excuses and stayed away. Strangely, I always knew from the start that Freda was different, that her invitations were genuinely to me and not because she wanted some jobs doing; and I was right.

I had been having Sunday lunch with Brian and Janet but now Freda started to ask me on a regular basis as our friendship grew stronger. At Easter we took a holiday together in Bournemouth and then another one in August when we went to Sherringham in Norfolk. I would meet Freda from work and drive her home, stopping at the chip shop on Friday evenings to pick up a fish supper, which we enjoyed at her house in Rothwell, accompanied by a bottle of white wine and Elgar's Enigma Variations, a story which I later related to Classic FM and won a box of chocolates for my trouble. Losing Ena had devastated me, but meeting Freda gave me a new life and new happiness. I would never forget Ena, but Freda took me forward.

All my friends knew about Freda and inevitably we were seen as a couple. More importantly, we saw ourselves as a couple and married on Saturday, 6th April 1991, with our honeymoon at Chipping Norton, where we visited Adlestrop, made famous by Edward Thomas's poem. We didn't need two houses, so we sold mine and lived in Freda's at Rothwell, a decision which worked very well since I had done all sorts of improvements for her there over the two years that we had known each other.

I had continued to keep close contact with all my RAF friends and now Freda was part of both the social and the formal events that I was involved with. The memorial at Birchwood naturally became the focus of our annual re-union weekend, but the residents of Skellingthorpe also made us very welcome in their village hall. Friday night was a buffet and 1940s dance at Skellingthorpe, and then on Saturday morning we held our Association AGM at the Leslie Manser School, where they would give us a buffet lunch followed by a very entertaining performance from the children echoing the 1940s.

Saturday evening was the formal dinner and dance in Lincoln's Assembly Rooms, attended by some of the City Council politicians and senior RAF officers from Waddington and other bases in the area. Finally, Sunday morning brought a church service and march past at the Birchwood Memorial, followed by a return to Skellingthorpe village hall for afternoon tea and a short service at the little memorial there. This has always been a very intimate service as the community, and especially the children, are closely involved with it.

In 1994, we sold Freda's house in Rothwell and moved to Kettering. Freda had by now retired, too, and we enjoyed many holidays, including one to Germany. Despite my tour of operations, I had never actually set foot in the country. I was very impressed with how clean the streets were and how well organised the traffic control. By comparison, Kettering, and many other parts of Britain, was just one big rubbish tip, and getting worse. I don't know why or how we have become such a slovenly dirty nation with so little pride in our country.

In Cologne, they were still working on the cathedral and I could see so many signs of the rebuilding that had taken place in the post-war years. It was quite a revelation to see how work had been undertaken to repair and replace the buildings which we had destroyed. It was long before I went to Germany that the nightmares started. I have had to live with my memories of the war years and of my time in the RAF in particular, but I do not regret what we did in Bomber Command. The reality is that after Dunkirk and before D-Day, whilst the 8th Army was fighting Rommel's Afrika

Korps, it was only the young men of the RAF who were able to take the war to the heart of the Third Reich.

When I started my wireless operators' course at Blackpool in 1941, seven of the twelve airmen who were billeted with Mrs Clegg in Charnley Road became good friends: Arthur Bromich, Keith Kenway, Robbie Robertson, Ron Boydon, George Plank, Tubby Melhuish, whose real name was Eric, and me. One day in 1995, I came to realise what a small world this is and how long the reach of coincidence when I received a letter from America. It had been written by Matthew Poole, whose mother was George Plank's widow. After completing his training, George married his sweetheart before being posted to India, where he lost his life whilst bombing the Japanese in Rangoon. He had been among twenty airmen killed in two Liberators lost that day. Towards the end of the war, Matthew's mother had met an American, Jim Poole, whom she married and moved to the States with when he returned home.

Even though she was happily married to Jim, she never forgot George and kept his letters to her which he had written from India and which she showed to her son Matthew when he grew up. I had also kept in touch with George after his posting and he must have mentioned me in some of his letters home. Matthew became fascinated with George, whose death had led to his own birth, and one day, in 1995, whilst browsing aviation books, he came across a photograph of me with the caption "Reg Payne at his home". He recognised my name from his mother's letters and the accompanying article confirmed my time with 50 Squadron. It didn't take Matthew long to contact our Association secretary for my address, and hence the letter from America.

Of the seven young friends who stayed with Mrs Clegg, Ron, George and Arthur didn't survive the war, and by now only Tubby and I were still alive. My reply to Matthew led to him coming over to stay with us, to a reunion with Tubby and his wife, Hilda, and a memorial service at the RAF Church Clement Danes in London for all those twenty Liberator airmen lost that day over Rangoon. It was ironic that I should have been posted there too.

Inevitably with the passage of time, someone in the Kettering branch of RAFA was going to be the last person to have seen operational service during the war, and by 1996, that person was me. So I was elected as president, a position which I soon discovered required Freda and me to attend many social events, although my great friend and branch chairman, George Bennett, and his wife, Mavis, always gave us a lot of help and support. Together with my Welfare Officer role for the Air Gunners' Association and my paintings, there was never a dull moment, but Freda and I still found time to enjoy our walking and holidays.

The 28th June 2012 dawned bright and clear, giving the promise of a beautiful day. Together with Kenneth Ballantyne, I travelled by train to London's Green Park where, beneath an unbroken crystal-blue sky, Her Majesty Queen Elizabeth II unveiled the seven stunningly poignant figures of the magnificent Bomber Command Memorial in their Portland stone setting. Sixty-seven years after the end of the most devastating war that this planet has ever endured, there is at last a fitting national memorial to the 55,573 young men of Bomber Command who gave their lives defending our freedom and democracy from tyranny and oppression. Men who came from Great Britain, Australia, Canada, South Africa, New Zealand and the further reaches of the Empire, every one of them a volunteer; there was no conscription into the aircrew of any Command.

The memorial has been paid for entirely by private subscription and has undoubtedly only come about through the great efforts of many people, although the commitment of the late Robin Gibb gave the campaign a very high public celebrity profile. Another who worked tirelessly, though so often unseen, was Sir Michael Beetham. Not as well known as Robin Gibb outside RAF circles, as the Marshal of the Royal Air Force who had completed a tour in Bomber Command during the Battle of Berlin, he was in a unique position to advocate the cause which has now so captured the public imagination and support in the same way that what we were doing as young airman all those years ago did.

On VE-Day, Winston Churchill spoke to the nation and praised everybody for winning the war; everybody except Bomber Command. He deliberately ignored Air Chief Marshal Harris and us; the 1945 election was coming. Atlee's government, like Churchill's before it and every one since, refused to strike a Bomber Command medal, even though we had taken the war to the enemy from the very beginning to the end. We did what we were asked to do and then we were treated as pariahs. Fortunately, for whatever reasons, nearly seventy years on, a new generation understands better, even reveres us, and Prime Minister David Cameron has ordered that Bomber Command aircrew be awarded a clasp to the 1939–45 Star in recognition of 'the extraordinary courage of the aircrew'.

Churchill knew the value of bombing in the preparation for an invasion of Europe, privately expressing, *"When I look round to see how we can win this war there is only one sure path… and that is an absolutely devastating, exterminating attack by very heavy bombers from this country upon the Nazi homeland."* In his famous September 1940 Battle of Britain speech, he publicly endorsed his private views by saying, *"The fighters are our salvation but the bombers alone provide the means of victory. We must therefore develop the power to carry an ever-increasing volume of explosives to Germany, so as to pulverise their entire industry and scientific structure on which the war effort and economic life of the enemy depends, whilst holding him at arm's length from our island."*

In the worst days of the war, the chance of survival for a bomber crew was around one in four; less than for an infantry subaltern on the Western Front in the 1914–18 war. On 14th May 1940, the Luftwaffe bombed the virtually defenceless Dutch city of Rotterdam, even though the government had formally surrendered, and in a ninety-minute daylight bombing frenzy, 30,000 civilians died and another 50,000 were injured.   The horror of modern warfare had truly arrived.

With the defeat of the immense French army, the largest in the world at the time, and the British Expeditionary Force in June 1940, Britain and its empire stood alone against the might of the world's most powerful army and air force, which now occupied northern Europe from Norway to the French border with Spain.   The German forces had swept away all that lay before them, rolled up to the English Channel and stopped.   No army had successfully crossed that narrow stretch of water for nearly a thousand years.   Hitler knew that he must crush the people of these islands or lose the war, and he also knew that air supremacy was the key to that victory; and so began the Battle of Britain.   In the summer of 1940, the burden of salvation lay upon the Royal Air Force, for only it stood between freedom and total defeat.

Outnumbered four to one, RAF Fighter Command took on the might of the Luftwaffe during the long hot summer days of 1940.   But they were not alone, because whilst the battle raged above southern England, Bomber Command was attacking the German landing barges, ships, ports and equipment that was needed for the invasion and stored along the French coast.   These were mostly daylight raids, carried out at low level in aircraft which were highly vulnerable to the coastal defences and the much superior German fighters.

Fighter Command may have had the finest of modern aircraft in the Hurricane and the Spitfire, but Bomber Command was for the most part operating slow, lightly armed bombers such as the Fairey Battle and the Bristol Blenheim.   To compound their troubles, our politicians believed they could prosecute the war by the rules of cricket and would only allow attacks on well-defended military targets.   Thus daylight raids were necessary with the consequent appalling and unsustainable loss of aircrew lives.

Eventually, some sense of reality emerged and night bombing was introduced, but navigation equipment was basic, often no more than a sextant and a map, both of which were useless in cloud. Crews were sent five or six hundred miles into enemy territory to find small specific targets in the middle of a huge land mass shrouded in total darkness and often cloud. Despite the courage, commitment and optimism of the crews, success rates were so abysmal that the enemy was often unable to identify what the intended target had been. In the summer of 1941, the government carried out a secret survey of bombing accuracy. The resultant Butt report concluded that only thirty per cent of bombers were getting to within five miles of their target; the number actually hitting the target was considerably less than that, whilst the loss of men and aircraft remained disproportionately high.

Following the Butt report, the Air Ministry adopted and refined the 'area-bombing' tactic. Essentially, it was the same tactic used by the Luftwaffe in the Blitz, but on a larger scale and much more difficult and dangerous to execute because the distances were so much greater. The strategy was whole-heartedly embraced by Churchill. The War Cabinet, containing Conservative, Labour and Liberal politicians, concluded that area bombing was the right strategy and approved the policy. It ordered the Air Ministry to carry it out, and in 1942, Air Chief Marshal Harris was appointed C-in-C Bomber Command. It fell to him to devise the tactics and to us to implement them. Harris has been consistently blamed for the strategy of area bombing; it was not Harris's strategy, it was not Bomber Command's; it was the government's, on behalf of its people. I can think of no better example of where the messenger has been repeatedly shot.

Until the latter stages of the war, Churchill was an ardent advocate of area bombing because he realised the importance of forcing the Germans to defend their homeland. They diverted 55,000 anti-aircraft guns and a million men to defend Germany, and Albert Speer, Hitler's Armaments Minister, described it as "the greatest lost battle on the German side."

Opponents of the area-bombing strategy most often quote the raid on Dresden to indict Bomber Command of culpability and even suggest it was a war crime; but again, it was not Harris's conception. Churchill was pressed by Stalin to relieve the pressure on the eastern front with a defining blow against the Germans. The Air Ministry had selected Dresden as a target as far back as 1941 because of the railway yards there, but Harris had avoided attacking it until he was ordered to do so by the Prime Minister in February 1945. Furthermore and so often overlooked, is the American USAAF's continued bombing of the city the next day. Dresden was one of four such selected targets, but when the news of the firestorm was reported, public opinion soured, the other targets were largely dropped and the politicians, Churchill in particular, with an eye to the inevitable General Election, left Harris and the young men of Bomber Command to take the blame.

As aircrew, we were not given the luxury of picking over the moral ethics of our orders in the quiet calm of peaceful surroundings with the benefit of hindsight. We were at war; we didn't know that it would end in May. We had been fighting for our very survival for years, for the survival of our families, and the RAF had been the only arm of the Services capable of striking at the German homeland on a regular basis. The whole purpose of area bombing was to disrupt industrial production, wear down morale and to force the enemy to divert resources, including troops from the battle areas, to the defence of their homeland. The price of success paid by the young men of Bomber Command was desperately high. Half our force were killed, a higher proportion than any other part of the Armed Forces on either side; only the devastated German U-boat crews of the Kriegsmarine came close to that level of loss.

We were at war with the German people. It was total war. It was irrelevant whether they were in uniform or not, they were all part of the German war machine, producing munitions and materials with which their army, air force and navy sought to defeat the British people. I cannot see a distinction between civilians and armed services in such circumstances. It was civilian scientists who developed Hitler's Vengeance weapons, the V-1 and V-2, which killed civilians in London, and who were trying to make an atomic bomb; it was civilian workers in the factories who produced the aircraft and bombs which shattered our cities and killed our women and children; it was civilian workers in the factories who built the fighters and made the flak shells which shot down and killed more than 55,000 RAF aircrew; it was civilian shipbuilders who built the *Bismarck*, which sank HMS *Hood* with the loss of her entire company bar three; it was civilian workers who made the torpedoes which sank the evacuation ship *City of Benares* with mostly women and children on board and which sank hundreds of merchant ships, claiming the lives of thousands of Merchant Navy sailors, and it was civilians who made the guns and tanks which killed our soldiers in North Africa, Italy and Normandy, at Dunkirk, El Alamein and Arnhem. Their factory overalls were their uniforms.

Of course, it was exactly the same here from the German point of view and the arguments apply equally. British civilian workers were employed making all the same weapons for us to fight them with. It demonstrates the wasteful futility of war, but also that total war cannot make distinctions between the clothes which people wear in prosecuting that war. A nation at war is just that, the whole nation, whatever individuals within that nation might think about it.

The Lancaster was a brilliant aircraft and today has a very romantic image, but when we flew them it was to face the most terrifying battle conditions imaginable, flying for hours at a time when at any moment cannon shells could rip into us, fire could engulf us, flak could blow us apart. It was the stress of waiting, of the unseen enemy lurking out there, of the predictive flak, of constantly being only moments away from death, that was so wearing. It was not enviable, it was not enjoyable and it was not avoidable. It broke a few men; I'm only surprised that it didn't break more.

Our heavy bombers were great aircraft in their day, but they were also noisy, cold, cramped, smelled of oil and aviation fuel and were highly dangerous places. Too many of my friends and tens of thousands I never knew died in burning aircraft, trapped by the G-forces as they spiralled 20,000 feet before crashing into the earth, their last few seconds of life a terrifying realisation of inevitability. It was so dangerous a task that only volunteers did it and we did it to secure freedom for ourselves, our children and future generations.

Whoever may have been to blame for causing the Second World War, I know that it was not the young men and women who served in Bomber Command. When we dropped our bombs on German cities, we were not criminals; we were doing what our country ordered us to do and what it had to do to win, because winning was the only way to survive. As we flew across Europe and bombed our targets, we were targets ourselves, as the graves of all those lost crews testify. Every mile of the way we were the hunted and hated enemy of the German people and they used every means to kill us.

Life on an operational station is often depicted as beer and raucous parties, but it was much more complex than that. Certainly we enjoyed ourselves whenever we could, because we never knew whether our next mission would be our last. But such antics were the results of living on adrenalin and fear, tainted by physical and emotional exhaustion; relief at having survived another mission when others did not, recognition that respite lasted only until the next mission.

There were stark reminders around the station to the loss of crews: a vacant dispersal area the next morning, an empty table at breakfast, a bicycle left propped up outside the briefing room, a motor car abandoned beside the Officers' Mess, even a new CO. Each a symbol of finality which struck hard at us, no matter how often they were repeated, but then they had to be locked away in the box labelled 'memories for another day'. We had to function as a crew for our own survival and could not dwell upon the loss of others.

The cars which were left behind were impounded to await instructions from the next of kin once the owner's fate was known. If he was never going to return, the family would often let it be sold to someone else on the base for a very reasonable sum, the money usually going into the Airmen's Benevolent Fund. Like chop girls, some cars changed hands many times. That was what it was like. A small but relentless loss of crews, week after week; some would be good friends, others only acquaintances, others still new to the squadron and on their first mission, but all kindred spirits. We felt their loss, but then had to move on; another mission, another target, another night of fear and death.

It is now in my later years that I miss the people I knew so well. Their faces still haunt my dreams, faces that were so young, lives that had lived so little. Some of these young men had never even kissed a girl, never known the pleasures of a relationship, killed too soon to have had that chance. These memories have always been with me, but as I get older they seem clearer; the noise, the smells, the flames, the fear, the names of those we lost, their faces still laughing, still so young, and then gone; but now I see them again. That's the trouble with nightmares, there's no control over them; only waking banishes them – until next time.

On 28th August 2012 my world collapsed for a second time when Freda unexpectedly died in Kettering Hospital. She had been unwell for some little time, but there was nothing to suggest how serious it was. Twenty-two years and ten days after I lost Ena, I lost Freda and became widowed for a second time. Slowly I have started to pick up the threads of my life and put it back together again, and once more I have found great solace and comfort in my painting. But even in the depths of despair, there is always a light, something to smile at if you can just find it. Not many weeks after I lost Freda, I had a telephone call from an acquaintance we had known for some time, a widow, who was inviting me to her house for a coffee and a chat. But even as she was speaking, I could hear the echo of Mary Donald's words from all those years ago: "Beware of widows, Reg. They are ruthless." Don't they ever give up! But I am much wiser now.

"Yes, I remember Adlestrop -
The name, because one afternoon
Of heat the express-train drew up there
Unwontedly. It was late June.

The steam hissed. Someone cleared his throat.
No one left and no one came
On the bare platform. What I saw
Was Adlestrop – only the name."

From '*Adlestrop*'; Edward Thomas

"6th April 1991. Reg and Freda on their wedding day"

"Reg and Ena relaxing in David's garden"

"Four generations, r-l, Reg, his son David, grandson David and great-grandson Max,"

"10th June 2012. Reg at the 50/61 Squadron Memorial, Birchwood, Lincoln"

"28th June 2012. Reg at the Bomber Command Memorial, Green Park, London"

"19th March 2013. Reg at East Kirkby"

"19th March 2013. Reg at East Kirkby with George Bennett [left] and the author"

"19th March 2013. Reg back at his wireless operator's position wearing his silk scarf"

"Warrant Officer Reg Payne"

MMXIII © Kenneth JS Ballantyne

The Author

Born to Army officer parents at Gibraltar Military Hospital in 1949, Kenneth Ballantyne was educated at schools across Europe, Scotland and England. His father, a career soldier with the Royal Artillery, had served throughout the Second World War, as had his mother, who trained as a nurse at the outbreak of war and then joined the First Aid Nursing Yeomanry.

Part of Kenneth's early years were spent living and playing amongst the bomb craters left in the German Ruhr by RAF Bomber Command. At seven, his parents took him and his brother Iain to the Reichswald Forest War Cemetery to educate them both about the true price that had been paid for their lives and freedom, an experience which became an indelible memory for him.

After several years as a police officer, Kenneth graduated and then practised law as a solicitor before retiring to combine his love of writing with his interest in the personal experiences of those who fought the Second World War, an interest which had grown out of that visit to the Reichswald Forest War Cemetery. A member of the Bomber Command Association, the Shropshire Aircrew Association, No50/61 Squadrons Association and No210 [Flying Boat] Squadron Association, he now spends much of his time collecting and recording the true stories and experiences of the men and women who served on the Home Front and in the Armed Services during the war as an important historical project for an enduring legacy.

By giving talks about his books to community groups across the country, Kenneth and his wife Elaine raise money to support several charities, including the Bomber Command Memorial Fund and the Severn Hospice in Shropshire. He established his own publishing business in 2005 in order to put his first book into print, and other titles have followed.